T0369782

Exploring the Public Effects of Religious Communication on Politics

EXPLORING THE PUBLIC EFFECTS OF RELIGIOUS COMMUNICATION ON POLITICS

Edited by Brian Calfano

University of Michigan Press
Ann Arbor

Copyright © 2021 by Brian Calfano
All rights reserved

For questions or permissions, please contact um.press.perms@umich.edu

Published in the United States of America by the
University of Michigan Press
Printed and bound by CPI Group (UK) Ltd, Croydon, CR0 4YY
First published August 2021

A CIP catalog record for this book is available from the British Library.

Library of Congress Cataloging-in-Publication data has been applied for.

Library of Congress Control Number: 2021937087

ISBN 978-0-472-07491-4 (hardcover : alk. paper)
ISBN 978-0-472-05491-6 (paper : alk. paper)
ISBN 978-0-472-12908-9 (e-book)

Cover image: Shutterstock.com / TeaGraphicDesign

Contents

Digital materials related to this title can be found on
the Fulcrum platform via the following citable URL:
https://doi.org/10.3998/mpub.11533900

ONE

Introduction

Communication as a New Path in Religion and Politics Research

Brian Calfano

Human behavior is powered by motivating factors, as Maslow's (1943) hierarchy of needs so eloquently describes. Faith (or religion) is about halfway up the hierarchy as part of the larger category of "love and belonging." Before one can enjoy the higher rungs of esteem and self-actualization, satisfying the need for group acceptance is paramount. Family and friendship are also part of this group-oriented rung. It is unsurprising, given its midpoint in the need hierarchy, that religion, with its claim to perhaps the ultimate experience in love and belonging ever devised, stays relevant to the human activities at the heart of social scientific inquiry. But religion, like family and friendship, is largely not an atomistic experience. It is shared with others, which means that assessing religion as a motive requires considering the human communication milieu in which faith is experienced or "lived out." And it suggests that beliefs and behaviors—the manifestations of "religion" as a social phenomenon—are subsumed in a larger, dynamic communication process between believers, elites, and institutions (and even nonbelievers in some cases). If a first-order requirement of religion is that its claims must be made known (including how people ought to think and behave), then it is communication—not belief, behavior, identity, or any other concept—that is the critical antecedent to all other religion-based outcomes that social scientists study.

Recognition of this reality is likely why scholars have broached the subject of religious communication before, ranging from the perspective of systems or social psychology theories (see Arens 2011; Luhmann 2013; Pace 2016) to the actual act of communicating religion (e.g., its teachings) through media platforms (Meyer and Moors 2005; Stout 2006). Missing, however, was a concerted political science treatment of religious communication. This volume extends the gaze of inquiry on religious communication to political topics and institutions and is in line with previous work joining the communication theme to a range of social scientific theories (see, e.g., Harris 2012).

The need for this volume is apparent in that religion's role as a basic motivator of thought and behavior logically extends its political relevance (Durkheim 1915; Weber 1930; Stark and Glock 1968; Wald, Owen, and Hill 1988; Stark and Finke 2000; Weilhouwer 2000; Guth et al. 2006). And politics, which, by definition, is about "the authoritative allocation of values for a society" (Easton 1953, 129), is never far removed from religion as a sphere to co-opt (or be co-opted by). Though the percentage of those claiming no religious affiliation in the U.S. has been on the rise in recent years (see Thiessen and Wilkins-Laflamme 2017), religious institutions still represent the largest of voluntary associations (Bellah et al. 1985). Indeed, a reason why the secularization thesis never realized the potential its proponents originally envisaged (Swatos and Christiano 1999; Norris 2004) likely has to do with the critical role religion still plays for many.

As Berger (1967) explains, the crux of religion's resilience is its role in creating plausibility structures to sort out life's challenges and puzzles. Geertz's (1973, 90) description of religion's importance shows a similarly wide scope as he observed that religion creates "powerful, pervasive, and long lasting moods and motivations in men by formulating conceptions of the general order of existence." Both scholars drew from Durkheim (1915), who argued that society uses religion to justify norms that underpin regularity or predictability in social interaction (see also Douglas and Wildavsky 1982). Culture, which Geertz (1973) defines as both symbols/traditions and a set of controls on behavior, is a related concept to norms and counts religion as a foundation.

But norms and culture notwithstanding, the exact direction in which religion influences politics (assuming the causal arrow points from sacred to secular; see Margolis 2018) will depend, in part, on what religion teaches about the natural and supernatural. As Leege (1993, 3) explains, religions

> make different assumptions about the innate goodness or depravity
> of humankind, formulate rationales for the design and purpose of

political systems, and generate expectations about the end of time and the outcomes of salvation. Some religious worldviews are world affirming, while others are world denying. Some churches and belief systems are universalistic and tolerant. Others are particularistic and shun all those who fail to follow in a singular way. Some show respect and compassion to all human beings, but others see the hand of a judging God in the misfortunes of others.

Religious experience is as psychological as it is sociological, with individuals deriving identity boundaries, norms, and potential motivations for individual and collective action in the political realm (though these motives and actions will certainly differ between and across individuals and groups). Importantly, Leege's (1993) insight undergirds the first basic condition or tenet that we accept for this volume: religion, as it is interpreted and lived out through the experiences of both religious elites and laypeople, is variable in its orientations, emphases, and effects. This is true in terms of both inter- and intra-faith comparisons and whether we focus on religion from a domestic or international perspective. A second tenet is that, while religion is not going away (inroads among the religious "nones" notwithstanding), it does not operate as a closed system. In the US especially, where economic influences on the nation's social and political structure have always existed (Irwin and Sylla 2011), religion is an influence on (and is influenced by) competing sources of ideation (including political identity and ideology).

Though not operating independently of political or economic factors, religion forged historic roles in developing political systems, parties, and policies—all affecting believers and nonbelievers alike. This is particularly true in the US, where scholars paid considerable attention to a variety of political phenomena at the intersection of religious belief and identity, including social movements, voting behavior, public opinion, and public policy (Kleppner 1970; Wilcox 1992; Noll and Harlow 2007). Along the way, certain approaches to understanding religion in the political realm held consistent sway, including a focus on religious traditions as explanations for political views and behavior (Green et al. 1996; Guth et al. 1997; Layman 2001), on local institutional context as causal influences on how faith is explained and experienced (Djupe and Gilbert 2009), and on religion as a basis for group identities that shape preferences (Jelen 1993).

But Leege and his colleagues, writing in what arguably became the seminal reader on religion from a social science perspective—*Rediscovering the Religious Factor in American Politics* (Leege and Kellstedt 1993)—also made a case that the social science of the time needed an updated perspective on religion and how to study it. Though today the religion and politics subfield is far more advanced (and pluralistic) in its approach to assessing religious phenomenon than it was almost thirty years ago, our work is premised on the notion that social science is at another crossroad in its assessment of religion as a political force. Indeed, Donald Trump's 2016 election, the extent to which white evangelicals shed prior concerns about candidate morality (see Djupe and Calfano 2018), and the growing insights from panel data suggesting that religious choices are partly the outcome of political influences (see Margolis 2018) point to a current opportunity to offer another assessment of religion and political factors. Herein we adopt a focus on religious communication.

The Religious Communication Factor

Any political influence that religion possesses is invariably linked to how religion makes claims about transcendent knowledge and "truth." This is because the plausibility structures that Berger (1967) described require communication to establish and maintain their influence in both the religious and political domains. Recognizing this, Djupe and Calfano (2019, 2) argue that "the link between religious variables and political choices is wrapped up in a communicative process of exposure and adoption." Exposure to religious views leads people to decide whether they will adopt said views and to what extent. But people do not make this adoption decision as blank slates, and the exposure process does not occur in a vacuum. Therefore, and though religious variables have can be causal factors in determining public views on foreign policy (Guth et al. 2005), nationalism (Shortle and Gaddie 2015), social welfare (Be'ery and Bloom 2015), political tolerance (Djupe 2015), abortion (Green et al. 1996), and gay rights (Haider-Markel and Meier 1996), and a host of other topics, scholars ignore the variable impacts of religious communication at their peril.

Understanding religion's relationship to political outcomes, including policy preferences and behavior, requires that we delve more deeply into the exposure and adoption process. As Djupe and Calfano (2019) summarize, religious communication exposure and adoption happen in three broad frameworks: (1) religious settings from religious elites, (2) secular settings from religious elites, and (3) secular settings from secular elites. A fourth framework—religious settings from secular elites—also exists, but with far less frequency than the other three. The nature of these frameworks recommends that we focus the study of religious communication exposure and adoption along two broad factors: (1) elite cue giving and

(2) identity boundary making among the religiously affiliated. Of course, the larger social movement and institutional (i.e., denominational) factors remain important, but this volume's collection of assessments represents an advance in how political scientists understand religious communication through elite cues and identity markers.

Just what does religious communication look like? Offering examples is always fraught with challenges in that it runs the risk of creating limits on what people recognize as the phenomena under study. Our position throughout the volume is that religious communication is broad in nature and includes everything from political statements from elected officials to what clergy tell their congregations to public smears made against discriminated outgroups. But the examples that perhaps most people think of regard religious communication from elites (e.g., elected officials and clergy) and organizations or groups with a religious mission. Communication from these sources can occur in both secular and sacred contexts, targeting audiences of specific characteristics. In fact, when thinking about the litany of opportunities people have to be exposed to communication (and to react to it in the form of adopting perspectives or behaviors), the examples are boundless. That said, there are certain, clearly political forms of religious communication that deserve mention.

For example, Kaylor (2011) compiled a few examples of presidential communication along religious themes.

> I deeply believe that the loving God who gave us this land should have never been expelled from America's classrooms. If the Congress can begin its day with prayer, children can, too. (Ronald Reagan, 1984)

> The Bible asks, "If you child asks for bread, would you give him a stone? If he asks for fish, would you give him a serpent? If he asks for an egg, would you give him a scorpion?" Our children are what we give them, what we teach them. We dare not forget that basic truth. Their lives and our common future depend on it. (Bill Clinton, 1996)

In terms of religious elites (e.g., clergy) engaging in communication of a political tenor, the examples are also legion. They also have a long trail in US history, as Clardy (2011) shows in this excerpt of a Dr. Martin Luther King Jr. speech from 1967.

And don't let anybody make you think that God chose America as his divine, messianic force to be a sort of policeman of the whole world. God has a way of standing before nations with judgment, and it seems that I can hear God saying to America, "You're too arrogant!"

Religious interest groups and similar organizations engage in religious communication perhaps even more frequently than clergy. And, like clergy communication exposure, religious interest group cues are wide-ranging, almost unlimited, in scope (examples of these cues alone could likely fill a separate volume). One of the more attention-grabbing forms of this type of religious communication comes in the targeting of scrutinized social out-groups or their supporters. This 2020 example from the American Family Association, an evangelical-based political interest and advocacy group, targets PBS programming that highlights LGBTQ Pride Month. The excerpt is from an invite to have group members sign a petition calling for PBS's removal of the programming.

PBS is going all out the month of June to celebrate LGBTQ-Pride Month by launching a six-episode series of short videos on a dedicated YouTube Channel created by its Digital Studios. . . . PBS's decision . . . to push the homosexual agenda is an unjust attack on Christianity and a mockery of the Bible and God's design for human sexuality.[1]

To be sure, scholars are not entirely sold on the idea that religious communication (in whatever form people are exposed to it) impacts public behavior, including civic engagement (see Scheufele, Nisbet, and Brossard 2003). But the contributors' work in this volume is not premised on the idea that religion, and religious communication, needs large-scale population effects to be of interest. The chapters herein examine religious communication outcomes representing an array of phenomena, some of which are limited in scope but still produce broader insights into religious exposure and adoption through the lens of the elite cue and identity boundary factors. These communication outcomes include the media's role in furthering religious narratives about minority groups, religious strategies that interest groups use to advance their appeals, the variable strength of

---

1. https://www.afa.net/activism/action-alerts/2020/pbs-celebrates-pride-month-pro-hom osexual-series/, accessed June 15, 2020.

Islamophobia in cross-national contexts, the determination of what qualifies as an "evangelical" identity, and clergy representation of religious and institutional teachings.

In addition to being of scholarly import, each of these lesser-studied topics (relative to the wider religion and politics literature in the American and comparative subfields) promises insight into how religion has changed in the Trump political era. While it is generally good to avoid viewing large-scale political developments through a lens associated with an individual, there is a strong case to make that Trump is different. The president uses religion as a unifying (and dividing) political force like perhaps no political leader before him (see Djupe and Claussen 2018). Even once he leaves office, Trump's political blueprint will likely see attempted replication across political campaigns and institutions. A critic might argue that Trump has done little different from his Republican predecessors in aligning political strategy with faith community (i.e., white evangelical and certain Roman Catholic) priorities. While this is true to an extent, it is inarguable that Trump's blatant public linking of his presidential actions to expected voting reciprocity from these faith communities lacks parallel in the last eighty years. At the same time, the political landscape for white religious communities has changed, as these voters now consider themselves victims of broader cultural and political attacks (see Jones 2016; Lewis 2017). Whether Trump caused, or merely exacerbated, this trend, his presidency represented a shift in elected officials' public use of religious communication (Domke and Coe 2008; Calfano and Djupe 2009).

Trump, as a political elite, has potential communication paths of influence. But religious elites have their own paths, which often overlap with the institutional settings in which these religious leaders operate. The frequency with which religious elites communicate in religious settings means a better understanding of communication exposure in religious institutions critical (Djupe and Gilbert 2003). For Christians, the church has long defined political community (Wald, Owen, and Hill 1988; Gilbert 1993)—one that inculcates values and perspectives about how to treat people both in and outside their religious community (for a similar dynamic regarding religious elites, see Djupe and Sokhey 2003). Jewish and Muslim communities enjoy a similar dynamic through their religious institutions and organizations (Lazerwitz and Harrison 1979; Jamal 2005). And a long line of scholarship documents the link between religious organization involvement and political participation more broadly (Verba, Schlozman, and Brady 1995; Djupe and Gilbert 2006; but see Scheufele, Nisbet, and Brossard 2003), though some raise concerns about the quality of the political deliberation within religious contexts (e.g., Mutz 2006). Of core concern to skeptics is that religious organizations indoctrinate.

But, by and large, deliberative political discussion does develop in churches (and, by extension, in other houses of worship). This is true across racial and ethnic lines as well as denominations and traditions (Calhoun-Brown 1996; Djupe and Gilbert 2009). While it is tempting to see the local faith institution as an opinion factory stamping parishioners with a uniform worldview, local congregants are more likely to bring a relatively diverse set of social and political experiences with them as they interact (Djupe, Sokhey, and Gilbert 2007). This diversity makes opinion homogenization difficult to create, including in traditions where it might be expected (e.g., evangelical Christianity) (Stark and Finke 2000). Indeed, Neiheisel, Djupe, and Sokhey (2009) push back on the notion that churches and other religious organizations produce opinion uniformity among self-selected publics by showing that small-group encounters in churches lead to deliberation. Thus, communication exposure in religious environments may incubate opinion diversity (even if some local congregations are less successful in this effort than others). And those exposed to political messages within religious environments may find the motive for political action as well (Wilcox and Siegelman 2001). Against this backdrop is the lingering question of whether, and to what extent, religious elites influence parishioners. Generally, there is the potential, but often not the realization, of such influence (see Djupe and Gilbert 2009; Djupe and Calfano 2013).

Since most believers live part of their lives outside of the religious context, inherent tension exists between religious identity boundaries—constituting "ingroup" and "outgroup" differences (Finke and Stark 2005). Given this tension, it is not surprising that communication within religious settings includes aspects of inclusive and exclusive values (the latter focusing on preserving a group's inherent sense of separation from those on the outside) (Djupe and Calfano 2013). Yet, as Schaffer et al. (2015) found, even white evangelical Christians exhibit far less "exclusive" tendencies than what one might expect if considering religious tradition as a generator of fixed opinion (see, e.g., Smidt, Kellstedt, and Guth 2009). Social networks are also key in the communication exposure-opinion-behavior link, as parishioners bring the perspectives of network discussions, social identities, and lived values to bear in their faith community activities (Djupe, Sokhey, and Gilbert 2007). Indeed, discussion, teaching, and interaction can produce alignment with both "liberal" and "conservative" political policies and values among community members.

There is also evidence that religious contexts exist outside of church walls, as is the case where religious elites offer cues in the secular realm or where secular elites offer religious cues to the public. For example, political activity by religious organizations motivates religiously inclined voters to increase their participation (Djupe and Conger 2012), while the proximate density of specific types of churches correlates with lawmakers' positions on signature "moral" issues like abortion (Calfano 2010). Meanwhile, the interactive dynamic that religious settings create helps shape the expectations parishioners have for clergy, particularly in terms of addressing local and community challenges (Djupe and Gilbert 2009). In addition, scholars show that the view that religious publics, particularly evangelicals, have of the so-called secular media's coverage of their community and beliefs impacts these believers' perceptions (Wills 1990; Kerr and Moy 2002; Muirhead et al. 2006). This volume's approach, however, focuses on new directions in understanding how elites leverage religious communication for group boundary maintenance, political cues, and related outcomes. This emphasis is in line with existing scholarship on the long history of religious media in America (see Schultze 2003; Denton 2005; Newman and Smith 2007).

Then there is the communication of religious appeals by secular political actors. This practice has been present throughout American history (Butler, Wacker, and Balmer 2007), especially in the form of presidential rhetoric featuring religious ideas and imagery to frame political events and policy (Chapp 2012). In some cases, religiously committed politicians, including William Jennings Bryan, played major party roles (see Calfano 2014), but the parties themselves were less directly tied to the overt or systematic use of religious appeals until after the New Deal. By the 1950s, Republicans, looking to break up the Roosevelt coalition by exacerbating cultural, racial, and religious wedges in the Democrat Party, turned much of their attention to Southern whites (Leege et al. 2002). Part of this effort has been Republican office holders' concertedness in resisting culturally progressive positions on issues like abortion and gay rights (Oldmixon 2005; Oldmixon and Calfano 2007).

To show policy responsiveness and gain acceptance by targeted constituencies, Republican political candidates eventually adopted what Calfano and Djupe (2009, 2013) called "God Talk" and included the deliberate use of coded religious appeals by politicians to serve as group identity appeals devised to go undetected by outgroup audiences (see also Domke and Coe 2008; Albertson 2011). Yet with Trump's communicative penchant for avoiding subtlety, the God Talk strategy appears in tatters, at least for Republican and conservative candidates. Instead, the door might be open for Democrats and progressives, who have long struggled to find an effective way to signal religious credentials, to find a way to leverage coded appeals for their electoral purposes. The stakes for success are high given the polarized responses stemming from religious appeals received by non-religious audiences (Adkins et al. 2013) and the extent to which the public stereotypes politicians based on the candidate's faith (real or perceived) (McDermott 2009; Hollander 2010).

Regardless of who is doing the religious communicating and with what content, the state of the literature suggests religious communication often comes from "above" (hence the "up in the air" reference in the next section), at least in terms of elite-based messages as provided through media. Therefore, the volume's first three empirical chapters extend consideration of communication from above by focusing on religious media and elite influence through three complementary studies that draw on experimental designs to assess how subjects respond to elite-based cues referencing the treatment of outgroups.

Up in the Air: Religious Communication via Media and Elites

The volume is loosely organized into three sections. The first section moves beyond the basic question of elite cue influence to assess how audiences perceive elites when the cues offered do not align with conventional expectations. Since religiously oriented communication has a prophetic tradition in America (see, e.g., Chappell 2004), it makes sense to assess the boundaries of what elites can say to audiences and still maintain their credibility. As such, the first three empirical chapters help to gauge reaction to elite statements that variably position religious elites' support of (or opposition to) scrutinized social groups or, in one case, an elite who is revealed to be a member of a scrutinized group. The three cases feature a mixture of religious and secular elites, but none serve as clergy in charge of local religious organizations.

Chapter 2, coauthored by Brian Calfano and Salvatore James Russo, assesses whether religious programming with a tangential political focus can shape viewers' political opinions. Calfano and Russo hypothesize that religious programming—and, more specifically, the elites featured in it—influences television viewers' feelings toward social and political outgroups. They test this hypothesis using both cross-sectional data assembled by General Social Surveys and two original experimental designs focusing on Pat Robertson's influence as host of *The 700 Club*. The authors demonstrate that increased viewing of religious television programs is significantly correlated with increased antipathy toward the LGBTQ community and that exposure to religious programming directly encourages lowered support for LGBTQ persons and gay marriage. Furthermore, the authors show that how elites explain their views of outgroup rights in society impacts those inclined to view religious programming in ways that conventional wisdom would not expect—by encouraging subjects to have more positive views of LGBTQ persons and gay marriage.

Chapter 3 builds on the insights from chapter 2 by focusing on the question of plausibility among religious and nonreligious elites when pushing the boundaries of how far a candidate might go in offering a new take on an existing political issue. The treatment is in the form of conciliatory language toward an ethnic group (Persians) in Iran whose religious and national identities the American public often assumes are a national security threat. Here, Calfano joins with Alexis Straka to leverage a 2019 survey experiment to determine how a subject pool of 880 adults responded to media-based claims attributed to a politician about Iranians as Persians *not* being a historic threat to the US and its interests. The experiment is based on language used in 2012 by then Republican presidential candidate Rick Santorum on the campaign trail when he made conciliatory remarks about Persians in Iran. Results show that respondents (including evangelicals) are willing to move in the candidate's articulated policy direction, even as the candidate refers to religious behavior in offering a reason for his view. This chapter offers some of the volume's clearest evidence that communication exposure effects are not necessarily as conventional wisdom assumes.

Calfano joins with Nazita Lajevardi and Melissa Michelson in chapter 4 to explore how media-based claims from political elites may, again, affect audience perceptions. Here, the elite is a local civic leader who is mentioned in a local news report as leading an organization that sponsors deliberative forums where residents can meet to discuss political candidates and policy. But this elite does not carry with him the usual credentials of a leader. In the experiment, he is variably described as an Arab, a Muslim, or an Arab Muslim. The idea, similar to the plausibility statement aspect of the Santorum experiment in chapter 3, is to see whether audiences—in this case, a subject pool of 1,500 Americans—respond positively to the civic leader (whose actions endorse a typical democratic norm—deliberation about candidates in advance of an election) when said leader also has the attributes of scrutinized outgroups. And, beyond the question of how audiences perceive the elite's signaling the importance of democratic deliberation, the authors are interested in the larger theoretical question of whether the public transfers any positive feelings about the elite to the larger identity group that he is associated with. The authors find that the public is willing to view the local civic leader somewhat positively but that these impressions are less likely to improve public perceptions of the identity groups with which he is associated (a finding that is pronounced when it comes to Muslims versus the other identity points).

Group Communication: Bounded Identity

In addition to religious communication from "above" through the media by elites with varying messages and personal characteristics, horizontally based communication within groups is also important to consider. Chapter 5 shifts the volume's focus to a more systems- or group-based perspective, while taking a comparative politics diversion into examining Muslim treatment by US and Indian societies. Here, Laura Dudley Jenkins and Rina Verma Williams find that comparing India and the US demonstrates that, despite starkly different demographic realities, Muslims and Islam are imagined, communicated about, and delegitimized in two of the world's largest secular democracies through a vilification of Islamic law and, therefore, Islamic identity itself. The chapter begins with a review of literature on Islamophobic communicative discourses and then explains how discourse and visual analyses allow us to interpret and compare these xenophobic narratives. The recent rise of anti-Muslim narratives in the US echoes the same increase that scholars of Indian politics have been observing in India for several decades.

The authors begin with demographic and legal overviews of Muslims and Islamic law in India and the US. They next introduce three common themes in the vilification of Muslim minorities via public discourses about Islamic law. Although each theme appears in both countries, their emphases vary. The first theme (gender threat) is prominent in both cases; the second (demographic threat) is more pronounced in India; the third (violent threat) is more prevalent in the US. Jenkins and Williams suggest that neither different demographics nor broader contextual similarities of secularism and democracy may protect Muslim minorities from the tactic of attacking Islamic law to "otherize" Muslims and Islam itself. The authors conclude with calls for further research to understand this tactic's impact on group-level attitudes and to trace the influence of transnational Islamophobic networks and organizations.

Part of the mechanism at work in chapter 5 is the attempted enforcement of group identity boundaries. For religious persons, these group boundaries have partially formed along denominational lines. While this volume does not leverage the religious tradition framework (see Steensland et al. 2000) to evaluate communication effects, denominational influence itself cannot be excluded. In chapter 6, Michael W. Wagner and Amanda Friesen extend insights into denominational identity by assessing its effect on political attitudes. Their focus is important because after the behavioral revolution in political science, the dominant explanation for how Americans approached faith and politics rested on denominational identity. The most obvious example is when the New Deal coalition's Roman Catholic contingent did ecclesiastical and political battle with Republican mainline Protestants for much of the twentieth century. However, more recent explanations about the comingling of faith and politics begin with exhortations about preferences on "culture war" issues (Hunter 1991) and generally end with the sorting of American Christians into categories like religious traditionalist and religious modernist (Layman 2001). The latter perspective, while the dominant one in current politics and religion research, is not without its critics (Djupe and Gilbert 2003; Leege et al. 2002; Friesen and Wagner 2012; McTague and Layman 2009).

Wagner and Friesen argue that one's perceived place in a religious denomination continues to play a crucial, independent role in the shaping of political attitudes. The authors show how one's self-reported sense of feeling like a prototypical member of a denomination is connected to political attitudes. Large-scale, replicated survey measures are certainly important contributions to this line of inquiry, but the authors' data are drawn from interacting with people of faith in their local networks to shed light on what it means for individuals to "belong." Wagner and Friesen leverage a series of focus group conversations conducted in eight adult Sunday school classes (across seven Christian denominations) in three large American cities. The authors captured how group communication in a religious setting impacts a sense of denominational identity. Results suggest that to comprehensively understand the ways in which Americans view the relationship between religion and politics, it is necessary to understand who thinks of themselves as prototypical members of their faith and what they think as a typical denomination member.

Of course, a denomination-based approach is not the only way to measure group identity, which brings up the question of how groups come to use certain terms to communicate their sense of collectiveness. Religion and politics scholars have long wrestled with measurement approaches to accurately capture individual identity and affiliation with religious movements, particularly related to terminology (see C. Smith 1998; Alwin et al. 2006; Smidt, Kellstedt, and Guth 2009). And, as Ryan Burge argues in chapter 7, the identity term "evangelical" may be the most controversial and consequential one.

"Evangelical" can be traced to the writings of the early Christian Church and through Martin Luther's ninety-five theses. It denoted committed followers of Jesus Christ who consistently endeavored to try to evangelize (i.e., convert) others to Christianity (Eskridge 2012). Evangelicalism picked up speed in the US through the Second Great Awakening and was transmitted to the masses through Jonathan Edwards and John Wesley (Noll 2010). Beginning in the 1950s, the term took on a new life with Billy Graham and his famous altar calls (Whalin 2014). Despite *Time* magazine's declaration of 1976 as "The Year of the Evangelical," no one was certain what that actually meant (*Time* 1976). Even Graham himself struggled with how to define the identity label. In a 1987 interview, he was asked, "What is an evangelical?" Graham's response perfectly encapsulates the confusion around the term: "That's a question I'd like to ask somebody, too" (Mattingly 2013).

Scholars have puzzled over this problem of religious identity for decades. Initial approaches divided Protestants up by geography (Stouffer 1955) or sorted all Christians into fundamentalist, moderate, or liberal camps (T. Smith 1990). More recent scholarship utilized a typology relying on church affiliation to sort individuals into religious traditions (Steensland et al. 2000). This process received wide use in the social science literature, although there have been several recent attempts to refine or extend it (Stetzer and Burge 2016; Burge and Lewis 2018). In addition, evangelical groups have tried to define the identity label themselves. For instance, Lifeway Research uses a series of four statements it considers to constitute the necessary components of evangelical belief (Smietana 2015; "What Is an Evangelical?" 2017). In some ways academics and evangelicals are competing to define evangelical identity.

There is a strong possibility that a disconnect exists between the way that the academic community talks about evangelicals and the way that the average person understands the term. Fortunately, the rise of social media gives observers of American religion an unprecedented look at how the internet talks about evangelicals. To that end, Burge scraped Twitter on four different occasions over the last eighteen months to collect tweets that contain the word "evangelical." He uses chapter 7 to analyze these tweets and to explore a series of questions. First, is the term "evangelical" more of a religious description or a political one? Second, who is driving the conversation about evangelicals online: evangelicals themselves or their critics? Finally, how has the tone of the discussion around evangelicals shifted as a result of Donald Trump's presidency? This chapter offers insights into how social media communicates about one of the most contentious group identity terms in twenty-first century politics.

Communication by Religious Organization Elites

This volume's third section returns to a focus on religious elites but situates them in the context of religious organizations—thereby combining elements of the vertical and horizontal foci from the previous sections. In terms of organizations carrying the banner for religious concerns about public policy, interest groups are a key example of communication nodes and elite-led vehicles for political change. The work of religious interest groups has come far since the efforts to repeal prohibition (Szymanski 2003). Today, these religious organizations operate in sophisticated ways to address policy and cultural grievances (Conger 2009). They function against the backdrop of competing theories of interest group influence and formation (see Truman 1951; Dahl 1961; Salisbury 1969). The new direction of interest here is one not of group formation or member motivation to support group interests (e.g., Olson 1965) but of the communication strategies that group elites leverage to make public appeals drawing on religious symbolism and activity.

In chapter 8, Kimberly H. Conger and J. Tobin Grant examine how the supernatural reality created by religion carries over into politics. The authors focus on one part of religion—prayer. Prayer is the quintessential religious act. Religions differ in their ontologies and teleologies of prayer, but few (if any) religions exist that do not include prayer. It is through prayer that humans communicate with the supernatural (Stark and Finke 2000; Giordan and Swatos 2011). In America, a majority of adults pray. In the 2014 General Social Survey, 58 percent of Americans said they pray every day; another 16 percent pray at least once a week. Prayer is ubiquitous in American religion.

Prayer is the most common religious act, but it is also a part of religion that remains understudied in social science (Giordan 2011). In political science, prayer is rarely included in studies of religion and politics. When it is included, it is treated as a distinctly religious act that may impact political behavior. Loveland et al. (2005), for example, find that those who pray are more likely to join some types of organizations but are not more likely to join political groups. In many studies of prayer and politics, the frequency of prayer is viewed as a proxy for private religious devotion (vis-à-vis communal acts such as attending a worship service). There is nothing wrong with this approach, but it ignores the meaning of prayer in the lives of those who practice it (Ammerman 2014; Paloma and Pendleton 1991). For those who pray, there is the belief that prayer "works." The 2007 Pew Religious Landscape Survey found that 90 percent of adults who pray say they have received a "definite answer to a specific prayer request." Prayer is viewed as an efficacious way to bring about results, change events, and shape the future.

Because many religious firms are not active in politics and often see involvement in the political process as distracting (at best) and corrupt (at worst), political groups can use prayer to put a gilded edge on otherwise seemly politics. By communicating the framing of action in terms of prayer, political actors are able to make political goals more tolerable; that is, it helps put a political goal in terms acceptable to a religious audience. Sharp (2013) finds that elites may use public references to prayer for several reasons. One is to justify actions that would otherwise be viewed negatively. A second is to demonstrate yearning, to show the importance of an issue. When a group calls on supporters to pray, they focus attention on an issue as a religious cause (even if the goal is political). Finally, prayer can show concern and compassion for others. A political group can demonstrate compassion by asking for prayer, for example, for victims of a natural disaster, when the group will not provide other assistance. In these ways, prayer advantages religious interest groups even if the actual prayers are ineffective.

Arguably, the most influential organization-based religious elites are clergy. As such, the volume's third section also includes a focus on clergy. Clergy communication efforts are critical for various religious and political reasons, not the least of which is the possibility that what clergy say about politics is less important in the overall context of political communication, including what believers might hear in their houses of worship. This is because of the degree to which partisanship may reinforce the long decline of religion in American public life. In chapter 9, Jason Adkins considers the effectiveness of religious elite cues attributed to leaders operating in decidedly religious contexts (a combination missing in chapters 2, 3, and 4).

Adkins focuses specifically on elite cue effects among those who identify as part of the Church of Jesus Christ of Latter-Day Saints (LDS) or the Roman Catholic Church. In following Campbell, Green, and Monson's (2014) Peculiar People Survey of Mormon political attitudes, Adkins designed an original survey experiment to test political cue effects from Catholic and LDS leaders on political attitudes. The LDS Church is heavily centralized. The First Presidency and the Quorum of Twelve Apostles make most financial and leadership decisions. All financial contributions collected in individual congregations are sent to LDS Church headquarters in Salt Lake City, Utah. The Catholic Church is decentralized compared to the LDS Church, as Catholic bishops have a large degree of authority over individual parishes, while the Vatican generally does not involve itself in administrative matters at the diocese level.

The survey included a series of questions about various issues. Issue selection corresponded with recent statements by religious elites within the Catholic Church and LDS Church. LDS respondents received questions about their attitudes toward marijuana legalization, religious freedom for business owners in accommodating LGBT customers, and refugee admission into the US based on religion. Catholic respondents fielded questions on climate change, immigration, and transgender bathrooms. In addition, two treatment groups were randomly assigned to receive political cues attributed to the church in which the respondent indicated membership.

Respondents in the first treatment group (i.e., coded treatment) received a statement from religious leaders outlining their church's principles on a given issue, without providing a clear yes-or-no stance. Respondents in the second treatment group (i.e., explicit treatment) received a statement from religious leaders from that church with a specific political cue on an issue. These explicit cues represented a more direct cue than those that the coded treatment group received. Results from the survey experiment indicate that political cues from religious elites offer a mixed bag in terms of effectiveness. For Catholic respondents, treatment exposure leads to a higher probability of indicating that climate change exists and is caused by humans. But, for LDS political cues, the effects are not particularly effective. Treatment effects are not statistically significant for the models with controls addressing attitudes toward marijuana legalization, refugee admission in the US, and religious freedom for those who identify as LDS Church members.

The variability in elite cue effects that Adkins finds is expounded on by Paul A. Djupe's analysis in chapter 10. There, Djupe documents just what religious audiences hear and the extent to which this hearing occurs. Drawing on several survey datasets from national samples in the last several years (in addition to clergy survey data from clergy), Djupe documents what religious Americans hear on a range of political issues and candidates and how those reports concentrate across partisan and religious categories. He focuses attention on immigration, drawing on detailed reporting from clergy of what specific arguments they agreed with and advanced in public.

Djupe suspects that while most have heard about some issues from their clergy, the address of issues is too idiosyncratic and too nuanced to make a meaningful difference in a raucous marketplace of elite communication.

Finally, chapter 11 concludes the volume with an overview of the insights provided by the previous chapters according to the vertical, horizontal, and combined emphases featured in each section. It recommends additional insights and research possibilities in the study of religious communication in the relevant social science literature.

REFERENCES

Adkins, Todd, Geoffrey C. Layman, David E. Campbell, John C. Green. 2013. "Religious Group Cues and Citizen Policy Attitudes in the United States." *Politics and Religion* 6:235–63.

Albertson, Bethany L. 2011. "Religious Appeals and Implicit Attitudes." *Political Psychology* 32:109–30.

Alwin, Duane F., Jacob L. Felson, Edward T. Walker, and Paula A. Tufis. 2006. "Measuring Religious Identities in Surveys." *Public Opinion Quarterly* 70:530–64.

Ammerman, Nancy T. 2014. "Finding Religion in Everyday Life." *Sociology of Religion* 75:189–207.

Arens, Edmund. 2011. "Religion as Communication." In *The Social Psychology of Communication*, edited by Derek Hook, Bradley Franks, and Martin W. Bauer, 249–65. New York: Palgrave Macmillan.

Be'ery, Gilad, and Pazit Ben-Nun Bloom. 2015. "God and the Welfare State: Substitutes or Complements? An Experimental Test of the Effect of Belief in God's Control." *PLoS ONE* 10:6.

Bellah, Robert N., Richard Madsen, William M. Sullivan, Ann Swidler, and Steven M. Tipton. 1985. *Habits of the Heart: Individualism and Commitment in American Life*. Berkeley: University of California Press.

Berger, Peter L. 1967. *The Sacred Canopy: Elements of a Sociological Theory of Religion*. New York: Doubleday.

Burge, Ryan P., and Andrew R. Lewis. 2018. "Measuring Evangelicals: Practical Considerations for Social Scientists." *Politics and Religion*, May, 1–15.

Butler, John, Grant Wacker, and Randall Balmer. 2007. *Religion in American Life: A Short History*. New York: Oxford University Press.

Calfano, Brian Robert. 2010. "The Power of Brand: Beyond Interest Group Influence in US State Abortion Politics." *State Politics and Policy Quarterly* 10:227–47.

Calfano, Brian. 2014. "Religion and Political Parties: Mediation in the Mass Party Era." In *Mediating Religion and Government*, edited by Kevin R. den Dulk and Elizabeth A. Oldmixon, 59–82. New York: Palgrave.

Calfano, Brian R., and Paul A. Djupe. 2009. "God Talk: Religious Cues and Electoral Support." *Political Research Quarterly* 62:329–39.

Calfano, Brian R., Melissa R. Michelson, and Elizabeth A. Oldmixon. 2017. *A Matter of Discretion: The Politics of Catholic Priests in the United States and Ireland*. Lanham, MD: Rowman and Littlefield.

Calhoun-Brown, Allyson. 1996. "African American Churches and Political Mobilization: The Psychological Impact of Organizational Resources." *Journal of Politics* 58:935–53.

Chapp, Christopher B. 2012. *Religious Rhetoric and American Politics: The Endurance of Civil Religion in Electoral Campaigns.* New York: Cornell University Press.

Chappell, David L. 2004. *A Stone of Hope: Prophetic Religion and the Death of Jim Crow.* Chapel Hill: University of North Carolina Press.

Claassen, Ryan L., and Paul A. Djupe. 2018. "What If . . . ? Evangelicals and the Future of American Politics. In *The Evangelical Crackup? The Future of the Evangelical-Republican Coalition,* edited by Paul A. Djupe and Ryan L. Claassen, 273–78. Philadelphia: Temple University Press.

Clardy, Brian K. 2011. "Deconstructing a Theology of Defiance: Black Preaching and the Politics of Racial Identity." *Journal of Church and State* 53:203–21.

Conger, Kimberly H. 2009. *The Christian Right in Republican State Politics.* New York: Palgrave.

Dahl, Robert A. 1961. *Who Governs?* New Haven: Yale University Press.

Denton, Robert E., Jr. 2005. "Religion, Evangelicals, and Moral Issues in the 2004 Presidential Campaign." In *The 2004 Presidential Campaign: A Communication Perspective,* edited by Robert F. Denton, 255–82. Lanham, MD: Rowman and Littlefield.

Djupe, Paul A. 2015. *Religion and Political Tolerance in America: Advances in the State of the Art.* Philadelphia: Temple University Press.

Djupe, Paul A., and Brian R. Calfano. 2013. *God Talk: Experimenting with the Religious Causes of Public Opinion.* Philadelphia: Temple University Press.

Djupe, Paul A., and Brian R. Calfano. 2019. "Communicating Dynamics in Religion and Politics." In *Oxford Encyclopedia of Politics and Religion,* edited by Paul Djupe, Mark Rozell, and Ted Jelen, 1–30. New York: Oxford University Press.

Djupe, Paul A., and Ryan L. Claussen. 2018. *The Evangelical Crackup? The Future of the Evangelical-Republican Coalition.* Philadelphia: Temple University Press.

Djupe, Paul A., and Kimberly H. Conger. 2012. "The Population Ecology of Grassroots Democracy: Christian Right Interest Populations and Citizen Participation in American States." *Political Research Quarterly* 65:924–37.

Djupe, Paul A., and Christopher P. Gilbert. 2003. *The Prophetic Pulpit: Clergy, Churches, and Communities in American Politics.* Lanham, MD: Rowman and Littlefield.

Djupe, Paul A., and Christopher P. Gilbert. 2006. "The Resourceful Believer: Generating Civic Skills in Church. *Journal of Politics* 68:116–27.

Djupe, Paul A., and Christopher P. Gilbert. 2009. *The Political Influence of Churches.* New York: Cambridge University Press.

Djupe, Paul A., and Anand E. Sokhey. 2003. "American Rabbis in the 2000 Election." *Journal for the Scientific Study of Religion* 42:563–76.

Djupe, Paul A., Anand E. Sokhey, and Christopher P. Gilbert. 2007. "Present but Not Accounted For? Gender Differences in Civic Resource Acquisition." *American Journal of Political Science* 51:906–20.

Domke, David, and Kevin Coe. 2008. *The God Strategy: How Religion Became a Political Weapon in America.* New York: Oxford University Press.

Douglas, Mary, and Aaron Wildavsky. 1982. *Risk and Culture: An Essay on the Selection of Technical and Environmental Dangers.* Berkeley: University of California Press.

Durkheim, Émile. 1915. *The Elementary Forms of Religious Life.* London: George Allen and Urwin.

Easton, David. 1953. *The Political System: An Inquiry into the State of Political Science.* New York: Knopf.

Eskridge, Larry. 2012. "Defining Evangelicalism | Wheaton." Wheaton College website. http://www.wheaton.edu/isae/defining-evangelicalism

Finke, Roger, and Rodney Stark. 2005. *The Churching of America, 1776–2005: Winners and Losers in Our Religious Economy.* New Brunswick, NJ: Rutgers University Press.

Friesen, Amanda, and Michael W. Wagner. 2012. "Beyond the 'Three Bs': How American Christians Approach Faith and Politics." *Politics and Religion* 5:791–818.

Geertz, Clifford. 1973. *The Interpretation of Cultures.* New York: Basic Books.

Gilbert, Christopher P. 1993. *The Impact of Churches on Political Behavior: An Empirical Study.* New York: Praeger.

Giordan, Giuseppe. 2011. "Toward a Sociology of Prayer." In *Religion, Spirituality, and Everyday Practice,* edited by Giuseppe Giordan and William H. Swatos, 33–44. New York: Springer.

Giordan, Giuseppe, and William H. Swatos. 2011. *Religion, Spirituality, and Everyday Practice.* New York: Springer.

Green, John C., James L. Guth, Corwin E. Smidt, and Lyman A. Kellstedt. 1996. *Religion and the Culture Wars: Dispatches from the Front.* Lanham, MD: Rowman and Littlefield.

Guth, James L., John C. Green, Corwin W. Smidt, Lyman A. Kellstedt, and Margaret M. Poloma. 1997. *The Bully Pulpit: The Politics of Protestant Clergy.* Lawrence: University Press of Kansas.

Guth, James, L., John C. Green, Lyman Kellstedt, and Corwin E. Smidt. 2005. "Faith and Foreign Policy: A View from the Pews." *Review of Faith and International Affairs* 3: 3–10.

Guth, James L., Lyman A. Kellstedt, Corwin E. Smidt, and John C. Green. 2006. "Religious Influence in the 2004 Presidential Election." *Presidential Studies Quarterly* 36:223–42.

Haider-Markel, Donald P., and Kenneth J. Meier. 1996. "The Politics of Gay and Lesbian Rights: Expanding the Scope of the Conflict." *Journal of Politics* 58:332–49.

Harris, Tina. 2012. *Religion and Communication: An Anthology of Extensions in Theory, Research, and Method.* New York: Peter Lang.

Hollander, Barry A. 2010. "Persistence in the Perception of Barack Obama as a Muslim in the 2008 Presidential Campaign." *Journal of Media and Religion* 9:55–66.

Hunter, James D. 1991. *Culture Wars: The Struggle to Define America.* New York: Basic Books.

Irwin, Douglas A., and Richard Sylla. 2011. *Founding Choices: American Economic Policy in the 1970s.* Chicago: University of Chicago Press.

Jamal, Amaney. 2005. "The Political Participation and Engagement of Muslim Americans." *American Politics Research* 33:521–44.

Jelen, Ted. 1993. "The Political Consequences of Religious Group Attitudes." *Journal of Politics* 55:178–90.

Jones, Robert P. 2016. *The End of White Christian America*. New York: Simon and Schuster.

Kaylor, Brian T. 2011. "Top 10 Over-the-Top Religious Quotes from Presidential Candidates." *Huffpost*, May 25.

Kerr, Peter A., and Patricia Moy. 2002. "Newspaper Coverage of Fundamentalist Christians 1980–2000." *Journalism and Mass Communication Quarterly* 79:54–72.

Kleppner, Paul. 1970. *The Cross of Culture: A Social Analysis of Midwestern Politics, 1850–1900*. New York: Free Press.

Layman, Geoffrey. 2001. *The Great Divide: Religious and Cultural Conflict in American Party Politics*. New York: Columbia University Press.

Lazerwitz, Bernard, and Michael Harrison. 1979. "American Jewish Denominations: A Social and Religious Profile." *American Sociological Review* 44:656–66.

Leege, David C. 1993. "Religion and Politics in Theoretical Perspective." In *Rediscovering the Religion Factor in American Politics*, edited by David C. Leege and Lyman A. Kellstedt, 3–25. Armonk, NY: ME Sharpe.

Leege, David C., and Lyman A. Kellstedt. 1993. *Rediscovering the Religious Factor in American Politics*. Armonk, NY: ME Sharpe.

Leege, David C., Kenneth D. Wald, Brian S. Krueger, and Paul D. Mueller. 2002. *The Politics of Cultural Differences: Social Change and Voter Mobilization Strategies in the Post-New Deal Period*. Princeton: Princeton University Press.

Lewis, Andrew R. 2017. *The Rights Turn in Conservative Christian Politics: How Abortion Transformed the Culture Wars*. New York: Cambridge University Press.

Loveland, Matthew T., David Sikkink, Daniel J. Myers, and Benjamin Radcliff. 2005. "Private Prayer and Civic Involvement." *Journal for the Scientific Study of Religion* 44:1–14.

Luhmann, Niklas. 2013. *A Systems Theory of Religion*. Translated by David A. Brenner with Adrian Hermann. Stanford: Stanford University Press.

Margolis, Michele F. 2018. *From Politics to the Pews: How Partisanship and the Political Environment Shape Religious Identity*. Chicago: University of Chicago Press.

Maslow, Abraham. 1943. "A Theory of Human Motivation." *Psychological Review* 50:370–96.

Mattingly, Terry. 2013. "Defining Evangelical, or Not, in 2013." Uexpress, January 11. http://www.uexpress.com/on-religion/2013/1/11/defining-evangelical-or -not-in-2013

McDermott, Monika L. 2009. "Religious Stereotyping and Voter Support for Evangelical Candidates." *Political Research Quarterly* 62:340–54.

McTague, John Michael, and Geoffrey C. Layman. 2009. "Religion, Parties, and Voting Behavior." In *The Oxford Handbook of Religion and American Politics*, edited by Corwin E. Smidt, James Guth, and Lyman Kellstedt, 330–70. New York: Oxford University Press.

Meyer, Birgit, and Annelies Moors. 2005. *Religion, Media, and the Public Square*. Bloomington: Indiana University Press.

Muirhead, Russel, Nancy L. Rosenblum, Daniel Schlozman, and Francis X. Shen.

2006. "Religion in the 2004 Presidential Election." In *Divided States of America: The Slash and Burn Politics of the 2004 Presidential Election*, edited by Larry J. Sabato. New York: Pearson Longman.

Mutz, Diana C. 2006. *Hearing the Other Side: Deliberative versus Participatory Democracy*. New York: Cambridge University Press.

Neiheisel, Jacob R., Paul A. Djupe, and Anand E. Sokhey. 2009. "Veni, Vidi, Disseri: Churches and the Promise of Democratic Deliberation." *American Politics Research* 37:614–43.

Newman, Brian, and Mark Caleb Smith. 2007. "Fanning the Flames: Religious Media Consumption and American Politics." *American Politics Research* 35:846–77.

Noll, Mark A. 2010. *The Rise of Evangelicalism: The Age of Edwards, Whitefield and the Wesleys*. Westmont, IL: InterVarsity Academic.

Noll, Mark A., and Luke E. Harlow. 2007. *Religion and American Politics from the Colonial Period to the Present*. 2nd ed. New York: Oxford University Press.

Norris, Pippa. 2004. *Sacred and Secular: Religion and Politics Worldwide*. New York: Cambridge University Press.

Oldmixon, Elizabeth Anne. 2005. *Uncompromising Positions: God, Sex, and the U.S. House of Representatives*. Washington, DC: Georgetown University Press.

Oldmixon, Elizabeth A., and Brian R. Calfano. 2007. "The Religious Dynamics of Decision Making on Gay Rights in the U.S. House of Representatives." *Journal for the Scientific Study of Religion* 46:55–70.

Olson, Mancur. 1965. *The Logic of Collective Action*. Cambridge, MA: Harvard University Press.

Pace, Enzo. 2016. *Religion as Communication: God's Talk*. New York: Routledge.

Paloma, Margaret M., and Brian F. Pendleton. 1991. "The Effects of Prayer and Prayer Experiences on Measures of General Well-Being." *Journal of Psychology and Theology* 19:71–83.

Salisbury, Robert H. 1969. "An Exchange Theory of Interest Groups." *Midwest Journal of Political Science* 13:1–32.

Schaffer, Joby, Anand E. Sokhey, and Paul A. Djupe. 2015. "The Religious Economy of Political Tolerance." In *Religion and Political Tolerance in America: Advances in the State of the Art*, edited by Paul A. Djupe, 151–64. Philadelphia: Temple University Press.

Scheufele, Dietram A., Matthew C. Nisbet, and Dominique Brossard. 2003. "Pathways to Political Participation? Religion, Communication, and Mass Media." *International Journal of Public Opinion Research* 15:300–324.

Schultze, Quentin J. 2003. *Christianity and the Mass Media in America*. East Lansing: Michigan State University Press.

Sharp. Shane. 2013. "How to Do Things with Prayer Utterances." *Symbolic Interaction* 36:159–76.

Shortle, Allyson F., and Ronald Keith Gaddie. 2015. "Religious Nationalism and Perceptions of Muslims and Islam." *Politics and Religion* 8:435–57.

Smidt, Corwin E., Lyman A. Kellstedt, and James L. Guth. 2009. *The Oxford Handbook of Religion and American Politics*. New York: Oxford University Press.

Smietana, Bob. 2015. "What Is an Evangelical? Four Questions Offer New Definition." ChristianityToday.com, November 19. http://www.christianitytoday.com

/gleanings/2015/november/what-is-evangelical-new-definition-nae-lifeway-re
search.html

Smith, Corwin. 1998. *American Evangelicalism: Embattled and Thriving.* Chicago:
University of Chicago Press.

Smith, Tom W. 1990. "Classifying Protestant Denominations." *Review of Religious
Research* 31:225–45.

Stark, Rodney, and Roger Finke. 2000. *Acts of Faith: Explaining the Human Side of
Religion.* Berkeley: University of California Press.

Stark, Rodney, and Charles Glock. 1968. *American Piety: The Nature of Religious
Commitment.* Berkeley: University of California Press.

Steensland, Brian, Jerry Z. Park, Mark D. Regnerus, Lynn D. Robinson, W. Bradford Wilcox, and Robert D. Woodberry. 2000. "The Measure of American Religion: Toward Improving the State of the Art." *Social Forces* 79:291–318.

Stetzer, Ed, and Ryan P. Burge. 2016. "Reltrad Coding Problems and a New Repository." *Politics and Religion* 9:187–90.

Stouffer, Samuel A. 1955. *Communism, Conformity, and Civil Liberties: A Cross-Section
of the Nation Speaks Its Mind.* Garden City, NY: Doubleday.

Stout, Daniel. 2006. *Encyclopedia of Religion, Culture, and Media.* New York: Routledge.

Swatos, William H., Jr., and Kevin J. Christiano. 1999. "Secularization: The Course
of a Concept." *Sociology of Religion* 60:209–28.

Szymanski, Ann-Marie. 2003. *Pathways to Prohibition.* Durham: Duke University
Press.

Truman, David B. 1951. *The Governmental Process.* New York: Knopf.

Time. 1976. "Religion: Counting Souls." Time.com, October 4. Accessed June 30,
2018. http://content.time.com/time/magazine/article/0,9171,918414,00.html

Verba, Sidney, Kay Lehman Schlozman, and Henry E. Brady. 1995. *Voice and Equality: Civic Volunteerism in American Politics.* Cambridge, MA: Harvard University
Press.

Wald, Kenneth D., Dennis E. Owen, and Samuel S. Hill. 1988. "Churches as Political Communities." *American Political Science Review* 82:531–48.

Weber, Max. 1930. *The Protestant Ethic and the Spirit of Capitalism.* New York: Routledge.

Weilhouwer, Peter W. 2000. "Releasing the Fetters: Parties and the Mobilization of
the African-American Electorate." *Journal of Politics* 62:206–22.

Whalin, W. Terry. 2014. *Billy Graham: A Biography of America's Greatest Evangelist.*
Garden City, NY: Morgan James Faith.

"What Is an Evangelical?" 2017. National Association of Evangelicals. Accessed
March 14, 2017. https://www.nae.net/what-is-an-evangelical/

Wilcox, Clyde, and Lee Sigelman. 2001. "Political Mobilization in the Pews: Religious Contacting and Electoral Turnout." *Social Science Quarterly* 82:524–35.

Wills, Gary. 1990. *Under God: Religion in American Politics.* New York: Simon and
Schuster.

TWO

Don't Join the Club?

Religious Television and Elite Influence
Bounds on Perceptions of LGBTQ Issues

Brian Calfano and Salvatore James Russo

Elite communication is effective in shaping audience political perceptions, although this influence is not absolute and may be issue specific (Yin 1999; Watts et al. 1999; Paul and Brown 2001; Druckman 2001). Other things being equal, pairing an elite with a media program should enhance the elite's potential to influence audience perceptions, particularly when the program contains a news-oriented product. In the post-broadcast era, political news comes in disparate forms from varying sources. Some sources may present political viewpoints as news by using a "hard news" format, but these sources have strong ideological agendas to advance with less interest in conforming to standard journalistic practices or formats. With the increased narrowcasting in television network programming (Lotz 2007; Chen and Suen 2008; Perren 2011), our focus here is on the political effect that the elite-based agenda advances within a specific niche of the television news landscape: religious programming featuring ideological views presented in a "hard news" and commentary format.

We use this chapter to investigate four questions. First, does the expectation of audience self-selection of media sources—which is well established for other media platforms (see Groseclose and Milo 2005)—hold for religious television? Second, what effect does religious television exposure have on viewers' perceptions of outgroups targeted for negative coverage? Third, is audience reaction to religious television merely a matter of partisanship (e.g., Republicans are more likely to watch and, therefore, viewer effects may be more appropriately attributed to party identity)? Fourth, can elite-based cues attributed to religious television programs shape viewer opinion differently from the elite's stated agenda?

Drawing on General Social Survey (GSS) data, we confirm the expectation that audiences self-select into religious television programming exposure. We also find confirmatory evidence regarding the second question; exposure to religious television news and commentary statistically impacts how viewers feel toward certain outgroups (which are often criticized during these programs). Interestingly, there is no support for the notion in the third question that religious television audiences are simply motivated by partisanship; religious television has an independent impact. Given the drawbacks with using cross-sectional data to measure media effects (see Behr and Iyengar 1985; Iyengar, Peters, and Kinder 1982; Ladd 2009), we follow up the GSS data analysis with findings from a randomized experiment that confirms the effects from these observational data. We touch on the fourth question again below.

The experimental results show that exposure to religious television content increases antipathy toward the outgroups that the programs target. In this case, watching a clip of *The 700 Club* regarding the then upcoming vote on California's Proposition 8 increases antipathy toward LGBTQ persons while lowering support for same-sex marriage. These findings bolster our argument that the feelings religious program viewers have about outgroups are not simply due to audience self-selection. Rather, religious news and information programs (a category that aptly describes *The 700 Club*) shape viewer opinion on social issues and about identity outgroups through program content. These outcomes help to explain the continuing political impact of religious media on audiences, even if many of these viewers find themselves in increasing isolation by resisting social and cultural changes (see Jones 2016).

That the religious television treatment shows an effect outside of self-selection, while interesting, also draws attention to our fourth question about the nature of elite-based influence in religious programming. Namely, and assuming religious media elites (like *700 Club* host Pat Robertson) motivate audience members to tune in, does offering information about how an elite arrives at the characterization of an outgroup impact regular viewers? Here, our focus is on expanding the elite effect from our first experiment to investigate elite plausibility boundaries in providing cues that are somewhat different from what the elite (Robertson in this case) is known for. In so doing, we build on Djupe and Calfano's (2013) finding that the revelation of elite process cues can move public opinion in unexpected directions. Results of the second experiment show that exposure to the decision process attributed to Robertson moves subject opinion toward more favorable outgroup impressions (thereby answering our fourth research question in the affirmative).

Television Effects and Videomalaise

The importance of understanding religious television effects is that the programming can present social groups in an "us versus them" manner, often exposing certain outgroups to hostility and posing threats to social tolerance (Bruce 1990; Hughey 1990; Straub 1988). Though religious audiences presumably seek to satisfy some spiritual desire rather than feed a political information appetite (Gerbner et al. 1984), viewers may find their political attitudes and beliefs shaped even while they do not overtly seek political information from religious television.

Baum and Jamison (2006) argue that political content, when communicated through an "entertaining context," can be "piggybacked" (i.e., attached) to information intended primarily to entertain and thereby can be consumed incidentally (948). Here, we expand the theoretical notion of "entertainment" beyond its humorous and escapist dimensions in the nonreligious media because the television production techniques used in religious programs such as Robertson's *The 700 Club* mirror those of top-notch secular content. The goal of adhering to these production values is to capture the viewer's attention through attractive visual and aural stimuli, not unlike the basic premise behind more general entertainment strategies (see Thussu 2008). Leveraging entertainment production values enables religious programming to inform audience political attitudes, including when these programs use a news and commentary format.

Television news politically frames and primes stories for audience consumption (DellaVigna and Kaplan 2007). Similarly, religious programming, including long-running shows like *The 700 Club*, contain segments devoted to reporting and analyzing political events, thereby exposing audiences to secular news content under the guise of religious instruction and information. Religious television audiences in the US tend to be older, lower income, less educated, blue collar, and female. Viewers are also more likely to be church members, participate in other religious activities, be evangelical, and hold conservative political and social outlooks (Abelman 1987b; Litman and Bain 1989).

Most of these characteristics suggest that religious audiences may be particularly susceptible to a modified version of Zaller's (1992) model of opinion articulation, whereby audiences readily adopt religious communication messages of a political nature because they both trust the religious elite facilitating the broadcast and have fewer countervailing political arguments to access. In other words, those who consume religious television content do so because they have confidence in applying the elite's cues about social and political issues to attitude formation along an array of items (i.e., well beyond the religious realm).

Some might argue that the "otherworldly" focus in religious television programming could lead to a disinterest in politics outright (see Campbell 2006). But the electronic church, which includes television audiences for shows like *The 700 Club*, is often overtly political and not at all withdrawn or insular (Abelman and Neuendorf 1987; Hadden 1987). Issues of the day may be discussed in the context of sermons as examples of America's "sinfulness" or presented in formats like the evening news (Abelman 1987a; Straub 1988). In fact, religious television audiences may be particularly susceptible to having their political outlooks and behavior molded given that political messages on religious programming are more entertaining than the typical news broadcast. Indeed, Parkin (2010, 13) suggests that "the entertaining aspects of unconventional news sources can have a real impact on what people know about politics and how they make their decisions."

We hypothesize that exposure to religious programs containing political messages increases antipathy toward outgroups mentioned in those broadcasts. This expectation stems from an understanding of videomalaise theory and its progeny (Forgette and Morris 2006; Martin 2008; Mutz 2007; Mutz and Reeves 2005; Robinson 1976). "Videomalaise" expects that exposure to television news programming increases audience cynicism and negativity (see Mutz and Reeves 2005). We take this effect a step further and posit that videomalaise applies not only to traditional television news programs but to any television program communicating political commentary or policy views (including those from a religious perspective).

Since one of the notable features of religious broadcasting is the overt "us versus them" ridicule of outgroups—including LGBTQ and atheists (Bruce 1990; Hadden 1983; Heinz 1983; Hughey 1990; Petersen and Donnenwerth 1998; Straub 1988)—we expect that exposure to messages contained in religious news stimuli will lead to antipathy (if not outright hostility) toward outgroups cast as "sinful" by religious programming. But we also anticipate that exposure to the religious news programming messages will not lead to a corresponding increase in warm feelings toward implied ingroups. This is, in part, because prior studies show that exposure to negative stimuli elicits greater audience arousal than the reception of pleasant or consonant messages aligning with audience preferences (Hutchinson and Bradley 2009).

As such, we expect that viewing programs targeting specific outgroups will cause audiences to feel negatively toward these outgroups without any corresponding positive ingroup effect (Meffert et al. 2006; Mutz 2007). And, despite the legalization of gay marriage in 2015, as Rogers (2020) explains, over one hundred anti-LGBT pieces of legislation were proposed in that same year alone. Rogers also argues that only by understanding the factors that go into making one opposed to equal rights for homosexuals can one hope to effectively advocate for equality.

Audience Self-Selection and Outgroup Impressions

The GSS question pertaining to watching religious television—"About how much time per week, in hours and minutes, do you normally spend watching religious shows on television?"—was asked in 1988–91 and again in 1998 (generating a total of 5,813 responses). These were the two panels in which respondents were asked how much time per week, in hours and minutes, they normally spent watching religious television shows. In addition to standard demographic and partisanship controls, we follow Olson and Warber (2008) and Layman (1997) in measuring respondent "religiosity" using biblical literalism and frequency of prayer questions. The controls include where a respondent lived, measured as a 10-point ordinal variable ranging from a metropolitan area/large city of over 250,000 (1) to "open country within a larger civil division, e.g., township division" (10). Sex was coded "0" for males and "1" for females. Income is a 12-point ordinal variable, with "1" representing the lowest end and "12" the highest GSS income bracket.

The outcome variable in each of the three models measures respondents' views about homosexuals and is based on consistent findings that the LGBTQ community is a frequent foil for religious television hosts (Bruce 1990; Hadden 1983; Heinz 1983; Hughey 1990; Petersen and Donnenwerth 1998; Straub 1988). GSS respondents were asked whether homosexuals should be allowed to speak in their community (model 1), whether homosexuals should be able to teach a college course (model 2), and whether books supporting homosexuals should be banned from their local library (model 3).

These initial findings allow us to address the first research question about audience self-selection of religious television programs and a preliminary assessment of the second question on programming effects on outgroup impressions, although these measures are not specific to either Robertson or *The 700 Club*. As seen across the three models in table 2.1, increased viewership of religious media makes one more hostile toward LGBTQ individuals. Specifically, an increase in the amount of time respondents watch religious television per week increases the probability of saying that gays should not be allowed to speak in their community by 45 percent, holding all other variables at their means. Meanwhile, an increase in consuming religious television per week increases the probability of saying that gays should not be allowed to teach a college course by 47 percent, holding all other variables at their means. Finally, the GSS respondents watching more religious television per week show a 50 percent probability increase of agreeing with banning books favoring homosexuality, holding all other variables at their means. These results largely support the video-malaise hypotheses presented earlier.

Concerning our third research question on whether response to outgroups is merely a partisan reaction, notice that party effects were absent in these GSS models. Though the observational nature of these data pre-

TABLE 2.1. Religious Media Effects on Tolerance of LGBTQ (GSS)

	Speak in Community		Teach Course		Ban Books	
	Coef./SE	Marginal Effect	Coef./SE	Marginal Effect	Coef./SE	Marginal Effect
Watches religious TV	.24/.06**	.45	.24/.06**	.47	.25/.06**	.50
Income	−.11/.02**	.24	−.10/.02**	.26	−.06/.02**	.15
Sex	−.41/.13**	.06	−.52/.12**	.22	−.52/.12**	.11
Age	−.02/.004**	.18	.02/.003**	.03	.02/.003**	.03
Urban	.12/.02**	.19	.11/.02**	.22	.08/.02**	.16
Religiosity	.15/.02**	.24	.12/.02**	.24	.17 (.02)**	.34
Republican	.14/.15	.02	.10/.13	.02	.05/.13	.01
Democrat	.12/.15	.02	−.03/.14	.001	.19/.14	.04
African American	−.20/.21	.03	.11/.19	.02	.17/.18*	.03
Constant	−1.96/.43**		−1.35/.40**		−1.86/.04**	
Chi²/Prob	195.3/.000		214.8/.000		211.1/.000	
Pseudo R²	.12		.11		.11	
N	1,617		1,581		1,579	

Note: Binary logit models with two-tailed tests. * $p < .05$, ** $p < .01$. "Marginal effect" represents the change in probability moving from the independent variable's minimum to maximum value, holding all other variables at their means.

vents us from conducting more direct tests of partisan and religious overlap, we consider whether the frequent consumers of religious television
are strong supporters of several issues of historic interest to the GOP.
These include gun control (model 1), the death penalty (model 2), and
marijuana legalization (model 3). Affinity for each of these issues was used
as the dependent variable in a series of logit models, with controls for
partisanship, ideology, and sociodemographic criteria included, as well as
religious television viewership.

As seen in table 2.2, increased viewing of religious television has no
statistically significant relationship with views on the legalization of marijuana, gun control, or the death penalty. These null findings lend support for the assertion that consumers of religious television are not simply
Republicans with peculiar television viewing habits; rather, consumers of
religious broadcasts are a unique subset of the American populace.

But a problem in determining media effects from observational data
like the GSS is the potential of audience self-selection. For example, it
could be that religious Americans who particularly dislike LGBTQ people
are also the religious Americans who tune in to watch religious television
(Bruce 1990; Hughey 1990; Straub 1988). An experimental design helps
to alleviate these concerns through the random assignment of a treatment
stimuli, and experiments in both laboratory and field settings demonstrate
that media messages can change in political attitudes and behaviors (For-

TABLE 2.2. Religious Media Effects on View of GOP Platform (GSS)

	Gun Permits		Death Penalty		Pot Legalization	
	Coef./SE	Marginal Effect	Coef./SE	Marginal Effect	Coef./SE	Marginal Effect
Watches religious TV	.07/.06	.10	−.003/.06	.01	.08/.10	.09
Income	−.03/.03	.05	.02/.02	.04	.01/.03	.02
Sex	−.87/.13**	.14	−.16/.13	.02	.48/.19**	.08
Age	−.001/.004	.01	.01/.004	.07	.01/.01*	.14
Urban	.11/.02**	.17	.04/.02	.06	.09/.04*	.12
Religiosity	−.04/.02**	.06	−.06/.02*	.09	.19 (.03)**	.32
Republican	.19/.15	.03	.36/.14	.06	.39/.20	.07
Democrat	−.27/.15	.04	−.31/.14*	.05	−.23/.21	.04
African American	−.14/.22	.02	−.99/.17**	.20	−.22/.60	.04
Constant	−.03/.43	.19	1.2/.42**	.77	−1.77/.60**	.79
Chi^2/Prob	92.3/.000		95.4/.000		90.1/.000	
Pseudo R^2	.06		.06		.10	
N	1,583		1,495		783	

Note: Binary logit models with two-tailed tests. * $p < .05$, ** $p < .01$. "Marginal effect" represents the change in probability moving from the independent variable's minimum to maximum value, holding all other variables at their means.

gette and Morris 2006; Hayes 2008; Iyengar 1987; Iyengar 1991; Iyengar and Kinder 1987).

Religious Television Experiment

We recruited subjects for this experiment via the Amazon service Mechanical Turk (MTurk) between November 12 and November 22, 2012, with the survey hosted through Qualtrics. MTurk is frequently used in political science studies for its affordable provision of representative subject pools (Berinsky, Huber, and Lenz 2012; Buhrmester, Kwang, and Gosling 2011; Schaffner 2011, but see Mullinix et al. 2015 for a countervailing viewpoint). After all subjects received the same pretreatment series of questions, the subjects were randomly divided into three groups.

The first group received a three-minute clip from *The 700 Club* featuring Robertson discussing California's Proposition 8, a ballot measure/ state constitutional amendment voted on in November 2008. The measure stated, in the part relevant to this research, "Only marriage between a man and a woman is valid or recognized in California." The clip features a newscaster's report on Proposition 8 from the June 16, 2008, episode. Robertson's commentary was from the December 12, 2007, episode. The two clips were spliced to make the transition from the newscaster's commentary to Robertson's commentary seamless, appearing to be from the same segment. The newscast ends with the commentator saying, "Pat?," requesting Robertson's input on the segment.

The second group received a three-minute clip of satirical media—a clip from Comedy Central's *The Daily Show with Jon Stewart* featuring liberal comedian Stewart discussing Proposition 8. The segment, entitled "I Now Denounce You Chuck and Larry," originally aired on November 3, 2008. The control group was assigned a three-minute clip of NBC's Sacramento affiliate, KCRA, reporting on Proposition 8 on October 20, 2008.

The reason for choosing *The Daily Show* is because of Stewart's ubiquity as a liberal political voice during his tenure, serving as a counterbalance to the well-known social conservative Pat Robertson in the first group's treatment (Baumgartner and Morris 2006; Cao 2008; Fox, Koloen, and Sahin 2007; Hollander 2005; LaMarre, Landreville, and Beam 2009). Late-night comedy shows tend to devote significant time and attention to political commentary more generally, sparking interest of late within the political communication literature (Baumgartner and Morris 2006; Fox, Koloen, and Sahin 2007; LaMarre, Landreville, and Beam 2009; Landreville, Holbert, and LaMarre 2010; Moy, Xenos, and Hess 2005, 2006; Young 2004). Additionally, the incidental by-product model (Baum 2005; Baum and Jamison 2006) argues that late-night comedy and other forms of humorous television and "soft news" can inform otherwise disinterested viewers by "piggybacking" information in the context of entertainment.

Subject age ranges from eighteen to sixty-seven years old (the average age is forty-one). Their partisanship skews more Democratic than the general population of the United States, with 31 percent of subjects considering themselves to be Republican or leaning Republican, 9 percent considering themselves independent, and 60 percent Democratic or leaning Democratic. Partisanship (binary measures for subjects identifying as Republican or Democrat), age (an interval variable where respondents wrote in their age), and religiosity (an index variable using questions asking respondents about their church attendance and their belief in biblical literalism) were controls. After exposure to one of the three video clips, subjects were then given a brief post-screening questionnaire to gauge their opinions on gay marriage and the selected outgroups that were featured within the visual materials.

We hypothesize that subjects' exposure to *The 700 Club* clip increases antipathy toward outgroups targeted for derision versus subjects in the satirical program or control group. Taking stock of negativity bias, we also expect that treatment exposure will not lead to a corresponding increase in warm feelings toward the implied ingroups for either program (Cacioppo and Gardner 1999; Hutchinson and Bradley 2009). In a short, single-dose experimental setting, the power of strong, negative emotional arousal will be more pronounced than any response to positive stimuli. This leads us to expect that the Robertson clip increases negative feelings toward LGBTQ and gay marriage policies (while exposure to satirical media should have no statistical effects on feelings toward homosexuals or gay marriage policies).

A total of 134 respondents were randomly assigned to one of the three treatments: 46 to *The 700 Club*, 43 to the *Daily Show*, and 36 to the KCRA clip. Note that key studies in the literature have used experimental designs to measure media effects with sample sizes of less than 100: 85 respondents were used in Iyengar's 1987 article, and only 28 to 29 respondents were used in Iyengar, Peters, and Kinder's 1982 article. Experimental designs most like the one utilized in this article have used sample sizes of 135 (Forgette and Morris 2006), 101 and 133 (White 2007), and 157 (Hayes 2008).

As seen in table 2.3, the dependent variable measures feelings toward homosexuals using a 100-point feeling thermometer, where respondents were told to place the thermometer on a scale of "0" (lowest) to "100" (highest). Compared to those in the control group, subjects exposed to *The 700 Club* clip have statistically significantly lower opinions toward homosexuals. The difference in group means drops from 63 for subjects exposed to the KCRA control to approximately 46 for those viewing *The 700 Club* clip (a 17.4-point difference significant at $p < .01$). And, as seen in table 2.5, even when additional controls are added, exposure to *The 700 Club* results in significantly lower feelings toward homosexuals, with treatment exposure causing a 17.6-point reduction in the thermometer score ($p < .01$), controlling for partisan affiliation, age, and religiosity.

We also predicted that *The 700 Club* exposure decreases support for same-sex marriage, while *The Daily Show* does not impact support for the same. We measured this outcome as a binary variable, with support for gay marriage coded as "1" and opposition as "0." As seen in table 2.4, subjects viewing the clip of *The 700 Club* had a higher percentage of opposition to gay marriage than those seeing the local news clip as the control ($p < .05$). A logit model incorporating controls in table 2.4 shows that exposure to *The 700 Club* causes statistically significant movement toward opposition to gay marriage. Other important control variables, such as religiosity and age, were statistically significant and ran in the anticipated directions.

The *700 Club* treatment increases the likelihood that subjects oppose same-sex marriage by 28 percent, while subject religiosity increases the probability of opposition by 50 percent. Meanwhile, older subjects show a 40 percent increase in opposition (holding all other variables at their means in each case). By contrast, Democratic subjects show a 41 percent reduction in the likelihood of opposing same sex-marriage, holding all other variables at their means. Overall, these results support the notion that Robertson's role as a religious elite offering cues about outgroups through his media platform affects subject preferences on issues relevant to the outgroup.

TABLE 2.3. *700 Club* Effects on Opposition to Gay Marriage

	N	Opposed % (N)	Difference from Control	Z Score (p value)
700 Club	49	53% (26)	21.5	2.00 (.02)
KCRA News (Control)	38	32% (12)		
Daily Show	43	44% (19)	12.6	1.2 (.24)

Note: Subjects were asked about their feelings toward homosexuals on a 100-point feeling thermometer, wherein 0 was the lowest, or lowest level of fondness toward homosexuals, and 100 was the highest, or most warmth toward homosexuals.

Elite Process Cue Experiment

Our first experiment's drawback is that, in overcoming the self-selection issue in detecting effects from Robertson's cues, questions arise as to how those with an affinity for Robertson and *The 700 Club* react to the kind of anti-LGBTQ cues offered in that treatment. It is not much of a leap to assume that anyone who watches Robertson regularly would respond in concert to anti-LGBTQ cues offered on *The 700 Club*. Robertson, after all, is the quintessential example of a religious television elite, having been on the air with his *700 Club* and Christian Broadcasting Network since the 1960s. What is more, with the death of Robert Schuller, Robertson is now the longest running of all religious television programmers in the US. Therefore, a more interesting question is whether communication attributed to Robertson about how he arrives at views about outgroups impacts how audiences think about these groups. This query is based on Djupe and Calfano's (2013) finding that exposure to religious elites' decision-making process impacts public opinion on political issues. In this case, while we expect Robertson's statements about outgroups (i.e., LGBTQ persons) to encourage negative reactions among self-selected viewers, it is also possible for Robertson to lead viewers away from these negative views by revealing his decision process in calling for social respect of a scrutinized outgroup.

In assessing this possibility, we look to advance what Calfano and Djupe (2015) describe as elite plausibility boundaries. Specifically, how far can elite go in offering cues that seem discordant with one's reputation (and what interested audiences would expect the elite to say on an issue or

TABLE 2.4. *700 Club* Effects on LGBTQ Feeling Thermometer

	LGBTQ Thermometer	Gay Marriage	
	Coef./SE	Coef./SE	Marginal Effect
700 Club	−17.6/6.8**	1.1/.39*	.28
Daily Show	−2.1/7.3	.82/.59	.20
Age	−.43/.20*	.03/.02*	.40
Republican	−6.9/.14.5	.54/.89	.13
Democrat	8.7/.14.0	−1.7/.83*	.41
Constant	82.9/16.9**	−2.00/1.1	
Chi²/Prob	37.9/.021	43.5/.000	
Adj./Pseudo R^2	.17	.27	
N	116	116	

Note: Thermometer model uses OLS, gay marriage uses binary logit with two-tailed tests. * $p <$ .05, ** $p <$ .01. "Marginal effect" represents the change in probability moving from the independent variable's minimum to maximum value, holding all other variables at their means.

about an outgroup)? In testing plausibility, it is important to maintain some degree of realism: attentive audiences are unlikely to believe that Robertson would offer a cue in favor of gay marriage legalization. But this is not the same as a somewhat softened stance from Robertson on the issue. So how might a less forceful objection affect these audience members' view of the LGBTQ outgroup and gay marriage?

The potential impact of a softened stance's effect is in how the elite presents it. The strategy Djupe and Calfano (2013) took positioned a statement by an evangelical elite (i.e., National Association of Evangelicals official Rich Cizik) in two basic forms: the first offered Cizik's views on global warming as simply his support for government policy to interdict climate change, while the second (the treatment) included a description of Cizik's decision process in arriving at his view: "after thoughtful prayer with others and reading scripture." Scholars, including Tilly (2006), theorize that the act of giving reasons for one's views provides an interpersonal dimension to the deliberative process (see also Cheng and Johnstone 2002). For an elite like Cizik to "show the spiritual work" performed in arriving at his position on a controversial issue sends a much stronger identity cue to ingroup members than simply raising the reality of nominal group ties. The question now is whether this same type of process cue impacts subject perception of Robertson, the LGBTQ community, and support for gay marriage. If communicating the decision-making process referencing spiritual reflection bolsters elite influence, it will have implications for both elites and the role of religious media as an audience cue giver.

For obvious validity reasons, tests of these types of message effects require subjects with an appropriate degree of prototypicality. In this case, subjects should be at least somewhat representative of the audience that Robertson addresses. Indeed, while knowing how less prototypical audiences might respond to Robertson (like our initial experiment in this chapter), understanding the reaction of sympathetic audiences to an elite is informative (particularly when the elite in question offers cues that test plausibility boundaries on political issues).

We assess the question of a countervailing elite effect for Robertson using an experiment in which audience self-selection was part of the experimental design. Specifically, to ensure a baseline level of audience prototypicality, we recruited subjects for an internet-based survey experiment where only those who claimed at least weekly viewership of a religious television program received random assignment to the treatment or control group. The subject pool recruitment came via online ads targeting southwest Missouri residents in spring 2016 (subjects received a nominal monetary amount for their participation).

Southwest Missouri, which is home to the world headquarters of the Assemblies of God denomination, is one of the nation's evangelical epicenters (see Chinni and Gimpel 2011). As such, the local population is ideal for the type of research design where homogeneity of religious experience is preferred over a more representative population sample. Of the 1,327 subjects who indicated an interest in participating, 665 stated that they "viewed religious television programs (such as *The 700 Club*)" at least once a week. These subjects were then randomly assigned to the treatment or control groups in the experiment. Note that 277 subjects indicated that they watch *The 700 Club* regularly, but we did not limit participation to only *The 700 Club* viewers. Theoretically, since Robertson includes some of the Pentecostal teachings associated with the Assemblies of God in his television program, those who do not watch *The 700 Club* as regularly as once per week may still have some affinity for Robertson.

To be sure, there are no known examples of Robertson softening his views on LGBTQ issues, so we could not use a video treatment featuring Robertson (as in our previous experiment). Instead, we randomly exposed subjects to one of two newspaper article mock-ups attributed to the *Springfield News Leader*, a local southwest Missouri newspaper. In the control condition, we reported that Magill University researchers conducted a content analysis of Robertson's statements on LGBTQ-related issues by examining scripts from every *700 Club* episode over the last twenty-five years. The article then provided a quote attributed to the researchers suggesting that Robertson's views on LGBTQ issues have not been consistent. At this point, the treatment and control articles diverged, with the treatment providing the decision-process language attributed to Robertson and the control lacking this language. Both articles contained a quote attributed to Robertson that softens his known anti-LGBTQ stance and references a *700 Club* episode from 1995.

PROCESS CUE Treatment ["After thoughtful prayer with others and reading scripture,"] All subjects: ["I have respect for gay people in this country. I don't agree with what their homosexual life choices, but we have to provide a level of fairness and decency to folks in this country. That extends to the law."]

By focusing the article content in a manner that does not reverse Robertson's known theological views related to homosexuality or gay marriage legality, we preserve the plausibility that Robertson said what the article states. The article text is provided in the appendix. One criticism of this approach is that we put words in Robertson's mouth as part of the treatment. But two arguments for this approach outweigh the drawbacks. The first is Robertson's reputation and familiarity among evangelicals. As one of the last evangelical elites of his generation, Robertson carries a level of name recognition and a socially conservative reputation unmatched except perhaps by James Dobson (who has all but retreated from public political activism at this point). The second is that using Robertson in the treatment provides some linkage to the insights drawn from the first experiment (our video-based design).

Our expectation, based on Djupe and Calfano's work (2013), is that subjects who are provided the process cue stating that Robertson came to his position "after thoughtful prayer and reading the Bible endlessly" will show a more positive view of the LGBTQ community and more support for gay marriage. But it is instead possible that these subjects—all of whom indicated regular exposure to religious media—will reject both the LGBTQ community and Robertson because this religious elite appears to depart from his reputational opposition to LGBTQ rights. Either way, the findings from this experiment are groundbreaking in that they shade in understanding how audiences perceive religious elites when they broach statements that are not clearly pro or con on controversial issues.

As we might expect, the characteristics of this subject pool are fairly different from those of the pool for our first experiment. In this pool, 41 percent identify as Republican, while only 22 percent claim to be Democrats. The average age is forty-seven, and 60 percent score highly on the religiosity index (introduced previously and featuring scores on church attendance and biblical literalism). The number of subjects randomly assigned to the treatment article was 318 (featuring process cues attributed to Robertson), with 337 assigned to the control. Table 2.5 reports the statistical findings.

Subjects are not put off by exposure to Robertson's decision-making process in the treatment (where he explains his reasons for calling for respect of LGBTQ persons). In fact, treated subjects show a 36.6-point increase in warmth toward Robertson ($p < .01$), suggesting that Robertson encourages a rather positive reaction as an evangelical elite by taking a position counter to his reputation for scrutinizing the LGBTQ community. The effect generally holds in the covariate model, with treatment exposure increasing subject feelings toward Robertson by 36 points ($p < .01$), while older subjects show a 2.39-point drop in warm feelings toward the elite. These effects are graphed in figure 2.1.

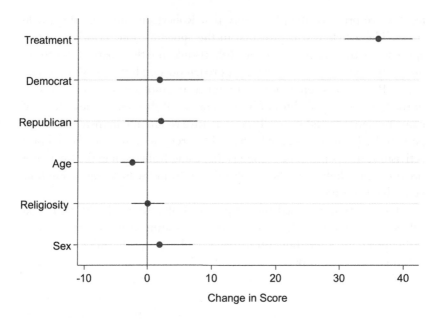

Fig. 2.1. Robertson Thermometer Score

TABLE 2.5. Effect of Robertson's Decision-Process Language

	Robertson Therm.	LGBTQ Therm.	Gay Marriage	
	Coef./SE	Coef./SE	Coef./SE	Marginal Effect
Treatment only	36.6/2.6**	11.6/2.3**	.70/.17**	.16
Constant	32.2/1.8**	54.9/18**	.31/.11**	
Covariate model				
Treatment	36.0/2.7**	11.5/2.3**	.76/.18	.15
Democrat	1.9/3.5	–2.1/3.0	–.14/.25	.03
Republican	2.1/2.9	–.11.8/2.5**	–1.45/.20**	.28
Age	–2.4/0.9**	.50/.82	–.03/.63	.004
Sex	1.9/.2.7	.42/2.3	–.17/.09*	.03
Religiosity	.05/1.3	1.3/1.1	.16 (.18)**	.03
Constant	38.4/6.0**	62.0/5.2**	–1.5/.41**	
Chi²/Prob	32.9/.010	25.0/.010	89.8/.000	
Adj./Pseudo R^2	.23	.04	.11	
N	655	655	655	

Note: Thermometer model uses OLS, gay marriage uses binary logit with two-tailed tests. * $p < .05$, ** $p < .01$. *** "Marginal effect" represents the change in probability moving from the independent variable's minimum to maximum value, holding all other variables at their means.

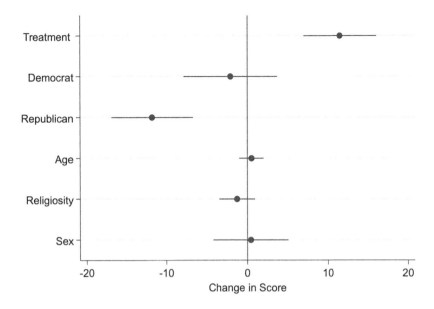

Fig. 2.2. LGBTQ Thermometer Score

The second round of models pivots away from Robertson to examine subject feelings about the LGBTQ community itself. The treatment-only model shows the continued effect from the decision-process language, with those exposed to the treatment showing an 11.6-point increase in warm feelings toward the LGBTQ community ($p < .01$), an effect that holds up in the covariate model, where treated subjects show an 11.5-point increase in warm feelings. Republican subjects show less warmth, registering an 11.8-point drop in warm feelings toward LGBTQ (although the interaction between treatment and Republican identity is not statistically significant). Effects from these first two models are graphed in figure 2.2.

The third set of models focuses on the potential policy impact that Robertson's decision-process language has among subjects in the form of supporting gay marriage. The treatment-only model shows that subjects exposed to the decision-process language have a 16 percent increase in likelihood of supporting gay marriage (holding all other variables at their means), and this same 16 percent increase sustains for the treatment in the covariate model. The marginal effects are graphed in figure 2.3. Meanwhile, Republican subjects show a 32 percent decrease in likelihood of supporting gay marriage (holding all other variables at their means). Again, there is no interaction effect between the treatment and the Republican

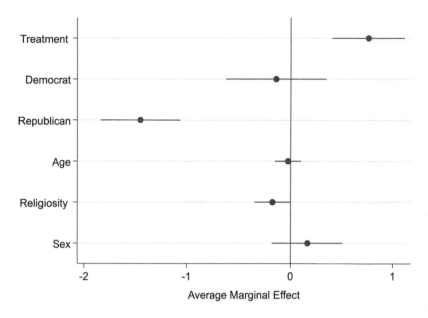

Fig. 2.3. Support for Same-Sex Marriage

control. And two obvious additions to these models are a covariate designating the subjects who claimed to regularly watch *The 700 Club* and an interaction between Republican subjects and the assigned treatment. In both cases, models featuring these two variables showed that neither had a statistically significant effect on any of the three outcomes, nor did they mute the direct treatment effect of Robertson's process cue.

Discussion and Conclusion

The treatment effects from the two experiments, though not large, are meaningful in that they show two facets of religious elite influence: the ability to reinforce existing negative views of targeted outgroups and the apparent flexibility that elites have in pushing audiences in a direction different from the one they are used to hearing the elite endorse. These results also underscore the influence of religious elites using television to broadcast their views. Yes, there is an element of self-selection in the process of consuming religious media like *The 700 Club*, but, as the second experiment demonstrated, the consequences of self-selection and audience prototypicality do not lead to a forgone conclusion about how viewers respond to elite cues. Process cues matter.

Of course, one might criticize our second experiment by pointing out the obvious: Robertson did not make the statement in our treatment vignette. While conceding this point, the bigger takeaway from the experimental effects is that treated subjects accepted Robertson's less than vitriolic approach to LGBTQ citizens enough to bolster their views of Robertson, the LGBTQ community, and gay marriage. This is no mean discovery, and it suggests that similar shifts in position from other religious elites might meet with the same reaction. Important to underscore here is the notion of plausibility. We did not make Robertson say something about the LGBTQ community that would be out of character for him. Had we attributed a pro–gay marriage quote to Robertson, it is likely the treated subjects would have found the information not believable. This is the essence of elite plausibility itself, shifting a position but only within certain bounds that maintain the elite's credibility in offering issue cues. Just where these boundaries lie likely differs for each religious elite and across issues. But scholars should be careful not to assume a lack of effect from cues pushing the plausibility bounds, especially when elites criticize other elites. Robertson's 2020 on-air rebuke of President Trump's response to protests following George Floyd's death while in Minneapolis police custody may have hurt Trump's standing among evangelicals more than it damaged Robertson's influence in communicating his perspectives. Such dynamism in the religious communication environment—and the extent to which audience exposure to these cues is variable—offers scholars a multitude of future research possibilities on elites both in and out of the religious media context. In terms of religious television effects and future research more broadly, there are qualities unique to television versus other media platforms that keep television at the forefront of inquiry (Forgette and Morris 2006; McLuhan 1964; Mutz 2007; Robinson 1975, 1976).

The potential for cross-national work in this subject area is also tantalizing, as religious media effects are not a strictly US phenomenon. For example, Amr Khaled, an Egyptian Muslim televangelist, preaches to audiences across Europe and the Middle East whose size any American televangelist would love to claim (Micklethwait and Woolridge 2009). It would therefore be fascinating to undertake a similar study utilizing data collected in the Islamic or Hindu world. Scholars should also consider ways to collaborate in collecting religious media data for use in future research. Though we could not find pro-LGBTQ statements from Robertson in our search, it is possible that something akin to our treatment in the second experiment exists, thereby providing more support for elite plausibility in pushing audiences beyond what they expect from a religious elite with a national television following. Overall, there is much more for scholars to uncover about this aspect of religious communication as it intersects political outcomes and outgroup appraisals.

APPENDIX

Academics Eye Robertson Reversal on LGBT Issues, by Sam Risom

Special to the News-Leader January 12, 2016

There are a few constants in the world. One of them is that famed religious broadcaster M.G. "Pat" Robertson, longtime host of the popular syndicated program *The 700 Club*, is critical of expanded rights for LGBT citizens, including gay marriage.

But the idea that Robertson is as anti-LGBT as some of his critics suggest may be in doubt. Researchers at Magill University in Canada have just completed a large task in understanding Robertson's perspective: they amassed entire transcripts of every *700 Club* episode since January 1991. If you're wondering, the exact count of shows, including special productions provided by Robertson's Virginia Beach-based Christian Broadcasting Network, comes to just over 6,600.

That's a lot of material to comb through, but Amanda Stephens, one of the religious studies professors at Magill working on the project, says "everything's easier when you have software to help comb through the information."

So what are the researchers looking to find? In actuality, nothing related to Robertson and LGBT issues. Instead, the original research path involved collecting *700 Club* scripts to examine how Robertson and his co-hosts explained crises facing the US and its allies through the prism of what Robertson calls "a biblical worldview."

In a phone interview, Stephens offered "The LGBT aspect was not on the agenda, but then we came across a transcript that got pulled from the stack for an automation issue our software had. That made us go over the transcript manually."

The show in question was a May 1995 episode in which Robertson provided a monologue about his view of the LGBT community in America. "My eyes just kinda fell on his statements, and then I re-read the quote to make sure I was reading it correctly."

Near the start of the episode, which includes a mix of daily news and commentary with CBN News reporters, Robertson says: "[Treatment: After thoughtful prayer with others and reading scripture] I have respect for gay people in this country. I don't agree with what their homosexual life choices, but we have to provide a level of fairness and decency to folks in this country regardless. That extends to the law."

On the surface, the quote looks like Robertson making what is (for him) a positive statement about the LGBT community and the legal rights of its members. That's how Stephens reads it also. But, she is quick to point out that gay marriage was just starting to brim as a political issue in 1995. President Clinton signed the Defense of Marriage Act (DOMA) in 1996. In 2003, Massachusetts was the first state where gay marriage became legal.

Given the timing, and evidence that Stephens and her colleagues found for Robertson supporting DOMA, coupled with his consistent negativity toward the LGBT community on *The 700 Club*, suggests to Stephens that Robertson wasn't referring to gay marriage in his 1995 statement. Still, she adds, "the 1995 show quote provides some nuance about Robertson's views. He is not calling for gay people to be abused at will, even if he doesn't support marriage for gay adults."

Attempts to get to the bottom of the matter by contacting Robertson directly were unsuccessful. The CBN press office, which handles all inquiries about Robertson, officially refused comment about the 1995 show and the Rev.'s positions on LGBT issues.

As for when we can expect to see more about Robertson and his LGBT views, Stephens says that her focus right now is on the original focus of her work, but "this Robertson/LGBT angle is really interesting." Indeed.

Risom is a local commentator on religion and public culture. His views do not necessarily reflect those of the Springfield News Leader.

REFERENCES

Abelman, Robert. 1987a. "Religious Television Uses and Gratifications." *Journal of Broadcasting and Electronic Media*. 31:293–307.

Abelman, Robert. 1987b. "Why Do People Watch Religious TV? A Uses and Gratification Approach." *Review of Religious Research* 29:199–210.

Abelman, Robert, and Kimberly Neuendorf. 1987. "Themes and Topics in Religious Television Programming." *Review of Religious Research* 29:152–74.

Baum, Matthew A. 2005. "Talking the Vote: Why Presidential Candidates Hit the Talk Show Circuit." *American Journal of Political Science* 49:213–34.

Baum, Matthew A., and Angela S. Jamison. 2006. "The Oprah Effect: How Soft News Helps Inattentive Citizens Vote Consistently." *Journal of Politics* 68:946–59.

Baumgartner, Jody, and Jonathan S. Morris. 2006. "The Daily Show Effect: Candidate Evaluations, Efficacy, and American Youth." *American Politics Research* 34:341–67.

Behr, Roy L., and Shanto Iyengar. 1985. "Television News, Real-World Cues, and Changes in the Public Agenda." *Public Opinion Quarterly* 49:38–57.

Berinsky, Adam J., Gregory A. Huber, and Gabriel S. Lenz. 2012. "Evaluating Online Labor Markets for Experimental Research: Amazon.com's Mechanical Turk." *Political Analysis* 20:351–68.

Bruce, Steve. 1990. *Pray TV: Televangelism in America*. London: Routledge.

Buhrmester, Michael D., Tracy Kwang, and Samuel D. Gosling. 2011. "Amazon's Mechanical Turk: A New Source of Inexpensive, yet High-Quality Data?" *Perspectives on Psychological Science* 6:3–5.

Cacioppo, John T., and Wendy Gardner. 1999. "Emotion." *Annual Review of Psychology* 50:191–214.

Calfano, Brian R., and Paul A. Djupe. 2015. "Going to Extremes: Stereotypes, Constitutional Violations, and Support for Religious Elites." In *Religion and Political Tolerance in America: Advances in the State of the Art*, edited by Paul A. Djupe, 200–210. Philadelphia: Temple University Press.

Campbell, David E. 2006. "Religious Threat in Contemporary Presidential Elections." *Journal of Politics* 68:104–15.

Cao, Xiaoxia. 2008. "Political Comedy Shows and Knowledge about Primary Campaigns: The Moderating Effects of Age and Education." *Mass Communication and Society* 11:43–61.

Chen, Jimmy, and Wing Suen. 2008. "A Spatial Theory of News Consumption and Electoral Competition." *Review of Economic Studies* 75:699–728.

Cheng, Martha S., and Barbara Johnstone. 2002. "Reasons for Reason-Giving in a Public Opinion Survey." *Argumentation* 16:401–20.

Chinni, Dante, and James Gimpel. 2011. *Our Patchwork Nation: The Surprising Truth about the "Real" America*. New York: Avery.

Cook, Thomas D., and Donald Campbell. 1979. *Quasi-Experimentation: Design and Analysis Issues for Field Settings*. Boston: Houghton Mifflin.

DellaVigna, Stefano, and Ethan Kaplan. 2007. "The Fox News Effect: Media Bias and Voting. *Quarterly Journal of Economics* August, 1187–234.

Djupe, Paul A., and Brian R. Calfano. 2013. *God Talk: Experimenting with the Religious Causes of Public Opinion*. Philadelphia: Temple University Press.

Druckman, James N. 2001. "On the Limits of Framing Effects: Who Can Frame?" *Journal of Politics* 63:1041–66.

Forgette, Richard, and Jonathan S. Morris. 2006. "High-Conflict Television News and Public Opinion." *Political Research Quarterly* 59:447–56.

Fox, Julia R., Glory Koloen, and Volkan Sahin. 2007. "No Joke: A Comparison of Substance in *The Daily Show with Jon Stewart* and Broadcast Network Television Coverage of the 2004 Presidential Election Campaign." *Journal of Broadcasting and Electronic Media* 51:213–27.

Gerbner, George, Larry Gross, Stewart Hoover, M. Morgan, N. Signorielli, and H. E. Cotungo. 1984. *Religion and Television: A Research Report by the Annenberg School of Communication, University of Pennsylvania*. Philadelphia: Annenberg School of Communication.

Gilson, Dave 2009. "Do Americans Really Watch 8 Hours of TV Daily?" *Mother Jones*, September 25.

Groseclose, Tim, and Jeffrey Milyo. 2005. "A Measure of Media Bias." *Quarterly Journal of Economics* 120:1191–237.

Hadden, Jeffrey K. 1983. "Televangelism and the Mobilization of New Christian Right Family Policy." In *Families and Religion*, edited by William D'Antonio and Joan Aldous, 247–66. Beverley Hills, CA: Sage.

Hadden, Jeffrey K. 1987. "Religious Broadcasting and the Mobilization of the New Christian Right." *Journal for the Scientific Study of Religion* 26:1–24.

Hayes, Daniel. 2008. "Does the Messenger Matter? Candidate-Media Agenda Convergence and Its Effects on Voter Issue Salience." *Political Research Quarterly* 61:134–46.

Heinz, Donald. 1983. "The Struggle to Redefine America." In *The New Christian Right*, edited by Robert C. Liebman and Robert Wuthnow, 133–48. New York: Aldine.

Hollander, Barbara A. 2005. "Late-Night Learning: Do Entertainment Programs Increase Political Knowledge for Young Viewers? *Journal of Broadcasting and Electronic Media* 49:402–15.

Hughey, Michael W. 1990. "Internal Contradictions of Televangelism: Ethical Quandaries of that Old Time Religion in a Brave New World." *International Journal of Politics, Culture, and Society* 4:31–47.

Hutchinson, David, and Samuel D. Bradley. 2009. "Memory for Images Intense Enough to Draw an Administration's Attention: Television and the 'War on Terror.'" *Politics and the Life Sciences* 28:31–47.

Iyengar, Shanto. 1987. "Television News and Citizens' Explanations of National Affairs." *American Political Science Review* 81:815–31.

Iyengar, Shanto. 1991. *Is Anyone Responsible? How Television Frames Political Issues.* Chicago: University of Chicago Press.

Iyengar, Shanto, and Donald R. Kinder. 1987. *News That Matters: Television and American Opinion, American Politics and Political Economy.* Chicago: University of Chicago Press.

Iyengar, Shanto, Mark D. Peters, and Donald R. Kinder. 1982. "Experimental Demonstrations of the 'Not-So-Minimal' Consequences of Television News Programs." *American Political Science Review* 76:848–58.

Jones, Robert P. 2016. *The End of White Christian America.* New York: Simon and Schuster.

Ladd, Jonathan M. 2009. "The Neglected Power of Elite Opinion Leadership to Produce Antipathy towards the News Media: Evidence from a Survey Experiment." *Political Behavior* 32:29–50.

LaMarre, Heather, Kristen D. Landreville, and Michael A. Beam. 2009. "The Irony of Satire: Political Ideology and the Motivation to See What You Want to See in *The Colbert Report*." *International Journal of Press/Politics* 14:212–31.

Landreville, Kristen D., R. Lance Holbert, and Heather L. LaMarre. 2010. "The Influence of Late-Night TV Comedy Viewing on Political Talk: A Moderated-Mediation Model." *International Journal of Press/Politics* 15:482–98.

Layman, Geoffrey C. 1997. "Religion and Political Behavior in the United States: The Impact of Beliefs, Affiliations, and Commitment from 1980 to 1994." *Public Opinion Quarterly* 61:288–316.

Leege, Davis C., Kenneth D. Wald, Brian S. Kruger, and Paul D. Mueller. 2002. *The Politics of Cultural Differences: Social Change and Voter Mobilization Strategies in the Post-New Deal Period*. Princeton: Princeton University Press.

Litman, Barry R., and Elizabeth Bain. 1989. "The Viewership of Religious Television Programming: A Multidisciplinary Analysis of Televangelism." *Review of Religious Research* 36:329–43.

Lotz, Amanda D. 2007. *The Television Will Be Revolutionized*. New York: New York University Press.

Martin, Paul S. 2008. "The Media as Sentinel: Why Bad News about Issues Is Good News for Political Participation." *Political Communication* 25:180–93.

McLuhan, Marshall. 1964. *Understanding Media: The Extensions of Man*. New York: Signet.

Meffert, Michael F., Sungeun Chung, Amber Joiner, and Jennifer Garst. 2006. "The Effects of Negativity and Motivated Information Processing during a Political Campaign." *Journal of Communication* 56:27–51.

Micklethwait, John, and Adrian Woolridge. 2009. *God Is Back: How the Global Rise of Faith Will Change the World*. New York: Penguin.

Moy, Patricia, Michael Xenos, and Verena K. Hess. 2005. "Communication and Citizenship: Mapping the Political Effects of Infotainment." *Mass Communication and Society* 8:111–31.

Moy, Patricia, Michael Xenos, and Verena K. Hess. 2006. "Priming Effects of Late Night Comedy." *International Journal of Public Opinion Research* 18:198–210.

Mullinix, Kevin J., Thomas J. Leeper, James N. Druckman, and Jeremy Freese. 2015. "The Generalizability of Survey Experiments." *Journal of Experimental Political Science* 2:109–38.

Mutz, Diana C. 1998. *Impersonal Influence: How Perceptions of Mass Collectives Affect Political Attitudes*. New York: Cambridge University Press.

Mutz, Diana C. 2007. "Effects of 'In-Your-Face' Television Discourse on Perceptions of a Legitimate Opposition." *American Political Science Review* 101:621–35.

Mutz, Diana C., and Byron Reeves. 2005. "The New Videomalaise: Effects of Televised Incivility on Political Trust." *American Political Science Review* 99:1–15.

Olson, Laura R., and Adam L. Warber. 2008. "Belonging, Behaving, and Believing: Assessing the Role of Religion on Presidential Approval." *Political Research Quarterly* 61:192–204.

Parkin, Michael. 2010. "Taking Late Night Comedy Seriously: How Candidate Appearances on Late Night Television Can Engage Viewers." *Political Research Quarterly* 63:3–15.

Paul, David M., and Clyde Brown. 2001. "Testing the Limits of Elite Influence on Public Opinion: An Examination of Sports Facility Referendums." *Political Research Quarterly* 54:871–88.

Perren, Alisa. 2011. "In Conversation: Creativity in the Contemporary Cable Industry." *Cinema Journal* 50:132–38.

Petersen, Larry R., and Gregory V. Donnenwerth. 1998. "Religion and Declining Support for Traditional Beliefs about Gender Roles and Homosexual Rights." *Sociology of Religion* 59:353–71.

Price, Vincent, and John R. Zaller. 1993. "Who Gets the News? Alternative Measures of News Reception and Their Implications for Research." *Public Opinion Quarterly* 57:133–64.

Robinson, Michael. 1976. "Public Affairs Television and the Growth of Political Malaise: The Case of the Selling of the Pentagon." *American Political Science Review* 70:409–32.

Rogers, Baker. 2020. *Conditionally Accepted: Christians' Perspectives on Sexuality and Gay and Lesbian Rights* New Brunswick, NJ: Rutgers University Press.

Schaffner, Brian F. 2011. "Racial Salience and the Obama Vote. *Political Psychology* 32:963–88.

Straub, Gerald T. 1988. *Salvation for Sale: An Insider's View of Pat Robertson*. Buffalo, NY: Prometheus Books.

Thussu, Daya K. 2008. *News as Entertainment: The Rise of Global Infotainment*. Thousand Oaks, CA: Sage.

Tilly, Charles. 2006. *Why? What Happens When People Give Reasons . . . and Why*. Princeton: Princeton University Press.

Watts, Mark D., David Domke, Dhavan V. Shaw, and David P. Fan. 1999. "Elite Cues and Media Bias in Presidential Campaigns: Explaining Public Perceptions of a Liberal." *Communication Research* 26:144–75.

White, Ismail K. 2007. "When Race Matters and When It Doesn't: Racial Group Differences in Response to Racial Cues." *American Political Science Review* 101:339–54.

Yin, Jun. 1999. "Elite Opinion and Media Diffusion: Exploring Environmental Attitudes." *International Journal of Press/Politics* 4:62–86.

Young, Dannagal G. 2004. "Late Night Comedy in Election 2000: Its Influence on Candidate Trait Ratings and the Moderating Effects of Political Knowledge and Partisanship. *Journal of Broadcasting and Electronic Media* 48:1–22.

Young, Dannagal G., and Sarah Esralew. 2011. "Jon Stewart a Heretic? Surely You Jest: Political Participation and Discussion among Viewers of Late-Night Comedy Programming." In *The Stewart/Colbert Effect: Essays on the Real Impact of Fake News*, edited by Amarnath Amarasingam, 99–116. Jefferson, NC: McFarland.

Zaller, John. 1992. *The Nature and Origins of Mass Opinion*. New York: Cambridge University Press.

THREE

What Did He Just Say?

Incongruent Candidate Cues across Constituencies

Brian Calfano and Alexis Straka

We saw when considering elite communication in the introductory chapter that secular political elites can effectively use religiously infused messages to shape political outcomes (Leege et al. 2002; Domke and Coe 2008; Claassen 2018). Sometimes, these appeals are "coded" or intentionally disguised to avoid detection while establishing credibility among intended audiences (Calfano and Djupe 2009; Albertson 2011). In more recent examples, however, politicians seeking to induce and advance polarization have all but abandoned attempts to hide their appeals to religious constituencies (see Djupe and Calfano 2019). As such, political elite cues containing ostensible religious content may be widely disseminated. The question we address in this chapter regards how public exposure to noticeable religious cues affects both impressions of the elite communicating them and preferences on the issues the cues raise.

The elite influence literature suggests that these leaders hold sway over the public because elite cues offer the provision of information about (and serve as indicators of) group-centric norms (see Zaller 1992; Hogg and Reid 2006). Elite cue influence has been attributed to the public's increasing reliance on heuristic or "peripheral route" processing (Petty and Cacioppo 1986) and the affective evaluations of candidates (Marcus et al. 2006. In addition, the likeability or affect heuristic (see Sniderman and

Brady 1984; Sniderman et al. 1991; Mondak 1993) suggests that public attitudes are shaped by mass impressions of the candidate as distinct from group-centered perceptions (e.g., political party).

As information enabling evaluation of an object in the absence of detailed knowledge, cues support electoral maximization by helping political candidates with impression management across varied constituencies (Mayhew 1974; Fenno 1978; Kinder and Herzog 1993; Eagly and Chaiken 1993; Lupia 1994; Delli Carpini and Keeter 1996; Sniderman 2000; Lau and Redlawsk 2001; Kam 2005; Arceneaux and Kolondy 2009). Upon exposure, people may change their views to match elite opinion cues on noncontroversial issues (Carsey and Layman 2006; Lenz 2009; Bergan 2012), although evidence is mixed on elite cues shaping public preferences and behavior on more contentious policies (Margolis 2018).

Indeed, elites have had varied success in deploying effective cues. One reason might be the cues themselves. Given the exigencies of exerting public influence in the American system, not all elite cues will have the desired effect. Some cues may compete with and undermine others, even when coming from the same elite. Hence, as elite appeals to multiple and disparate constituencies increase, so may the probability of deploying cues that do not provide the expected effects (Mondak 1993; Rahn 1993; Kuklinski and Hurley 1994; Druckman 2001; Goren 2004). While much remains to be understood about the psychological effects of both source and information cues on their receivers (Bolce, de Maio, and Muzzio 1992; McDermott 1998; Mendelberg 2001; Leege et al. 2002; Fiorina, Abrams, and Pope 2006; Kidd et al. 2007), one question stands out in regard to elite cues, including in the religious communication context: does cue information that is inconsistent or incongruent with what audiences expect to hear from an elite alter how audiences respond to the cue?

This question is born from the reality that one of the more intriguing, if underdeveloped, areas of the elite cue literature concerns what we might term "plausibility boundaries." These boundaries reflect how far an elite can go in offering cues that counter public expectations of what she or he will say before the public begins to reject the elite's perspective. Perhaps the most studied area of elite cue incongruence is public response to perceived invalid statements about well-informed or "expert" opinion. Most notably, as Darmofal (2005) found, the public follows cues from leaders they like, even if said cues are diametrically opposed to commonly known expert opinion (in this case, elites were political leaders, while "experts" were domain-specific specialists). But this insight does not directly address our question regarding elite cues that offer views different from what group members likely expect an elite to provide. Furthermore, what effect do these incongruent cues have on how the public perceives elite characteristics in terms of trust, electability, and related outcomes?

Religion and politics scholars have focused on the effects of cues from religious elites, although perhaps the best example of these leaders (i.e., clergy) has actually never been shown to hold direct influence over parishioner political views (see Djupe and Gilbert 2008). That said, when broadening the communication context to include more general audiences, religious elite cues can sway public reaction. This is especially the case when the elite offers varying pieces of information, including the articulation of specific values (Djupe and Calfano 2013), a religious justification for the outcome (Djupe and Gwiasda 2010; Wallsten and Nteta 2016), and allusion to a broader consensus among elites (Campbell and Monson 2003). But religious elite cues may also be inherently ineffective at inducing influence in this way (Robinson 2010; Adkins et al. 2013). Margolis (2018) provides additional nuance by showing that incongruent religious elite cues (relative to targeted audience expectations) can impact public attitudes, but this influence does not extend to political behavior.

Political elites, especially those running for elected office, are perhaps more adroit at offering cues for public consumption. This partly has to do with the exigencies of the US political system. Both the ideological pivot that political candidates often make between their primary and general election efforts and the median voter's importance for victory leave candidates vulnerable to alienating one or more key constituencies. This makes figuring out how to achieve cue acceptance a priority for candidates and their campaigns. Political elites offering religious cues in electoral contexts are in a similar situation in that the signals they send are likely intended to appeal to audiences with specific faith orientations and policy preferences (which might not be shared by the larger public to which the candidate must also appeal).

One way to thread this needle is to offer cues with narrow-casted content intended to avoid broader audience detection. This was the approach tested by the "God Talk" experiments a decade ago (see Calfano, Djupe, and Wilson 2010). But, to some extent, the expectation of message targeting associated with the God Talk literature (Calfano and Djupe 2013; Calfano and Paolino 2010) is out of step with the blunt appeals to religious publics seen in the Trump era. Yet it is improbable to expect that all political candidates will offer cues with the same unabashed overtness that characterizes Trump's communication style. Depending on the circumstances, candidates may wish to return to the use of coded appeals. Ironically, it is the social media age, with its alluring promise of message microtargeting, that makes successfully narrowcasting an elite cue more problematic than ever given the ease with which messages may spread across social media platforms. Political elites now must be prepared for the possibility that their targeted message may "go viral," thereby defeating the purpose of most narrowcasted cues.

When offering political cues, candidates (and political elites more generally) have to prioritize their goals. Given the increasingly polarized nature of American politics, along with the political system's first-past-the-post and winner-take-all election rule characteristics, perhaps the first rule of offering political cues is to not lose one's base of support, no matter what else happens with the cue and the unintended audiences exposed to it. Messages intended only for one's base (e.g., often those with which an elite has strong name recognition, ideological overlap, ingroup status, and even religious influence) are less problematic in that if the cue ends up being noticed by people beyond the base, one's core support group is unlikely to be alienated. And, following a Downsian (1957) perspective, an elite can make later forays into broadening a coalition to include the median voter once one's base is intact.

The goal in this scenario is to not lose the base, and an elite may offer signals to first solidify credentials with base constituents in addition to the issue-specific cue content provided. To do so, candidates need to embody prototypical behavior associated with the base as their political ingroup (Tyler and Lind 1992; Hogg 2001). This prototypical behavior, as recognized by the audience, positions the elite as a credible source offering trusted cues. Candidates may also benefit by revealing the decision process used in reaching their stated issue positions, thereby reinforcing the source cue effect (Cheng and Johnstone 2002; Tilly 2006; Calfano and Djupe 2009; Djupe and Gwiasda 2010). The underlying assumption behind these actions is that people have an appreciation of the groups to which they belong. This enables candidates to exploit social identity—ingroup versus outgroup—attachments as protective tools against any negative constituent responses to other cues not intended for them (Tajfel 1970; Tajfel and Turner 1986; Iyengar, Sood, and Lelkes 2012). Since the US party nomination process requires candidates to first address primary voters anyway, forging strong ingroup credentials through source cues is a logical initial strategy. And, assuming that most people use simplistic or heuristic processes in making their political evaluations (see Barker and Hansen 2005), candidates may be especially interested in offering ingroup appeals based on their source credentials. Having secured the base, candidates may assume they are then free to pivot toward other constituencies, perhaps by offering moderate-sounding (or even incongruent) cues.

This two-part appeal strategy works to a candidate's benefit *if* the ingroup members remain influenced by their anticipated heuristics (e.g., group identity, partisanship, etc.). But there is reason to expect that they may not. Heuristic users may be motivated toward systematic processing when exposed to cues containing incongruent information. Since many voters are, in fact, interested in politics and know reasonable amounts of political information (Delli Carpini and Keeter 1996), the wall between heuristic reliance and systematic processing of candidate cues may be quite thin (Maheswaran and Chaiken 1991; Barker and Hansen 2005). Nicholson's (2011) findings only add to the uncertainty by suggesting that information policy cues touting group benefits outperform source cue effects and encourage systematic processing (something candidates facing diverse constituencies may want to avoid). Hence, in offering the varied mix of information and source cues for the different constituencies needed for electoral success, candidates may inadvertently trigger systematic processing in both ingroup and outgroup targets, thereby affecting support from both constituencies.

To expand on Nicholson's (2011) findings, we evaluate the cognitive effects of candidate cues that elites offer when communication is directed to a targeted audience but the broader public is also exposed to it. From the perspective of an elite attempting the balancing act of not alienating broader publics beyond those targeted for cue transmission, a strong and credible source cue (e.g., from an elite with credentials and a reputation known by the targeted audience) may inoculate candidates against the effects of offering cues palatable to broader audiences. And, from a religious communication standpoint, since religious source cues may be particularly effective among constituencies on the political right (Maarek 1995; Weinberger 1995; De Landtsheer 1998; Anderson 2004; Luke 2004), cues attributed to the perspective of a conservative Republican candidate offering both source and variable (i.e., incongruent) information cues may provide the greatest insight into how effective these cues are. The variable cue information is designed to test the plausibility boundaries discussed above—namely, whether political elites appealing to religious constituencies can offer incongruent cues challenging the status quo framing of a political issue. In making this assessment, we build on the narrowcasting religious group cue literature by making religious voters the candidate's ingroup target (e.g., Domke and Coe 2008; Calfano and Djupe 2009; Albertson 2011; Weber and Thornton 2012).

An Incongruent Cue Experiment

Our experiment contains a treatment and control version of a cue that is intended for conservative and religious audiences but that is exposed to other constituencies as well (mirroring the reality of political message communication more generally). Our cue content leverages Blogowska and Saroglou's (2011) finding that religious conservatives harbor negative attitudes toward perceived cultural threats (which may be international in nature) and recommends inclusion of a real-world cue example from a former political candidate. The incongruent policy cue is taken from an actual spring 2012 GOP presidential primary campaign event hosted by former Pennsylvania senator Rick Santorum that one of the authors attended as a participant in local media coverage.

Santorum, a conservative Roman Catholic popular among evangelicals for his opposition to abortion and gay marriage, offered prototypical partisan and ideological credentials to a crowd of several thousand during a campaign stop in southwest Missouri. Interestingly, during his stump speech, Santorum veered off into a short discourse about Iran. Santorum began this section of his speech by talking about the need for the US to protect Israel, which is a staple position of Republican conservatism. He then mentioned Iran but did not call for war or another strong response to Tehran's escalating nuclear development program. Instead, Santorum pushed the plausibility boundaries of his elite credibility with the largely white, conservative audience by questioning why people would believe that Iran, a Persian state, would have a deeply held hatred for Israel. Santorum made the historical argument that Persians were not part of the Arab-Jewish conflict. Santorum then called for supporting Iranian "moderates" to overthrow the current government.

Throughout this two- to three-minute detour in an otherwise predictable stump speech, the GOP crowd became noticeably quiet, providing only reserved applause until Santorum returned to more predictable, and congruent, policy arguments. It is impossible to know what most in the crowd thought of Santorum's cue, but its silence suggested some degree of information processing. We believe that this episode with the then GOP presidential candidate shows the potential danger candidates face when attempting to stake out new policy ground that challenges conventional wisdom or predominant policies favored by the base constituency, including white evangelicals.

Of course, US policy toward Iran took a much harder line under the Trump administration than when Santorum ran for office (Belal 2019), including dropping out of the nuclear deal the Obama administration negotiated in 2015. That Trump, like Santorum, is a Republican elite who offers cues to conservative and religious constituencies sets up a useful natural control for our experiment in that most evangelicals, who are highly supportive of the forty-fifth president (Jones et al. 2019), are likely not conditioned to view Iran with the same nuance found in Santorum's 2012 cue. Against this backdrop, Santorum's speech is situated as the incongruent elite cue. And since scholars have already provided insight into the effects of religious source and process cue exposure (see Djupe and Calfano 2013), we can make these cue types part of the control condition (thereby freeing up the treatment to isolate effects from the incongruent policy cue).

We list below both the incongruent and the religious source cues from our experiment (the appendix contains the full treatment vignette). Note that both the treatment and control groups contained the partisan source cue reflecting the fact that the candidate was a Republican (we did not use Santorum's name), a religious decision process cue, and, for the treatment, the incongruent cue about American policy toward Iran. Since we target an oversample of self-identified evangelicals in our subject pool, and based on the insights derived from prior studies, we are confident that the decision process cue will serve as an effective ingroup (i.e., conservative and/or evangelical) credential that, along with the partisan source cue, can then be played against the incongruent cue information offered in the treatment. The material below appeared as part of a newspaper story vignette that subjects were asked to read.

> **Incongruent information cue [TREATMENT]:** "There is no historical reason for a Persian people like the Iranians to have a problem with Israel. Iranians are a moderate people who do not want conflict in their region. We need to reach out to them in our American foreign policy." **Religious process cue [BOTH CONDITIONS]:** "I have prayed and talked to a lot of believers about this issue." **Political Source Cue [BOTH CONDITIONS]:** "We have to deal effectively with Iran. Time is of the essence in order to ensure peace in this region that has not known it for centuries."

To include as many white evangelicals as possible, we asked the survey sampling firm Lucid to procure an oversample of adults with an evangelical affinity from its national panel of survey respondents. The sample of 880 adults who participated in the September 2019 survey-embedded experiment includes 436 self-identified evangelicals, which is almost 50 percent of the subject pool. Of the self-described evangelicals in the sample, 91 percent are Anglo, which allows us to avoid getting into the complexities of how African American and Latino Christians view political issues and policy differently from their Caucasian counterparts (McDaniel and Ellison 2008). Treatment assignment was not statistically predicted by subject race, gender, partisanship, or evangelical affiliation, and open-ended protocols asking respondents about the news article suggest general awareness of the article's topic.

Looking first at the subset of evangelical subjects, the treatment condition was randomly assigned to 219 subjects, with the control condition going to 217, resulting in a virtually even distribution. Across the entire subject pool, 460 subjects were assigned the control versus 420 who received the treatment. In terms of treatment effects, we first report on how the evangelical identifiers responded to the elite cue versus their nonevangelical counterparts. To make this comparison, we report response outcomes between the assigned groups using difference of median tests first on the entire subject pool and then among self-identified evangelicals receiving the treatment. Our outcome measures include a range of items focusing on subject appraisal of the elite as a political leader and of the views that subjects have about Iran and US policy toward that country. Measuring the dimensions on which candidates personally appeal to constituencies has become common in the literature (Holian and Prysby 2014; Redlawsk and Lau 2006). The attribute items include subject appraisals of whether the elite featured in the vignette (1) is weak or strong, (2) is trustworthy, (3) is electable, and (4) represents one's "group" (broadly defined). The "represents" item comes from Hains, Hogg, and Duck's (1997) work on perceptions of leader prototypicality (relative to group members), which is central in assessing how respondents view the candidate offering cues that cut across constituencies. And, because these cues are meant to be noticed by all, we leave the nature of group composition open in this question given that the cue is offered across groups, regardless of exposure intent. The second group of outcome measures focusing on Iran and US policy includes (1) the perception of Iran as the greatest threat to US national security, (2) agreement that the US should conduct a preemptive strike against Iran, (3) views of the 2015 deal between Iran and Western powers to limit Iran's nuclear program, and (4) the view of Iran as an imminent threat to national security.

Cue Effects: The Evangelical versus Nonevangelical Response

For ease of interpretation, we collapsed the ordinal scales into binary measures as indicted.[1] Overall, 529 respondents (60 percent of the overall subject pool) considered the political candidate in the vignette to be "strong," but there were clear differences in terms of which subjects viewed him in this manner. Of the 420 treated respondents (regardless of religious identity), 298 (71 percent) considered the candidate to be "strong." By contrast, 231 (50 percent) of the 460 control subjects considered him "strong" (since we are using binary outcomes for the analysis, the remaining subjects considered the elite to be "weak"). This treatment/control group difference is statistically significant (Pearson Chi^2 = 39.4, p < .00).

In terms of the subset of treated evangelicals, 157 (71 percent) of the 219 treated considered the candidate "strong" versus 100 (48 percent) of the 217 control group evangelicals, a difference that is also statistically significant (Pearson Chi^2 = 26.8, p < .00). But since each version of the news vignette contained religious process language—something that the traditional God Talk literature suggests Republicans might want to avoid because it undermines coded messaging (see Calfano and Djupe 2009)—an equally important question is how nonevangelicals perceived the candidate.

At least on the question of being "strong," nonevangelicals appear unphased by the religious language. Its presence does not drive down a positive impression of the candidate. Of the 201 treated nonevangelicals, 141 (70 percent) considered the candidate "strong" versus 127 (52 percent) of the 243 nonevangelicals in the control group, a statistically significant difference (Pearson Chi^2 = 8.62, p < .00). These findings show that nonevangelicals were swayed in their candidate impression much like their nonevangelical counterparts. Though the first of the outcome measures we evaluate, this effect pattern is promising for what it suggests about candidate cues pushing plausibility boundaries and offering religious language to less (or non-) religious voters in the process.

In terms of candidate trustworthiness, 541 respondents (61 percent of the overall subject pool) said the candidate was "trustworthy," though there were differences in which subjects viewed him as such. Of the 420 treated respondents (regardless of religious identity), 281 (67 percent) considered the candidate to be "trustworthy." By comparison, 260 (57 percent) of the 460 control respondents considered the candidate to be the same. This

---

1. For recoding dependent variable ordinal scales: 1–5 original scale (1–3 = 0, 4–5 = 1). See appendix for original variable coding.

treatment/control group difference is statistically significant (Pearson Chi^2 = 9.6, $p < .00$). In terms of treated evangelicals, 148 (68 percent) of the 219 considered the candidate "trustworthy" versus 116 (56 percent) of the 217 control group evangelicals, a difference that is also statistically significant (Pearson Chi^2 = 6.0, $p < .01$). Among the 201 treated nonevangelicals, 135 (67 percent) viewed the candidate as trustworthy versus 141 (58 percent) of the 243 nonevangelicals in the control (a difference that is not statistically significant). This lack of significance notwithstanding, that majorities of evangelicals in both the treatment and the control groups considered the candidate "trustworthy" indicates that the incongruent cue information is not dragging down constituent impressions more broadly.

But perceiving an elite or political candidate to be "strong" or "trustworthy" may be different from considering this person to be politically effective. To assess whether there are differences in subject evaluation along this dimension, we asked about electability perceptions. The number of respondents who considered the candidate "electable" was 569 (65 percent of the overall subject pool), but, as seen in the previous two instances, there were differences in terms of which respondents viewed him as such. Of the 420 treated (regardless of religious identity), 302 (72 percent) considered him "electable." In contrast, 267 (58 percent) of the 460 control respondents had the same view. This treatment/control group difference is statistically significant (Pearson Chi^2 = 17.9, $p < .00$). For treated evangelicals, 162 (70 percent) of the 219 indicate the candidate was "electable" compared to 110 (53 percent) of the 217 in the control, a difference that is also statistically significant (Pearson Chi^2 = 19.6, $p < .00$). Among treated nonevangelicals, 142 (71 percent) of the 201 thought the candidate to be electable compared to 156 (64 percent) of the 243 control nonevangelicals. But as with the "trustworthy" outcome, this difference is not statistically significant—even as the majority of nonevangelicals are positive in their impression of the candidate.

The fourth and final attribute appraisal is perhaps the most indicative of the effect that elite revelation of incongruent information may have—to the extent that the public considers an elite as prototypical of their group (however defined). This outcome says much about group member willingness to view political candidates (and other elites) as in comportment with points of members' personal identity. Recall that we opted to make the elite featured in the experiment a Republican (without using Santorum's name specifically). And, despite that the candidate matched Trump's party identity, his position on Iran represented a general departure from the Trump administration's hardline rhetoric. The outcome question about the candidate in this instance read, "How representative is the political candidate in the story of your group?"

The number of respondents who considered the political candidate to be representative of their group was 401 (46 percent of the overall subject pool), but, in terms of treatment effects, 222 (52 percent) of the 420 treated respondents (regardless of religious identity) considered the candidate to be representative. This compares with 179 (39 percent) of the 460 in the control who considered the leader to be the same. This treatment/control group difference is statistically significant (Pearson Chi^2 = 16.7, p < .00) and is intriguing given that respondents appear more willing to see the candidate as representative when exposed to the incongruent (for Republicans at least) cue information. This trend was found among evangelicals as well. In terms of treated evangelicals, 131 (60 percent) of the 219 considered the candidate to be representative, compared to 76 (37 percent) of the 217 in the control, a difference that is also statistically significant (Pearson Chi^2 = 22.3, p < .00). For treated nonevangelicals, 93 (46 percent) of the 201 considered the candidate to be representative versus 101 (42 percent) of the control—a nonsignificant difference.

And, in an expanded comparison given the open-ended nature of the group representation question, Republicans, as a whole, were like the larger subject pool. Of the 346 self-identified Republicans, 155 (45 percent) agreed that the candidate represented their group. Among treated Republicans, 97 (56 percent) of the 172 considered the candidate representative of their group compared to 58 (33 percent) of the 174 control Republicans; this difference is statistically significant (Pearson Chi^2 = 13.3, p < .00). Interestingly, Democrats were roughly as likely as Republicans to consider the candidate representative, that is, 153, or 48 percent, of the 318 Democratic respondents. This is fascinating given that the candidate had an ostensibly different party affiliation. But unlike for Republicans, the treatment (24 percent) and control (24 percent) differences were not statistically significant among Democrats, suggesting that the incongruent treatment, while affecting Republican appraisals of candidate representativeness, did not do the same for Democrats. This may be because Democrats were less open to considering an opposing candidate's policy argument but may have been influenced by other aspects of the candidate's speech (apart from the treatment language).

It is difficult to know what to make of the roughly equal percentage of Republican and Democratic responses in that the question's drawback is that we do not know exactly which group the respondents were thinking of when answering. However, it seems that among treated evangelicals and Republicans, the candidate's language about US policy toward Iran pushes them closer to considering the candidate as representative of their group. Indirectly, this may indicate that incongruent policy cues do not necessarily damage voter perception of candidates when testing plausibility boundaries.

Moving to the series of policy-related outcomes, we first examine response effects on subject appraisal of Iran as the greatest threat to US national security (from a list of countries—see the appendix). A total of 322 respondents (37 percent of the overall subject pool) answered that they thought Iran posed the greatest national security threat. In terms of treatment effects, 90 (21 percent) of the 420 treated respondents (regardless of religious identity) considered Iran to be the greatest threat. This compares with 232 (50 percent) of the 460 in the control who viewed Iran in this manner. This treatment/control group difference is statistically significant (Pearson Chi^2 = 78.4, p < .00). In terms of treated evangelicals, 38 (18 percent) of the 219 considered Iran to be the greatest US national security threat compared to 125 (56 percent) of the 217 in the control, a difference that is also statistically significant (Pearson Chi^2 = 78.9, p < .00). Importantly, this effect pattern is the same for nonevangelical respondents—those treated with the incongruent information were also less likely to view Iran as the greatest threat (27 percent of the treated nonevangelicals versus 42 of nonevangelicals in the control—Pearson Chi^2 = 4.2, p < .05). This means that respondents were generally receptive to the treatment information pushing back on the notion that US conflict with Iran was inevitable or overtly necessary.

Even if one does not consider Iran to be the "greatest" threat to US national security, it is possible to view Iran as an imminent one, which is the notion posed in the next outcome measure. A total of 511 respondents (58 percent of the overall subject pool) answered that they thought Iran was an imminent national security threat (as originally measured on a 1–5 Likert scale and collapsed into a binary outcome; see footnote 1). Breaking this into treatment effects, 218 (52 percent) of the 420 treated (regardless of religious identity) considered Iran to represent an imminent threat. This contrasts with 293 (64 percent) of the 460 in the control who viewed Iran in this way. The treatment/control group difference is statistically significant (Pearson Chi^2 = 12.5, p < .00) and shows that the incongruent cue moves respondents away from viewing Iran in the kind of stark national security terms the Trump administration advanced. Among treated evangelicals, however, the effect breaks down. Of the 219 treated, 117 (54 percent) considered Iran to be an imminent national security threat compared to 139

(55 percent) of the 217 control group evangelicals, but this difference is not statistically significant. Differences among nonevangelicals in terms of viewing Iran's threat as imminent (52 percent for the treated, 62 percent for the control) were just outside the standard significance threshold.

A corollary notion stemming from the view of Iran as a national security threat is the idea that the US should conduct a preemptive strike against it. A total of 465 respondents (53 percent of the overall subject pool) answered that they thought the US should conduct a preemptive strike. Of the 420 treated respondents (regardless of religious identity), 198 (47 percent) agreed with the preemptive strike policy. This contrasts with 267 (58 percent) of the 460 control respondents agreeing with preemption. The treatment/control group difference is statistically significant (Pearson Chi^2 = 10.0, $p < .00$). Among treated evangelicals, 103 (48 percent) of the 219 agreed with preemption versus 117 (52 percent) of the 217 control group evangelicals, a difference that falls just outside standard significance bounds. For nonevangelicals, 59 percent of the treated and 61 percent of the control agreed with a preemptive strike, which means the evangelicals were more responsive overall to the elite's argument.

The fourth and final policy question regards respondent views of the 2015 deal that the Obama administration, along with Russia and European allies, negotiated to limit Iran's nuclear program. The outcome measure is coded to reflect subject agreement with the deal, which the US was no longer party to per Trump administration policy. A total of 527 respondents (60 percent of the overall subject pool) answered that they support the nuclear deal. Of the 420 treated (regardless of religious identity), 274 (65 percent) support the deal. This contrasts with 253 (55 percent) of the 460 in the control group who do so. This treatment/control group difference is statistically significant (Pearson Chi^2 = 9.2, $p < .00$). Among the treated evangelicals, 143 (65 percent) of the 219 support the Iran nuclear deal versus 113 (52 percent) of the 217 in the control, a statistically significant difference (Pearson Chi^2 = 5.1, $p < .024$). Nonevangelicals show a similar effect, with 67 percent of the treated favoring the deal versus 56 percent of the control, a statistically significant difference (Pearson Chi^2 = 4.9, $p < .03$).

Clearly, communication of the incongruent cue information powers positive appraisals of the candidate's personal attributes, electability, and group representativeness, especially among evangelical respondents (with some of the effects also evident among nonevangelicals). This communication also seems to make a statistical difference in how both evangelicals and nonevangelicals respond to various statements about US policy

TABLE 3.1. Treatment Effects on Perceived Candidate Attributes

	Strong		Trustworthy		Electable		Representative	
	Coef./Robust SE	Marginal Effect	Coef./Robust SE	Marginal Effect	Coef./Robust SE	Marginal Effect	Coef./Robust SE	Marginal Effect
Treatment only	.88/.14**	.20	.40/.14**	.09	.62/.14**	.14	.57/.14**	.14
Constant	.01/.09		.47/.10**		.32/.10		-.45/.10**	
Covariate model								
Treatment	.81/.20**	.17	.57/.22**	.12	.31/.21	.06	.19/.19	.05
Sex	-.28/.15	.06	.33/.15*	.07	.52/.15**	.11	.10/.15	.02
Nonwhite	-.18/.23	.04	-.48/.22*	.11	.17/.23	.04	-.13/.22	.03
Evangelical	-.14/.21	.03	-.12/.22	.03	-.49/.22*	.10	-.09/.22	.02
Education level	.03/.07	.01	.27/.09	.04	.12/.07	.03	-.14/.07	.03
Age	-.13/.09	.03	.27/.09**	.06	.31/.08**	.07	.05/.08	.01
Political interest	-.01/.10	.01	.02/.10	.01	.04/.10	.01	-.02/.10	.01
Republican	.24/.17	.06	.18/.18	.04	-.14/.18	.03	-.06/.17	.01
Democrat	.33/.18	.07	.11/.19	.02	.01/.19	.01	.29/.18	.07
Evangelical*treatment	.26/.29	.06	-.29/.29	.06	.68/.30*	.14	.76/.28**	.18
Constant	.54/.48		-1.6/.47**		-1.6/.49**		-.19/.45	
Wald Chi²/prob	48.1/.000		46.6/.000		60.5/.000		33.3/.001	
Log-Likelihood	-566.61		-540.7		-538.2		-588.3	
N	880		880		880		878	

Note: Binary logit models with two-tailed tests. * $p < .05$, ** $p < .01$. "Marginal effect" represents the change in probability moving from the independent variable's minimum to maximum value, holding all other variables at their means.

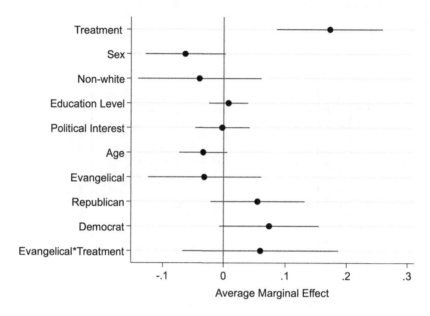

Fig. 3.1. Perception of Candidate as Weak/Strong

toward Iran—all while including the religious decision process language as a baseline across respondents. The question now regards how these treatment effects hold up in covariate models that include controls for gender (women = 1), race (non-Anglo = 1), education level (ordinal scale, higher values indicate higher levels of education), age (ordinal scale, higher levels indicate older age brackets), political interest (ordinal scale, higher levels indicate increased interest), and partisanship (binary variables for Republican and Democratic identifiers). Given the overall response differences that evangelicals showed between those assigned to the treatment and those assigned to the control in the prior analysis, we incorporate a multiplicative interaction term representing those evangelicals exposed to the treatment version of the news article.

Results are reported for binary logit models in tables 3.1 and 3.2, and average marginal effects for each model are graphed in figures 3.1–3.8. Specific marginal effects are reported while holding all other variables at their means. In keeping with determining average treatment effects in randomized experiments, we report a "treatment only" version of each model in the tables but focus here on the treatment effects as adjusted for covariate influence. Beginning with respondent appraisal of the elite on the weak/strong scale, those treated with the incongruent cue information have a 17

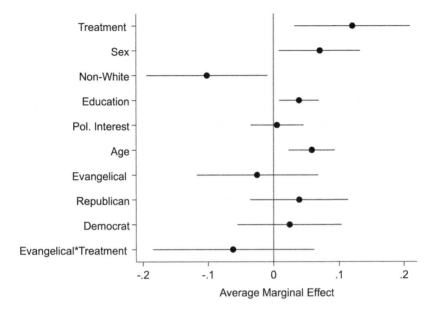

Fig. 3.2. Perception of Candidate as Trustworthy

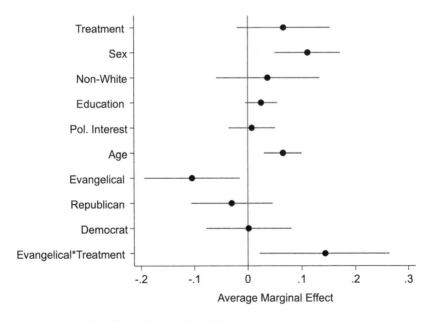

Fig. 3.3. Perception of Candidate as Electable

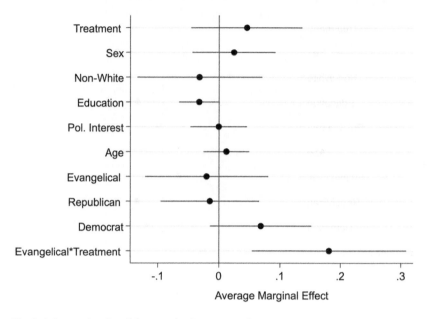

Fig. 3.4. Perception Candidate Leader Represents Group

percent higher probability of viewing the candidate as "strong" compared to the control group, holding all other variables at their means. Note that, when modeled as a covariate, neither the evangelical base variable nor the interaction term with treatment assignment is statistically significant, suggesting that the candidate's personal appeal as "strong" is found across the subject pool, irrespective of respondent religious identity.

A similar effect pattern is found for the "trustworthy" measure, with treated respondents showing a 12 percent higher probability of viewing the candidate as "trustworthy" compared to those in the control group, holding all other variables at their means (again, with no statistical significance for the evangelical/treatment interaction). In terms of covariate effects, older respondents are 6 percent more likely to consider the candidate as "trustworthy," while non-Anglos show an 11 percent decrease in this appraisal.

Moving to consideration of the elite as "electable," female respondents are 11 percent more likely to view the candidate as electable than their male counterparts, while older subjects have a 7 percent higher probability of doing the same. Meanwhile, the evangelical/treatment interaction is statistically significant for the first time in these models, with evangelicals exposed to the incongruent cue more likely to consider the candidate electable compared to evangelicals in the control. Finally, the last of the elite

TABLE 3.2. Treatment Effects on Perceptions of Iran

	Greatest Threat		Preemptive Strike		Iran Deal		Imminent Threat	
	Coef./Robust SE	Marginal Effect	Coef./Robust SE	Marginal Effect	Coef./Robust SE	Marginal Effect	Coef./Robust SE	Marginal Effect
Treatment only	-1.3/.15**	.28	-.44/.14**	.11	.43/.14**	.10	-.49/.14**	.12
Constant	.01/.10		.32/.09**		.20/.10*		.56/.10**	
Covariate model								
Treatment	-.70/.22**	.13	-.49/.19**	.11	.51/.20**	.11	-.39/.20*	.09
Sex	.24/.16	.05	-.26/.14	.06	.26/.15	.06	.13/.15	.03
Nonwhite	.64/.25*	.12	-.21/.22	.05	.36/.23	.08	.01/.23	.01
Evangelical	.20/.23	.04	-.21/.21	.05	-.24/.22	.05	-.07/.23	.02
Education level	.03/.08	.01	-.06/.07	.01	.30/.08**	.07	.34/.08**	.07
Age	.09/.10	.02	-.12/.09	.03	.22/.09**	.05	.08/.08	.02
Political interest	.13/.11	.02	-.13/.10	.03	.27/.10**	.06	.28/.11**	.06
Republican	-.21/.19	.04	-.15/.16	.04	.13/.18	.03	-.03/.18	.01
Democrat	-1.5/.21**	.28	-.12/.18	.03	-.23/.19	.05	-.60/.19**	.13
Evangelical*treatment	-1.5/.32**	.28	.10/.27	.02	-.08/.29	.02	-.26/.28	.06
Constant	-.70/.50		1.97/.53**		-3.1/.49**		-2.05/.49**	
Wald Chi²/prob	140.7/.000		23.5/.010		69.1/.000		66.0/.000	
Log-Likelihood	-488.1		-594.8		-553.8		-559.8	
N	880		880		880		880	

Note: Binary logit models with two-tailed tests. * $p < .05$, ** $p < .01$. "Marginal effect" represents the change in probability moving from the independent variable's minimum to maximum value, holding all other variables at their means.

appraisal measures respondent views of the candidate as representing their group. As with the previous outcome, treated evangelicals show a statistically significant increase in viewing the elite positively, in this case being 18 percent more likely to consider the candidate as representative (compared to control group evangelicals). None of the other covariates in the model are significant.

Turning now to the policy outcomes, subjects' views of Iran as the greatest threat to US national security appear affected by both partisanship and, among evangelicals, treatment exposure. Democrats in the subject pool are 28 percent less likely to agree that Iran is the US's greatest national security threat compared to non-Democrats, while evangelicals receiving the treatment vignette are 28 percent less likely to agree with the sentiment about Iran versus evangelicals in the control group. Substantively, this interaction effect is provocative in that it suggests that an evangelical perspective on a policy issue framed as adversarial by party and religious elites is somewhat malleable. This does not mean that treated evangelicals have abandoned concern about Iran entirely or are in favor of wholesale policy change in how the US deals with the republic. But the effect does indicate that religious communication offering incongruent (and nuanced) policy cues can have an impact on members of political groups not conditioned to expect these kinds of elite-level statements.

Concerning the remaining three policy outcome questions, it is interesting that the evangelical/treatment interaction is not significant in any of those cases but the base treatment variable is—again underscoring that the incongruent policy cue impacts policy views across religious identities. Specifically, and in terms of the US waging a preemptive strike against Iran, treated respondents are 11 percent less likely to agree with preemption compared to those in the control group (none of the model's other covariates are statistically significant). Meanwhile, and in terms of viewing Iran as an imminent threat to US national security, treated respondents (regardless of religious identity) are 9 percent less likely to consider Iran's threat to be imminent versus the control. Interestingly, however, better-educated respondents are 7 percent more likely to view Iran's threat as imminent, while those with higher levels of political interest are 6 percent more likely to hold this view. Perhaps not surprisingly, given that the nation's current posture toward Iran is generally the product of Republican policy views, subject partisanship cuts against these effects, with Democrats 13 percent less likely to consider Iran's threat to be imminent compared to non-Democrats.

Speaking of policy, the cue treatment also affected agreement with the

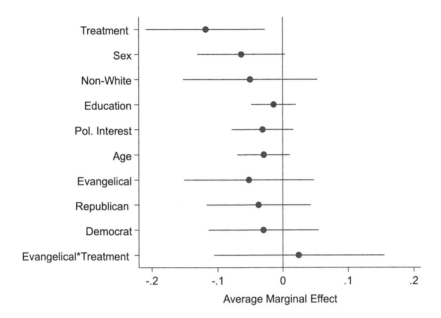

Fig. 3.5. Perception Iran Is Greatest Threat

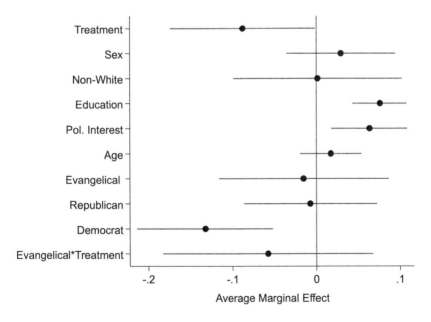

Fig. 3.6. Perception Iran Is Imminent Threat

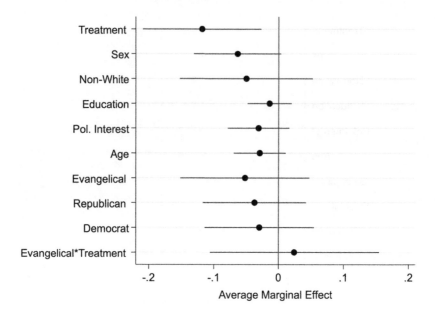

Fig. 3.7. Preemptive Strike on Iran

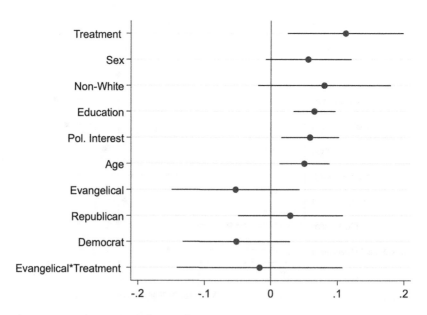

Fig. 3.8. Favor 2015 Iran Nuclear Deal

Iran deal, again regardless of subject religious identity. Treated subjects are 11 percent more likely to agree with the 2015 Iran deal versus those in the control group. In terms of covariate effects, those with a higher education level (who also were more likely to view Iran as an imminent threat) are 7 percent more likely to agree, while older subjects are 5 percent and those with higher political interest are 6 percent more likely to agree.

Discussion

Overall, these findings suggest a number of tentative conclusions about exposure to elite cues that feature incongruent information (relative to what one would normally expect given attributes like party affiliation). First, elites can successfully push against plausibility boundaries in terms of what political leaders say about contentious issues. In this case, the push-back seemingly brought respondents, including most self-identified evangelicals, closer to the kind of less confrontational Iran policy the candidate referenced in the vignette. But, unlike previous studies where the religious process language was randomly assigned, all respondents—evangelical and nonevangelical—heard that the candidate came to his position on Iran after praying about the issue. This is critical in that communication of this kind of overt religious reference by a candidate for secular office was previously considered anathema because it was believed to turn away nonevangelicals. But this did not occur.

Indeed, in terms of perceived candidate attributes, both evangelical and nonevangelical respondents generally perceived the candidate in a positive light. In a situation where a candidate attempts to thread a needle between constituencies of different perspectives (and likely different issue preferences), moving opinion away from the hawkish stance of the current Republican president (while not encountering resistance from constituencies exposed cues meant for another voter group) is noteworthy. It is also (again) worth underscoring that our analysis shows a Republican candidate espousing a view on Iran that is far more conciliatory than current US (and Republican) policy toward that nation. This is no mean finding given its potential implications for how Republicans articulate revised policy agendas in post-Trump politics.

Of course, and as with any research design, there are various limitations inherent in assessing public reaction to candidate cues. Perhaps the most obvious has to do with the nature of a foreign policy issue in terms of affecting respondent preferences. Iran is certainly important, but one might argue that it does not rise to the same level of cultural salience as other issues that motivate evangelicals (including abortion and LGBTQ rights). If a Republican offered an unorthodox view on a culture issue, the outcome might have been quite different. But even on Iran, respondents, especially evangelicals, might have chaffed if the candidate said something like, "We should let Iran have nuclear weapons to protect itself from regional threats, including Israel." There is also the nature of the cues from political opponents to consider, which we did not incorporate into this research design. For example, if the incongruent cue a Republican candidate offers essentially matches that of the Democrat, does this overlap trigger a sense among Republican voters that they are moving toward the opposing party's preferences (and thereby undermining the Republican cue)? This is but one of the additional research avenues for scholars to build on from our findings.

Overall, incongruent cue effects are likely more a matter of degree than a predetermined outcome whereby targeted audiences respond one way to religious cues and untargeted audiences another. The God Talk strategy, therefore, may not be needed in the future if voters are generally accustomed to encountering forms of religious communication not meant for them. Trump's overtness in appealing to evangelicals likely changed that dynamic from one of coded appeals to overt solicitation. The willingness of evangelicals to go along with incongruent cue information undergirds Djupe's argument in chapter 10: relative exposure to messages determines much how people think and act about politics. Santorum's original gamble was in taking a conciliatory posture toward Iran. There is no evidence that these cues mattered in the former Pennsylvania senator's failed 2012 presidential bid. But our chapter presents evidence that exposure to his incongruent message about Iran might have had a sympathetic audience among evangelical constituents. Our findings suggest that, at the least, politicians should not immediately limit the views and arguments they share with voters. Under the right conditions, exposure to these cues may actually help.

APPENDIX: DEPENDENT VARIABLES (WITH ORIGINAL CODING)

"Do you perceive the candidate to be weak or strong?" (1 = Weak,
    5 = Strong)
"Do you perceive the candidate to be trustworthy or untrustworthy?"
    (1 = Untrustworthy, 5 = Trustworthy)
"Do you perceive the candidate to be electable or unelectable?"
    (1 = unelectable, 5 = electable)

"How representative is the political candidate in the story of your group?" (1 = not at all, 5 = completely)

"As you may know, the US and other countries have announced a deal to lift economic sanctions against Iran in exchange for Iran agreeing not to produce nuclear weapons. International inspectors would monitor Iran's facilities, and if Iran is caught breaking the agreement economic sanctions would be imposed again. Do you support or oppose this agreement?

"In your opinion, should the US conduct a preemptive attack on Iranian military interests?"

"On a scale of 1–5, with one being no threat and 5 being an imminent threat, how much of a threat does Iran pose to the United States?"

"What one country anywhere in the world do you consider to be the United States' greatest enemy today?" [Selection options (percentage response): Russia (10), Iran (37), China (19), North Korea (14), Iraq (2), Syria (1), Saudi Arabia (3), Pakistan (2), Mexico (2), Venezuela (2), The Palestinian Authority (1), Japan (> 1), Libya (> 1), Cuba (1), Afghanistan (4), Israel (2)]

I consider myself a "born again" or evangelical Christian.

(Strongly Disagree / Disagree / Neither Agree nor Disagree / Agree / Strongly Agree)

Sparks Offers New Specifics on US Policy Toward Iran

Jamie Moorehouse, Associated Press

April 30, 2019

Updated at 9:25 pm

NORTH PASS—References to foreign policy were early often during Republican U.S. Senate candidate Doug Sparks' campaign rally last night at the Central Fairgrounds Hall. The twenty-minute speech included several pauses while Sparks received applause from the crowd police estimated at over 4,000.

Sparks' speech touched on issues ranging from the candidate's views on the Trump administration's tough stance to China to rapprochement with North Korean leader Kim Jung Un.

The candidate referenced his campaign theme of "Tough for Tomorrow," which Sparks describes as building on President Trump's foreign policy posture. Sparks told the crowd his campaign was "getting strong and speaking loud" for "our nation's best interest."

Sparks also touched on U.S. relations with Iran, long a hot spot for Trump administration officials. He offered an historical take on the relationship between the two countries.

"There is no historical reason for a Persian people like the Iranians to have a problem with Israel. Iranians are a moderate people who do not want conflict in their region. We need to reach out to them in our American foreign policy."

Sparks also offered the audience some of the reasoning behind his thinking before claiming the matter is urgent.

"I have prayed and talked to a lot of believers about this issue. We have to deal effectively with Iran. Time is of the essence in order to ensure peace in this region that has not known it for centuries."

Sparks' campaign spokesperson Linda Vesser told reporters after the rally that the Republican looks forward to contrasting his foreign policy perspective with Democrat James Kelley in next month's series of debates sponsored by the League of Women Voters.

The Kelley campaign was unavailable for comment by press time.

© 2019 The Associated Press. All Rights Reserved.

REFERENCES

Adkins, Todd, Geoffrey C. Layman, David E. Campbell, and John C. Green. 2013. "Religious Group Cues and Citizen Policy Attitudes in the United States." *Politics & Religion* 6.

Albertson, Bethany. 2011. "Religious Appeals and Implicit Attitudes." *Political Psychology* 32:109–30.

Anderson, Richard D., Jr. 2004. "The Causal Power of Metaphor. Cueing Democratic Identities in Russia and Beyond." In *Metaphorical World Politics: Rhetorics of Democracy, War, and Globalization,* edited by Francis A. Beer and Christ'l De Landtsheer, 91–110. East Lansing: Michigan State University Press.

Arceneaux, Kevin, and Robin Kolodny. 2009. "Educating the Least Informed: Group Endorsements in a Grassroots Campaign." *American Journal of Political Science* 53:755–70.

Bang-Petersen, Michael. 2010. "Distinct Emotions, Distinct Domains: Anger, Anxiety and Perceptions of Intentionality." *Journal of Politics* 72:357–65.

Barker, David C., and Susan B. Hansen. 2005. "All Things Considered: Systematic Cognitive Processing and Electoral Decision-Making." *Journal of Politics* 67:319–44.

Belal, Kulsoom 2019. "Uncertainty over the Joint Comprehensive Plan of Action: Iran, the European Union and the United States." *Policy Perspectives* 16:23–39.

Bergan, Daniel E. 2012. "Partisan Stereotypes and Policy Attitudes." *Journal of Communication* 60:1102–20.

Blogowska, Joanna, and Vassilis Saroglou. 2011. "Religious Fundamentalism and Limited Prosociality as a Function of the Target." *Journal for the Scientific Study of Religion* 50:44–60.

Bolce, Louis, Gerald de Maio, and Douglas Muzzio. 1992. "Blacks and the Republican Party: The 20 Percent Solution." *Political Science Quarterly* 107:63–79.

Brady, Henry, and Paul Sniderman. 1984. *Floors, Ceilings, Guessing, and other Pitfalls in Survey Research—The Case of Left Shift*. Manuscript.

Calfano, Brian Robert, and Paul A. Djupe. 2009. "God Talk: Religious Cues and Electoral Support." *Political Research Quarterly* 62:329–39.

Calfano, Brian R., and Paul A. Djupe. 2011. "Not in His Image: The Moderating Effect of Gender on Religious Appeals." *Politics and Religion* 4:338–54.

Calfano, Brian Robert, Paul A. Djupe, and Angelia R. Wilson. 2013. "God Save This "Broken" Land: The Efficacy of Closed-Circuit Voter Targeting in a UK Election." *Politics & Religion* 6:50–73.

Calfano, Brian R., and Philip Paolino. 2010. "An Alan Keyes Effect? Examining Anti-Black Sentiment among White Evangelicals." *Political Behavior* 32:133–56.

Campbell, David E., and J. Quin Monson. 2003 "Following the Leader? Mormon Voting on Ballot Propositions." *Journal for the Scientific Study of Religion* 42:605–19.

Carsey, Thomas M., and Geoffrey C. Layman. 2006. "Changing Sides or Changing Minds? Party Identification and Policy Preferences in the American Electorate." *American Journal of Political Science* 50:464–77.

Cheng, Martha S., and Barbara Johnstone. 2002. "Reasons for Reason-Giving in a Public-Opinion Survey." *Argumentation* 16:401–20.

Claassen, Ryan L. 2018. "The GOP, Evangelical Elites, and the Challenge of Pluralism." In *The Evangelical Crackup? The Future of the Evangelical-Republican Coalition*. Philadelphia: Temple University Press.

Colleau, Sophie M., Kevin Glynn, Steven Lybrand, Richard M. Merelman, Paula Mohan, and James E. Wall. 1990. "Symbolic Racism in Candidate Evaluation: An Experiment." *Political Behavior* 12:385–402.

Conover, Pamela J., and Stanley Feldman. 1989. "Candidate Perception in an Ambiguous World: Campaigns, Cues, and Inference Processes." *American Journal of Political Science* 33:912–40.

Darmofal, David. 2005. "Elite Cues and Citizen Disagreement with Expert Opinion." *Political Research Quarterly* 58:381–95.

De Landtsheer, Christ'l. 1998. "The Political Rhetoric of a Unified Europe." In *Politically Speaking: A Worldwide Examination of Language Use in the Public Sphere*, edited by Ofer Feldman and Christ'l De Landtsheer, 129–48. Westport, CT: Praeger.

De Landtsheer, Christ'l, Philippe De Vries, and Dieter Vertessen. 2008. "Political Impression Management: How Metaphors, Sound Bites, Appearance Effectiveness, and Personality Traits Can Win Elections." *Journal of Political Marketing* 7:217–38.

Delli Carpini, Michael, and Scott Keeter. 1996. *What Americans Know about Politics and Why It Matters*. New Haven: Yale University Press.

Devine, Patricia G. 1989. "Stereotypes and Prejudice: Their Automatic and Controlled Components." *Journal of Personality and Social Psychology* 42:116–31.

Djupe, Paul A. and Brian R. Calfano. 2013. *God Talk: Experimenting with the Religious Causes of Public Opinion*. Philadelphia: Temple University Press.

Djupe, Paul A., and Brian R. Calfano. 2019. "Communication Dynamics in Religion and Politics." In *Oxford Research Encyclopedia of Politics*.

Djupe, Paul A., and Christopher P. Gilbert. 2008. *The Political Influence of Churches*. Cambridge: Cambridge University Press.

Djupe, Paul A., and Gregory W. Gwiasda. 2010. "Evangelizing the Environment: Decision Process Effects in Political Persuasion." *Journal for the Scientific Study of Religion* 49:73–86.

Domke, David, and Kevin Coe. 2008. *The God Strategy: How Religion Became a Political Weapon in America*. New York: Oxford University Press.

Druckman, James N. 2001. "On the Limits of Framing Effects: Who Can Frame?" *Journal of Politics* 63:1041–66.

Eagly, Alice H., and Shelly Chaiken. 1993. *The Psychology of Attitudes*. New York: Harcourt Brace Jovanovich.

Evans, John H. 2011. "Epistemological and Moral Conflict between Religion and Science." *Journal for the Scientific Study of Religion* 50:707–27.

Federico, Christopher M., and James Sidanius. 2002. "Sophistication and the Antecedents of Whites' Racial Policy Attitudes." *Public Opinion Quarterly* 66:145–76.

Fenno, Richard. 1978. *Home Style: House Members in Their Districts*. New York: HarperCollins.

Fiorina, Morris P. 1989. *Congress: Keystone of the Washington Establishment*. New Haven: Yale University Press.

Fiorina, Morris P., Samuel Abrams, and Jeremy C. Pope. 2006. *Culture War? The Myth of a Polarized America*. 2nd ed. New York: Pearson Longman.

Fox, Richard L., and Jennifer L. Lawless. 2005. "To Run or Not to Run for Office: Explaining Nascent Political Ambition." *American Journal of Political Science* 49:642–59.

Goren, Paul. 2004. "Political Sophistication and Policy Reasoning: A Reconsideration." *British Journal of Political Science* 34:589–610.

Green, John C. 2007. *The Faith Factor: How Religion Influences American Elections*. New York: Praeger.

Hains, Sarah C., Michael A. Hogg, and Julie M. Duck. 1997. "Self-Categorization and Leadership: Effects of Group Prototypicality and Leadership Stereotypicality." *Personality and Social Psychology Bulletin* 23:1087–99.

Hogg, Michael A. 2001. "A Social Identity Theory of Leadership." *Personality and Social Psychology Review* 5:184–200.

Hogg, Michael A., and Scott A. Reid. 2006. "Social Identity, Self-Categorization, and the Communication of Group Norms." *Communication Theory* 16:7–30.

Holian, David B., and Charles Prysby. 2014. "Candidate Character Traits in the 2012 Presidential Election." *Presidential Studies Quarterly* 44:484–505.

Iyengar, Shanto, Gaurav Sood, and Yphtach Lelkes. 2012. "Affect, Not Ideology: A Social Identity Perspective on Polarization." *Public Opinion Quarterly* 76:405–31.

Jacobson, Gary C. 1980. *Money in Congressional Elections*. New Haven: Yale University Press.

Jones, Edward Ellsworth, and George R. Goethals. 1972. "Order Effects in Impression Formation: Attribution Context and the Nature of the Entity." In *Attribution: Perceiving the Causes of Behavior,* edited by Edward E. Jones and David E. Kanouse, 27–46. Mahwah, NJ: Lawrence Erlbaum.

Jones, Robert P., Natalie Jackson, Diana Orces, Ian Huff, Oyindamola Bola, and Daniel Greenberg. 2019. "Fractured Nation: Widening Partisan Polarization and Key Issues in 2020 Presidential Elections." Public Religion Research Institute. https://www.prri.org/wp-content/uploads/2019/10/PRRI_Oct_AVS-web.pdf

Kam, Cindy D. 2005. "Who Toes the Party Line? Cues, Values, and Individual Differences." *Political Behavior* 27:163–82.

Kazee, Thomas A. 1983. "The Deterrent Effect of Incumbency on Recruiting Challengers in U.S. House Elections." *Legislative Studies Quarterly* 8:469–80.

Kidd, Quentin, Herman Diggs, Mehreen Farooq, and Megan Murray. 2007. "Black Voters, Black Candidates, and Social Issues: Does Party Identification Matter?" *Social Science Quarterly* 81:1027–35.

Kinder, Donald R., and Don Herzog. 1993. "Democratic Discussion." *Reconsidering the Democratic Public* 347.

Kuklinski, James, and Nathan Hurley. 1994. "On Hearing and Interpreting Political Messages: A Cautionary Tale of Citizen Cue-Taking." *Journal of Politics* 56:729–51.

Kuo, David. 2006. *Tempting Faith: An Inside Story of Political Seduction.* New York: Free Press.

Lau, Richard R., and David P. Redlawsk. 2001. "Advantages and Disadvantages of Cognitive Heuristics in Political Decision Making." *American Journal of Political Science,* 951–71.

Leege, David, Kenneth D. Wald, Brian Krueger, and Paul Mueller. 2002. *The Politics of Cultural Differences: Social Change and Voter Mobilization Strategies in the Post-New Deal Period.* Princeton: Princeton University Press.

Lees-Marshment, Jennifer. 2004. *The Political Marketing Revolution: Transforming the Government of the UK.* Manchester: Manchester University Press.

Lenz, Gabriel S. 2009. "Learning and Opinion Change, Not Priming: Reconsidering the Priming Hypothesis." *American Journal of Political Science* 53:821–37.

Luke, Timothy W. 2004. "Megametaphorics. Rereading Globalization and Virtualization as Rhetorics of World Politics." In *Metaphorical World Politics: Rhetorics of Democracy, War, and Globalization,* edited by Francis A. Beer and Christ'l De Landtsheer, 217–36. East Lansing: Michigan State University Press.

Lupia, Arthur. 1994. "Shortcuts versus Encyclopedias: Information and Voting Behavior in California Insurance Reform Elections." *American Political Science Review* 88:63–76.

Maarek, Philippe. 1995. *Political Marketing and Communication.* London: John Libby.

Maheswaran, Durairaj, and Shelly Chaiken. 1991. "Promoting Systematic Processing in Low-Motivation Settings: Effect of Incongruent Information on Processing and Judgment." *Journal of Personality and Social Psychology* 61:13–25.

Marcus, George E., Michael MacKuen, Jennifer Wolak, and Luke Keele. 2006. "The Measure and Mismeasure of Emotion." In *Feeling Politics: Emotion in Political Information Processing,* edited by David P. Redlawsk, 31–45. New York: Palgrave Macmillan.

Margolis, Michele F. 2018. "How Far Does Social Group Influence Reach? Identities, Elites, and Immigration Attitudes." *Journal of Politics* 80:772–85.

Mayhew, David. 1974. *Congress: The Electoral Connection*. New Haven: Yale University Press.

McDaniel, Eric L., and Christopher G. Ellison. 2008. "God's Party? Race, Religion, and Partisanship over Time." *Political Research Quarterly* 61:180–91.

McDermott, Monika. 1998. "Race and Gender Cues in Low Information Elections." *Political Research Quarterly* 54:895–918.

Mendelberg, Tali. 2017. *The Race Card: Campaign Strategy, Implicit Messages, and the Norm of Equality*. Princeton: Princeton University Press.

Mondak, Jeffrey. 1993. "Public Opinion and Heuristic Processing of Source Cues." *Political Behavior* 15:167–92.

Newman, Bruce. 1999. *The Mass Marketing of Politics*. Thousand Oaks, CA: Sage.

Nicholson, Stephen P. 2011. "Dominating Cues and the Limits of Elite Influence." *Journal of Politics* 73:1165–77.

Petty, Richard E., and John T. Cacioppo. 1986. *Communication and Persuasion: Central and Peripheral Routes to Attitude Change*. New York: Springer-Verlag.

Plasser, Fritz, Christian Scheucher, and Christian Senft. 1999. "Is There a European Style of Political Marketing?" In *Handbook of Political Marketing*, edited by Bruce Newman, 89–112. Thousand Oaks, CA: Sage.

Rahn, Wendy. 1993. "The Role of Partisan Stereotypes in Information Processing about Political Candidates." *American Journal of Political Science* 37:472–97.

Redlawsk, David P., and Richard R. Lau. 2006. "I Like Him, But . . . : Vote Choice When Candidate Likeability and Closeness on Issues Clash." In *Feeling Politics: Emotion in Political Information Processing*, edited by David P. Redlawsk, 187–208. New York: Palgrave MacMillan.

Robinson, Carin. 2010. "Cross-Cutting Messages and Political Tolerance: An Experiment Using Evangelical Protestants." *Political Behavior* 32:495–515.

Sellers, Patrick J. 1997. "Fiscal Consistency and Federal District Spending in Congressional Elections: A District Analysis." *American Journal of Political Science* 41:1024–41.

Sherif, Muzafer, O. J. Harvey, B. Jack White, William R. Hood, and Carolyn W. Sherif. 1961. *Intergroup Conflict and Cooperation: The Robbers Cave Experiment*. Norman: University of Oklahoma Press.

Sniderman, Paul M. 2000. "Taking Sides: A Fixed Choice Theory of Political Reasoning." *Elements of Reason: Cognition, Choice, and the Bounds of Rationality*, 67–84.

Sniderman, Paul M., Thomas Piazza, Philip E. Tetlock, and Ann Kendrick. 1991. "The New Racism." *American Journal of Political Science* 35 (2): 423–47.

Tajfel, Henri. 1970. "Experiments in Intergroup Discrimination." *Scientific American* 232:96–102.

Tajfel, Henri, and John C. Turner. 1986. "The Social Identity Theory of Intergroup Behavior." In *Psychology of Intergroup Relations*, edited by William G. Austin and Stephen Worchel, 276–93. Chicago: Nelson.

Tilly, Charles. 2006. *Why? What Happens When People Give Reasons . . . and Why*. Princeton: Princeton University Press.

Tyler, Tom R., and E. Allan Lind. 1992. "A Relational Model of Authority in Groups." *Advances in Experimental Social Psychology* 25:115–91.

Wallsten, Kevin, and Tatishe M. Nteta. 2016. "For You Were Strangers in the Land of Egypt: Clergy, Religiosity, and Public Opinion toward Immigration Reform in the United States." *Politics and Religion* 9:566–604.

Weber, Christopher, and Matthew Thornton. 2012. "Courting Christians: How Political Candidates Prime Religious Considerations in Campaign Ads." *Journal of Politics* 74:400–413.

Weinberger, Ota. 1995. "Argumentation in Law and Politics." *Communication and Cognition* 28:37–54.

Wildavsky, Aaron B. 1987. "Choosing Preferences by Constructing Institutions: A Cultural Theory of Preference Formation." *American Political Science Review* 81:3–21.

Zaller, John R. 1992. *The Nature and Origins of Mass Opinion*. New York: Cambridge University Press.

FOUR

The Public Perceptions of Arabs and Muslims Supporting a Social Norm

Brian Calfano, Nazita Lajevardi,
and Melissa Michelson

As discussed in this volume's introduction, religious communication can take various forms. Aside from specifics related to content and location, who or what does the communicating may be critical for ensuring message effectiveness. In the previous two chapters, we saw that cues from both religious and political elites featuring incongruent information (i.e., unexpected statements from leaders relative to their reputation and/or ideology) cause audiences to move toward opinions consonant with the elite's statements when featuring religious decision process language. But in both sets of cue experiments, the elite was a white male Christian. This is arguably the strongest social identity position an elite can have when communicating political views in the US. The question we address in this chapter is whether communicating unexpected or incongruent cue information as an elite lacking dominant racial and religious characteristics garners a similarly positive audience response.

Our assessment involves public reaction to an elite characterized as a member of a religious outgroup facing discrimination and government scrutiny. Here, we do not test religious communication as cues featuring religious content like decision process language. Instead, we assess a leader with religious outgroup characteristics making statements that, other things being equal, should be acceptable to dominant social and religious groups. Understanding religious communication effects in this context is critical for evaluating the extent to which religious aspects help or hinder the cause of minority or scrutinized groups in the eyes of dominant social majorities.

The reality that individuals make up groups is self-evident, but the challenge for dominated social and political groups is that collective stigmas may stymie individual elite attempts to change the intergroup status quo, to say nothing of improving the elite's standing among dominant outgroup members. To be sure, harassed outgroups may address grievances through the political process, although success in this endeavor is highly variable. Another option is for individual outgroup elites to improve conditions through actions that appeal to the wider society (and are consonant with its social values). Dominated groups have incentives to improve their standing and look for ways of gaining greater acceptance by dominant social groups. Acceptance in this instance represents progress. And it suggests that how dominant groups perceive outgroup elites can be improved. Much of this mechanism is premised on symbolic interactionism.

An assumption of sociology's symbolic interactionism theory is that establishing identity is an ongoing communication process for everyone (see Goffman 1959). Through communication, identities are situated and maintained. Signaling or self-promotion of characteristics believed to result in being liked or respected is critical in the identity communication process (Jones and Pittman 1982). Mapping this motive onto the situation confronting religious outgroup elites suggests that performing behavior perceived to be consonant with dominant social group norms may effectively signal a desire for acceptance. Such signaling is aimed, in part, at gaining the elite access into secular social and political hierarchies (and, by extension, other group members). Scholars have found this signaling dynamic at work in cases where the outgroup's relative status to the ingroup was pronounced, leading outgroups to accentuate characteristics considered desirable to the socially dominant group. In this way, members of the dominated group can, as Alexander and Lauderdale (1977, 226) put it, "create the most socially desirable situated identity for himself or herself" (see also Clement and Noels 1992).

Part of this signaling involved impression management, whereby people adopt behaviors to create favorable impressions from others (see DePaulo 1992). But the difficulty for dominated outgroup members is that, even when signaling complimentary (if unexpected or incongruent) information/characteristics to gain wider social acceptance, misinformation persistence makes achieving said acceptance a challenge (see Kuklinski et al. 2001; Nyhan and Reifler 2010). Furthermore, it is not clear if individual-level desirability signaling (even by group elites) leads to bettering the dominated outgroup's position as a whole or if it simply garners individual-level goodwill. As with contact theory, the key is whether the elite is considered representative or prototypical of the larger group or is considered an exception (Pettigrew and Trope 2006; Dixon et al. 2010).

We address this puzzle by testing the signaling effectiveness of America's political deliberation norm by an outgroup elite. Using a randomized survey–embedded experiment, we vary the signaler's desirable identity attributes (from the dominant outgroup's perspective) according to ethnicity (i.e., Arab) and religion (i.e., Muslim). Results show that while the outgroup signaler gains some positive feedback as an individual, these positive effects do not translate into warmer evaluations of Arabs and Muslims by the dominant ingroup (i.e., white Christians). This suggests that the nominal identity linking an elite to a scrutinized outgroup is not overcome even by impression management attempts featuring desirability signaling in the form of dominant norm endorsement.

Arab Muslim Signaling

Both Arab and Muslim Americans strive for equality and justice for their communities. Elites and group members often must work to counteract negative attitudes pervasive among the general public and explicitly encouraged by certain political leaders and media elites (Calfano et al. 2016). Indeed, in the Trump era, the legitimacy of Muslim Americans (and, by extension, Arabs) has been questioned with unprecedented intensity (Calfano, Lajevardi, and Michelson 2017). Today, Arab and Muslim Americans find themselves targeted directly and indirectly by policies restricting their travel, speech, and participation in American political institutions (Collingwood, Lajevardi, and Oskooii 2018; Oskooii, Lajevardi, and Collingwood 2019; Hobbs and Lajevardi 2019).

Such group maltreatment took clearer dimensions in the two years following 9/11 (Lajevardi 2020). Initially, the wars "on terror" and in Iraq coupled with the long-standing US tradition of stereotyping Arabs as terrorists made ethnicity the primary point of negative public focus (Shaheen 2014). It was not until the increased proliferation of what was referred to as Islamic terrorism (also sometimes referred to as ISIS, ISIL, or Daeesh) and, more recently, the Syrian refugee crisis that the public political focus settled on Muslims and Islam. Over time, and with the 2016 presidential election, US legislators, media, and the public focused negative attention on Muslim identity with intensity (Lajevardi 2020).

Trump's election corresponded with increases in hate crime rates against, negative public attitudes toward, and the implementation of government policies targeting Arab Americans and Muslim Americans. Although Trump's Muslim immigration ban faced significant legal and popular resistance, the effort also fueled Islamophobia and negative attitudes about Muslim and Arab Americans. These negative attitudes lower Muslim American and Arab American social status and are inseparable from Muslim American political participation and feelings of belonging (Lajevardi et al. 2020; Ocampo, Dana, and Barreto 2018; Oskooii 2016; Dana et al. 2018).

Relative to Muslims, less is known about Arab Americans, who likely are equally afflicted in today's climate. Interestingly, Arabs are considered white by the US government; they are directed to check the "white" box for race on the US Census and other government forms. Historically, this enabled Arab Americans to own land and receive rights and privileges only afforded to whites, including citizenship. Official "whiteness" notwithstanding, Arab Americans in the US encountered both public and private discrimination (Tehranian 2008; Shaheen 2014). Systemic racial profiling in the post-9/11 world generated something akin to acceptable discrimination in the name of patriotism and national security—a phenomenon perhaps aptly described as toxic patriotism (see Raghunathan 2017).

An irony is that, given the extent to which Arabs are considered "white," the public generally conflates Arabs and Muslims (Tessler 2003; Haddad 2011). And scholars have largely focused on attitudes toward one or the other group, with little comparison of how the groups are differently perceived, if at all. This includes research on Arab Americans (Salaita 2005), Middle Eastern Americans (Tehranian 2007; Wald 2008), and Muslim Americans (Barreto, Masuoka, and Sanchez 2008; Jamal 2005, 2009). Generally speaking, the American public views Muslims and Arabs unfavorably (Panagopoulous 2006; Lajevardi and Oskooii 2018; Calfano and Lajevardi 2019), which suggests that members of both groups are motivated to send cues that promote intergroup permeability and the public acceptance this promises (Brittingham and de la Cruz 2005; Calfano 2018).

Therefore, what we examine empirically in this chapter is (1) the degree to which the public holds distinctive attitudes about Arabs and Muslims and (2) whether those attitudes can be manipulated through desirable signaling by a member of those groups. To address both items, we randomly manipulate information in a purported news article about a planned forum for city council candidates, sometimes identifying the organizer (i.e., the political elite who is the focus of our assessment) as Muslim, sometimes as Arab, sometimes as an Arab Muslim, and sometimes without information about his ethnicity or religious affiliation. As such, there is nothing expressly communicated about religion or religious teaching in the design aside from the nominal identity.

Even with this limited information available to respondents, we find clear differences in how the organizer is perceived, reflecting different public attitudes about Muslims and Arabs. We also find that a positive response to the elite organizer as an individual does not reduce public prejudice toward Muslims—thereby undermining traditional contact theory expectations and the logic behind impression management and desirability signaling.

But why should a vignette signaling otherwise desirable, prosocial behavior by an outgroup elite negatively affect public impressions of the elite's nominal identity group? Generally speaking, people do not evaluate outgroups positively, especially when differences in religion are salient (Tajfel and Turner 1979; Johansson-Stenman, Mahmud, and Martinsson 2009). Yet, and perhaps reflecting impression management efficacy, researchers consider desirability signaling a promising avenue for bettering how religious minorities are perceived. Hall et al. (2015) suggest an additional dimension related to Muslims beyond basic impression management to involve how the outgroup perceives cost to the cue giver. Specifically, the researchers found that the perceived trustworthiness that Christians feel toward individual Muslims increased for those Christians who were told that a Muslim engaged in costly religious commitment signals (including either religious charitable giving or adherence to religious dietary restrictions).

While what constitutes "costly" behavior is somewhat relative, the act of doing something costly may be fundamentally different from the impression management cues that scholars have previously assessed regarding one's acceptance by dominant groups. And, in pivoting toward a political topic, examples of "costly" behavior may be especially noticeable in situations where someone uses private resources to provide a public good. Since the elite signaler in our study is variably associated with a scrutinized religious minority (i.e., Islam), religion is likely not a useful basis either for the prosocial signaling or the public good provision. Given this, we focus on public perceptions of religious outgroup members engaging in a costly, nonreligious prosocial behavior—organizing a local political forum.

The elite organizer mentioned in the vignette (and whose ethnicity and religion are randomly manipulated in the experiment) is seen as signaling his commitment to democracy rather than a commitment to his religion and/or ethnicity (which is variably described as being Muslim and/or Arab). This signaling suggests, among other things, an undertaking of assimilation, integration, and related activities that might make majority ingroup members look favorably on the elite and, by extension, on the identity outgroup group he is associated with (Arends-Toth and Van de Vijver 2003; Zagefka et al. 2007). Importantly, and different from the prior two chapters' experiments, communicating about religion is a liability for the elite in this case. Whereas the elites in the prior experiments stood at least an average chance of benefiting from their decision process cues, the discrimination American Muslims and Arabs confront suggests that communicating this identity information will blunt positive evaluations.

In our experiment, the organizer was variably described as a member of a scrutinized outgroup (i.e., Arab, Muslim, or Arab Muslim), thereby allowing for a direct test of whether this norm signal is overwhelmed by an association with attributes the majority ingroup considers negative. If the participants in our experiment see the organizer as trustworthy, and not representative of his larger identity group (religious or ethnic), then the positive evaluations they have of the organizer will not spill over to affect attitudes toward his larger identity group.

The literature is of mixed perspective when it comes to outgroups' perception of ingroup members as prototypically the same (see Medin 1989; Oakes, Turner, and Haslam 1991; Turner et al. 1994). Generally, and as Haslam et al. (1995) argue, group members will exhibit differing degrees of group prototypicality and will, therefore, be seen as variable representatives of their identity group. Related work on the ability of interpersonal contact to reduce prejudice toward outgroup members finds that the contact must be perceived as intergroup rather than interpersonal (Hewstone and Brown 1986; Brown, Vivian, and Hewstone 1999). Effectiveness also depends on the degree to which an outgroup representative is considered typical according to an individual's prior attitudes (Skipworth, Garner, and Dettrey 2010).

In terms of how this relates to Arabs and Muslims in the US, we suggest that, in the process of offering signals to improve dominant social group perceptions, a signaler with a scrutinized identity may promote more positive perceptions of herself or himself by offering incongruent information in the form of costly behavior. However, these positive perceptions will not necessarily transfer to their larger identity group. Indeed, the public may be pleased to evaluate the signaler positively without changing their views of the target identity group long an object of suspicion and discrimination. This may be because evaluating an individual target positively is less costly for the socially dominant group than updating perceptions about entire scrutinized social outgroups. But, on the other hand, an elite undertaking costly action to uphold nonpartisan democratic norms may be strong enough to overcome negative predispositions and to engender positive generalization to the larger group. This is the general takeaway that Zagefka et al. (2007) describe in the concluding remarks of their study: public impressions of scrutinized outgroups might become more positive through the offering of information about a minority group's preferences and behavior (and, we would add, particularly when this information aligns with the majority public's preferences).

We therefore hypothesize that when an elite from a socially stigmatized group offers incongruent information (from the socially dominant group's perspective) by signaling support for dominant social norms (i.e., deliberation over political candidates), this boosts favorable attitudes toward both the elite and the outgroup to which he belongs. At the same time, and based on the previous discussion about how Arabs tend to be ignored in the study of Muslims, we test whether the public conflates Muslims and Arabs by comparing responses in each of the three treatment conditions. Logically, if respondents do not distinguish between Arabs and Muslims, their evaluations of the elite organizer will not vary between treatment conditions, and neither will their attitudes about Muslims vary between assigned groups. Conversely, if respondents do distinguish between Arabs and Muslims, their evaluations of the elite organizer will vary between treatment group conditions, as will their attitudes about Muslims. Note that, across the hypothesized outcomes, we do not propose that intergroup permeability occurs. Specifically, positive perceptions of the elite and/or his larger identity group will not be on par with how the dominant social group perceives its own ingroup members. Indeed, while the elite's costly signaling may improve how the dominant group perceives him and his identity compatriots, the dominant group will still consider the elite and his fellow Muslims and/or Arabs as outgroup members.

Procedure

To help control for varying degrees of relative contact frequency the general public has with Muslims and Arabs: Michigan (high), California

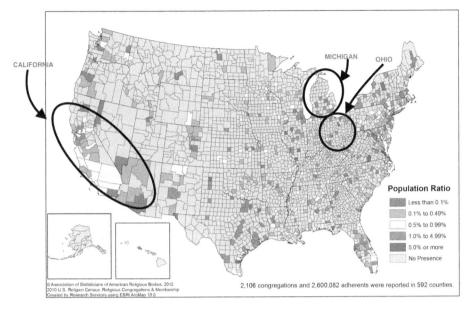

Fig. 4.1. Population Penetration, Estimated Muslim Adherents in the United States (2010)

(medium), and Ohio (low). Though not an exact match, figure 4.1 shows the relative concentration of the estimated number of Muslims across US counties, which we used as a proxy for determining which states to use as examples of high, medium, and low contact frequencies with Muslims (and, by extension, Arabs). We conducted an online vignette experiment using a purported newspaper article about a local community leader (i.e., elite) endorsing civil discourse in political deliberation by hosting a local political candidate forum through the organization he leads (i.e., the costly behavior). Deliberation is a hallmark value that the general public espouses (Durr, Gilmour, and Wolbrecht 1997), thereby aligning the elite with an activity signaling a consonant value held by the dominant social group. Subjects were randomly assigned to one of four conditions, which identified the local leader as (1) Arab, (2) Muslim, or (3) Arab Muslim or (4) provided no mention of his ethnic or religious outgroup identity. The survey firm Lucid, an online marketplace of opt-in respondents, provided subject recruitment. Lucid samples are a viable replacement option for Amazon's Mechanical Turk and provide the advantages of a less professionalized respondent pool (see Coppock and McClellan 2019). Data were collected through Qualtrics during the period July 18–23, 2018. Table 4.1 lists treatment and control condition assignments by state.

TABLE 4.1. Treatment and Control Group Assignments, by State

	Michigan	California	Ohio	Total
Control	122	127	119	368
Muslim	124	121	137	382
Arab	137	149	132	418
Arab Muslim	126	128	126	380
ALL	509	525	514	1,548

Note: Data collected July 18–23, 2018, by Lucid.

Subjects first answered demographic questions regarding their sex, race, and state of residence. These were used to ensure that the Lucid state subject pools matched US Census demographics for each state, which they did along these three dimensions. Subjects were then shown one of four vignettes about the "Be Civil, Be Heard" city council candidate forum organized by local resident Ralph Georgy (see appendix, where the manipulated language is shown in bold). After reading the vignette, subjects were asked to evaluate Georgy on their perception of him regarding a variety of individual-level attributes: (1) weak or strong, (2) lenient or harsh, (3) soft or hard, (4) cold or warm, (5) distant or caring, (6) their rating of him on a feeling thermometer, and (7) trustworthiness. Subjects were next posed a series of questions about whether they have personal contact with members of various groups, including Muslims and Arabs (masked by similar questions about contact with African Americans, Latinos, Asians, Jews, Hindus, Muslims, and atheists), and then given a variety of questions about their attitudes about Muslims, mosques, and the spread of sharia law. Finally, as a manipulation check, subjects answered an open-ended question recalling the news vignette topic and then a series of demographic questions including age, employment status, education, ideology, and political interest. Random assignment was not correlated with any subject demographic characteristic, and there was no evidence of nonrandom attrition across the assigned groups.

Results

We first examine whether subject evaluations of Georgy differ across the variable identity information in the treatment conditions. Our dependent variables are the seven questions about Georgy's personal attributes that immediately followed exposure to the manipulated news vignette: (1) weak or strong, (2) lenient or harsh, (3) soft or hard, (4) cold or warm, (5) distant or caring, (6) their rating of him on a feeling thermometer, and (7) perceived trustworthiness. Results are shown in table 4.2.

In terms of the general evaluation of Georgy's attributes, subject response across the three treatment conditions shows they were not statistically more likely to evaluate Georgy positively when exposed to information about his membership in scrutinized identity groups. Instead, there is an opposite effect when Georgy is described as a Muslim—he is considered harsher, colder, more distant, and less trustworthy relative to the other two treatment conditions and the control group. As such, there is no support for the expectation that incongruent cue information (in the form of a costly behavior) can make a positive impression for the individual performing the act when scrutinized religious identity information is communicated as part of an elite's biography. Perhaps the positive aspect in these findings is that subjects were comparatively more likely to not view Arab identity as harshly, including when paired with the Muslim identity (although the experiment does not have enough statistical power to detect significance in these ratings).

Note that there is mixed evidence that respondents distinguish between Muslims, Arabs, and Arab Muslims. Those assigned to the Muslim condition say Georgy was more lenient, colder, more distant, and less trustworthy compared to those assigned to the Arab condition (suggesting a more negative evaluation of Georgy as a Muslim). And, subjects considered Georgy colder, more distant, and less trustworthy when assigned

TABLE 4.2. Evaluations of Georgy, by Treatment Condition

	Muslim Mean		Arab Mean		Arab Muslim Mean		Control Mean	
Weak/strong	5.77	(1.41)	5.83	(1.52)	5.78	(1.50)	5.76	(1.33)
Lenient/harsh	4.58	(1.61) **ab *c	4.25	(1.47)	4.20	(1.52)	4.34	(1.40)
Soft/hard	4.64	(1.48)	4.49	(1.36)	4.59	(1.38)	4.69	(1.30)
Cold/warm	4.68	(2.00) **abc	5.44	(1.51)	5.20	(1.76)	5.31	(1.40)
Distant/caring	5.10	(2.07) **ac	5.81	(1.57)	5.23	(1.97)	5.65	(1.57)
Thermometer	50.20	(20.8) *c	50.00	(20.90)	50.60	(21.10)	53.60	(18.90)
Trustworthy	6.23	(2.90) **ac	7.28	(2.21)	6.53	(2.66)	7.07	(2.23)
N	382		418		380		368	

Note: Standard errors in parentheses. * $p < .05$, ** $p < .01$, two-tailed. The first five items are coded from 0 (low) to 8 (high); thermometer ratings range from 0 to 100; trust is coded from 0 (low) to 11 (high). Significance is noted as a for Muslim vs. Arab, b for Muslim vs. Arab Muslim, and c for Muslim vs. Control.

to the Arab Muslim condition compared to the Arab condition. Finally, those given the Arab Muslim treatment found Georgy more lenient and colder compared to the Muslim condition. These findings also suggest that being both Arab and Muslim presents the greatest challenge to generating positive individual-level appraisals from dominant outgroup members (even when offering incongruent information that aligns with the dominant group's norms or shows costly behavior in doing so). We checked the robustness of these results with analyses that eliminated respondents who took either less than ten seconds or more than one hour to complete the survey and those who were unable in the open-ended response at the end to recall the content of the news vignette. The results are similar, but not identical, as shown in table 4.3.

We also theorized that any positive impressions directed at the elite as an individual might transfer to the identity group with which he is associated. But with no significant movement toward positive views of Georgy when he is described as Muslim, we are left to leap into consideration of whether treated subjects report more favorable attitudes toward Muslims more generally compared to those in the control group. We model this with an attitude index composed of responses to nine different dependent variable items, controlling for demographic characteristics, ideology, and self-reported contact with Arabs and Muslims.

TABLE 4.3. Evaluations of Georgy, by Treatment Condition, Dropping Outliers on Duration

	Muslim Mean		Arab Mean		Arab Muslim Mean		Control Mean	
Weak/strong	5.76	(1.35)	5.93	(1.42)	5.86	(1.35)	5.82	(1.29)
Lenient/harsh	4.52	(1.56) **ab	4.21	(1.39)	4.18	(1.40)	4.33	(1.39)
Soft/hard	4.59	(1.43)	4.48	(1.28)	4.54	(1.29)	4.69	(1.29)
Cold/warm	4.68	(1.90) **abc	5.54	(1.42)	5.23	(1.70)	5.36	(1.37)
Distant/caring	5.12	(2.01) **ac	5.91	(1.49)	5.31	(1.96)	5.73	(1.51)
Thermometer	49.30	(20.10) *c	48.50	(20.40)	49.7	(20.80)	53.00	(19.20)
Trustworthy	6.27	(2.84) **ac	7.39	(2.12)	6.55	(2.57)	7.15	(2.22)
N	297		336		296		311	

Note: Standard errors in parentheses. * $p < .05$, ** $p < .01$, two-tailed. The first five items are coded from 0 (low) to 8 (high); thermometer ratings range from 0 to 100; trust is coded from 0 (low) to 11 (high). Significance is noted as a for Muslim vs. Arab, b for Muslim vs. Arab Muslim, and c for Muslim vs. Control.

The nine items are as follows:

1. Most Muslims integrate successfully in American culture (reverse coded).
2. Muslim Americans sometimes do not have the best interests of Americans at heart.
3. Muslims living in the US should be subject to more surveillance than others.
4. Muslim Americans, in general, tend to be more violent than other people.
5. Most Muslim Americans reject jihad and violence (reverse coded).
6. Most Muslim Americans lack basic English language skills.
7. Most Muslim Americans are not terrorists (reverse coded).
8. Wearing headscarves should be banned in all public places.
9. Muslim Americans do a good job of speaking out against Islamic terrorism (reverse coded).

Given the way these nine items are coded, positive coefficients mean subjects have more negative attitudes about Muslims in America. Note that we found no state-level effects for any of the reported outcomes in this chapter, and, as an example of these null effects, we included state-

TABLE 4.4. Muslim Attitudes Index

	Model 1 (all respondents)		Model 1 (with state dummies)		Model 2 (drop outliers & manipulation check fails)	
Treatment	0.01	(0.04)	0.00	(0.04)	0.01	(0.05)
Female	−0.06	(0.04) +	−0.06	(0.04) +	−0.04	(0.04)
White	−0.08	(0.04) *	−0.10	(0.04) *	−0.11	(0.05) *
Age	−0.00	(0.00)	−0.00	(0.00)	−0.00	(0.00)
Education	−0.11	(0.02) ***	−0.11	(0.02) ***	−0.12	(0.02) ***
Republican	0.46	(0.04) ***	0.45	(0.04) ***	0.50	(0.05) ***
Arab contact	0.00	(0.02)	0.00	(0.02)	0.00	(0.03)
Muslim contact	−0.34	(0.04) ***	−0.34	(0.04) ***	−0.34	(0.04) ***
CA dummy	−		−0.06	(0.05)	−0.08	(0.05)
MI dummy	−		−0.07	(0.04) +	−0.08	(0.05) +
Constant	2.99	(0.11) ***	3.04	(0.12) ***	3.08	(0.13)***
Adj. *R*-Squared	0.157		0.158		0.175	
N	1,530		1,530		1,227	

Note: Standard errors in parentheses. $+ p < .10$, $* p < .05$, $** p < .01$, $*** p < .001$, two-tailed.

level dummies for California and Michigan in table 4.4 (with Ohio as the excluded category). We find no evidence that attitudes about Muslims vary by exposure to any of the three treatments. Instead, subjects' education, partisanship, and level of interpersonal contact with Muslims affect attitudes. Perhaps unsurprisingly, Republican subjects have more negative attitudes about Muslims, while more educated subjects and those who report increased levels of Muslim contact have more positive attitudes.

Next, we examine whether subjects distinguish between Muslims and Arabs. We first look for differences on the items evaluating Georgy's attributes, as shown in table 4.5. There is no statistical difference on the attitudes index about Muslims across the full set of subjects. Instead, and as with the results just reported on in table 4.4, education, partisanship, and personal contact predict subject response. Republicans have less positive attitudes, while those with more education and more frequent Muslim contact are more positive. But results differ when dropping individuals who are outliers on duration and who fail the manipulation check that asked them to recall the news vignette topic. As table 4.6 shows, subjects give more positive (i.e., negatively signed) answers about Muslims when assigned to the Arab condition compared to the Muslim condition. They also have more positive views when assigned to the Arab Muslim condition versus the Muslim condition. These findings suggest that the public has some ability to distinguish between the groups. And, critically, from the standpoint of individual signaling as a way to improve impressions of one's identity group, subjects have less negative attitudes toward Arabs compared to their attitudes about Muslims. Hence, in terms of the larger question of

TABLE 4.5. Muslim Attitudes Index (Treatment Group Comparison Models)

	Model 1 (Muslim vs. Arab)		Model 2 (Muslim vs. Arab Muslim)		Model 3 (Muslim vs. Control)	
Muslim Treatment	0.02	(0.05)	−0.06	(0.05)	−0.00	(0.05)
Female	−0.04	(0.05)	0.07	(0.05)	−0.09	(0.05) +
White	0.02	(0.06)	−0.25	(0.06) ***	−0.11	(0.06) *
Age	−0.00	(0.00)	−0.00	(0.00)	−0.00	(0.00)
Education	−0.10	(0.02) ***	−0.11	(0.02) ***	−0.11	(0.02) ***
Republican	0.40	(0.06) ***	0.53	(0.06) ***	0.38	(0.06) ***
Arab contact	−0.01	(0.04)	0.01	(0.04)	0.00	(0.03)
Muslim contact	−0.30	(0.05) ***	−0.36	(0.05). ***	−0.39	(0.05) ***
Constant	2.87	(0.15) ***	3.15	(0.16) ***	3.09	(0.16) ***
Adj. R-Squared	0.126		0.174		0.148	
N	793		755		740	

Note: Standard errors in parentheses. $+ p < .10$, $* p < .05$, $** p < .01$, $*** p < .001$, two-tailed.

TABLE 4.6. Muslim Attitudes Index (Treatment Group Comparison Models, Dropping Outliers on Duration)

	Model 1 (Muslim vs. Arab)		Model 2 (Muslim vs. Arab Muslim)		Model 3 (Muslim vs. Control)	
Muslim Treatment	−0.03	(0.06)	−0.09	(0.06)	−0.03	(0.06)
Female	−0.00	(0.06)	0.11	(0.06) *	−0.08	(0.06)
White	0.01	(0.06)	−0.26	(0.06) ***	−0.08	(0.06)
Age	−0.00	(0.00)	−0.00	(0.00) +	−0.00	(0.00)
Education	−0.12	(0.03) ***	−0.12	(0.03) ***	−0.11	(0.03) ***
Republican	0.46	(0.07) ***	0.55	(0.07) ***	0.40	(0.07) ***
Arab contact	−0.01	(0.04)	−0.02	(0.04)	−0.02	(0.04)
Muslim contact	−0.28	(0.06) ***	−0.36	(0.06) ***	−0.38	(0.06) ***
Constant	3.00	(0.18) ***	3.23	(0.18) ***	3.08	(0.18) ***
Adj. R-Squared	0.146		0.195		0.157	
N	628		590		601	

Note: Standard errors in parentheses. $+ p < .10$, $* p < .05$, $** p < .01$, $*** p < .001$, two-tailed.

how Muslims are perceived and treated in America, the act of signaling dominant norms appears not to transfer from the individual to the group.

Discussion and Conclusion

These findings are noteworthy for what they do not show about elite-level communication from one holding a scrutinized religious identity. Despite some modest evidence that a local political forum organizer who is Arab receives a modicum of positive public evaluation, this same positivity is not afforded when the organizer is identified as Muslim. In addition, while positive, individual-level appraisals of the local organizer generate some positive impressions for Arabs and Arab Muslims in general, the same is not true for positive individual appraisals of Muslims. Subjects in our experiment were less likely to generalize their positive evaluation of the elite organizer to the broader group when he was identified as a member of a strongly stigmatized religious minority (even when knowing that this elite engaged in costly behavior to signal a dominant social group norm). The finding's implication is that there might be little that Muslims in America can do to systematically improve public perceptions of their identity group. Indeed, this may be an example where religious communication in the form of signaling dominant norm congruence meets with the lingering effects of negative group stereotypes regarding Muslims (see Calfano et al. 2016). If this is the case, then conventional wisdom about group-level benefits to

Muslims from demonstrating efforts to integrate or assimilate according to the public's expectations needs reconsideration.

Another takeaway may be that there is little that individual Muslims, even those in elite positions, can do to push back against stigmatization in the absence of a larger societal pivot, perhaps spurred by national political leaders or the media. But this pivot requires non-Muslim initiative and, even then, may have limited effects. As Collingwood, Lajevardi, and Oskooii (2018) found, dominant media narratives can move public opinion toward positions sympathetic to Muslims, although this is not the same as embracing Muslims more broadly as part of society (see also Lajevardi 2021). Still, the authors' finding is instructive in that it points to ways in which a scrutinized religious outgroup might find assistance from social and political institutions.

At the same time, and from a research design standpoint, it is possible that the issue here is not so much that the public is slow to move off its generally negative Muslim impression but, instead, that there is a problem with the norm we focused on. Specifically, it might be that signaling another dominant group norm has a more positive impact on public impressions of Muslim elites and, by extension, Muslims more generally. But while additional assessment of the effects from different types of signals is warranted, it is also hard to imagine how Muslim signaling of a different dominant norm might meet with a more positive public appraisal. What would this signaling include? Displaying the American flag? Singing patriotic songs? These kinds of ostensible, performance-oriented cues may have localized impacts, but they are not panaceas for how the dominant public views this identity group.

Perhaps part of the issue is that our assigned treatments were devoid of partisan cues, but finding positive evaluation of Muslim Republicans (for example) by non-Muslims in the GOP would suggest that the mechanism is more about partisan tribalism than it is public recognition that Muslims embrace the nation's dominant political norms. It would also point to the reality that, as scholars have started to recently argue with increased fervor (i.e., Margolis 2018), much of the causal power that religion was thought to occupy in determining political outcomes was, in fact, misappropriated—politics influences religion. In the case of Muslim signaling, it might be that public perceptions are only malleable when politics is meted out as partisan cues. Communicating norm congruity with the general public is simply not enough for scrutinized religious minorities.

APPENDIX—NEWS VIGNETTE ABOUT RALPH GEORGY

Jamie Moorehouse, Associated Press

April 30, 2018

Updated at 9:25 pm

With attacks ramping up between city council candidates, at least one organization hopes to bring opponents together to focus on substantive policy proposals.

Ralph Georgy, curator of Be Civil, Be Heard, announced Monday that seven of the nine registered candidates for three open council seats accepted invitations to appear at Be Civil, Be Heard's candidates forum on Thursday at 7:30 pm. The forum will be held at the Dickerson Elementary School auditorium on Ridgemont Road.

Be Civil, Be Heard describes itself in its promotional materials as "a place for city residents to deliberate on the issues that affect us all."

In a press release, Georgy said "We are excited about the opportunity for the public to hear from council candidates, and to make up their own minds about those who might best lead the city in the coming years."

Georgy has used Be Civil, Be Heard events to highlight the importance of community cohesion. "**[As a Muslim American/As an Arab American/As an Arab and Muslim American]** I know the challenges of bringing people together to see our common purpose, and this event can help us realize this opportunity as a city."

Georgy says the forum is free and open to all, although he recommends arriving early to find convenient parking.

© *2018 The Associated Press. All Rights Reserved.*

REFERENCES

Alexander, C. Norman Jr., and Pat Lauderdale. 1977. "Social Identities and Social Influence." *Sociometry* 40: 225–33.

Arends-Toth, Judit, and Fons J.R. Van De Vijver. 2003. "Multiculturalism and Acculturation: Views of Dutch and Turkish-Dutch." *European Journal of Social Psychology* 33: 249–66.

Brittingham, Angela, and G. Patricia De la Cruz. 2005. *We The People of Arab Ancestry in the United States.* Washington, DC: U.S. Census Bureau.

Brown, Rupert, James Vivian, and Miles Hewstone. 1999. "Changing Attitudes through Intergroup Contact: The Effects of Group Membership Salience." *European Journal of Social Psychology* 17:131–42.

Calfano, Brian R. 2018. *Muslims, Identity, and American Politics*. New York: Routledge.

Calfano, Brian R., Paul A. Djupe, Daniel Cox, and Robert P. Jones. 2016. "Muslim Mistrust: The Resilience of Negative Public Attitudes after Complimentary Information." *Journal of Media and Religion* 15:29–42.

Calfano, Brian R., and Nazita Lajevardi, eds. 2019. *Understanding Muslim Political Life in America: Contested Citizenship in the Twenty-First Century*. Philadelphia: Temple University Press.

Calfano, Brian Robert, Nazita Lajevardi, and Melissa Michelson. 2017. "Trumped Up Challenges: Limitations, Opportunities, and the Future of Political Research on Muslim Americans." *Politics, Groups, and Identities* 7:477–87.

Clement, Richard, and Kimberly A. Noels. 1992. "Toward a Situated Approach to Ethnolinguistic Identity: The Effects of Status on Individuals and Groups." *Journal of Language and Social Psychology* 11: 203–32.

Collingwood, Loren, Nazita Lajevardi, and Kassra Oskooi. 2018. "A Change of Heart? Why Individual-Level Public Opinion Shifted against Trump's 'Muslim Ban.'" *Political Behavior* 40:1035–72.

Coppock, Alexander, and Oliver McClellan. 2019. "Validating the Demographic, Political, Psychological, and Experimental Results Obtained from a New Source of Online Survey Respondents." *Research & Politics* https://doi.org/10.1177/2053168018822174

Dana, Karam, Nazita Lajevardi, Kassra A. R. Oskooii, and Hannah L. Walker. 2018. "Veiled Politics: Experiences with Discrimination among Muslim Americans." *Politics and Religion* 12:629–77.

DePaulo, Bella M. 1992. "Nonverbal Behavior and Self-Presentation." *Psychological Bulletin* 111: 203–43.

Dixon, John, Kevin Durkheim, Colin Tredoux, Linda Trapp, Beverley Clack, Liberty Eaton. 2010. "A Paradox of Integration? Interracial Contact, Prejudice Reduction, and Perceptions of Racial Discrimination." *Journal of Social Issues* 66: 401–16.

Durr, Robert H., John B. Gilmour, and Christina Wolbrecht. 1997. "Explaining Congressional Approval." *American Journal of Political Science* 41:175–207.

Goffman, Erving. 1959. *The Presentation of Self in Everyday Life*. Garden City, NY: Anchor Books.

Haddad, Yvonne Yazbeck. 2011. *Becoming American? The Forging of Arab and Muslim Identity in Pluralist America*. Waco, TX: Baylor University Press.

Hall, Deborah, Adam Cohen, Kaitlin K. Meyer, Allison H. Varley, and Gene Brewer. 2015. "Costly Signaling Increases Trust, Even across Religious Affiliations." *Psychological Science* 26:1368–76.

Haslam, S. Alexander, Penelope J. Oakes, Craig McGarty, John C. Turner, and Rina S. Onorato. 1995. "Contextual Changes in the Prototypicality of Extreme and Moderate Outgroup Members." *European Journal of Social Psychology* 25:509–30.

Hewstone, Miles, and Rupert J. Brown. 1986. "Contact Is Not Enough: An Intergroup Perspective on the 'Contact Hypothesis.'" In *Contact and Conflict in Inter-*

group Encounters, edited by Miles Hewstone and Rupert J. Brown, 1–44. New York: Basil Blackwell.

Hobbs, William, and Nazita Lajevardi. 2019. "Effects of Divisive Political Campaigns on the Day-to-Day Segregation of Arab and Muslim Americans." *American Political Science Review* 113:270–76.

Jones, Edward E., and Thane S. Pittman. 1982. "Toward a General Theory of Strategic Self-Presentation." In *Psychological Perspectives on the Self*, vol. 1, edited by Jerry Suls, 231–62. Hillsdale, NJ: Lawrence Erlbaum.

Kuklinski, James H., Paul J. Quirk, Jennifer Jerit, and Robert F. Rich. 2001. "The Political Environment and Citizen Competence." *American Journal of Political Science* 45: 410–24.

Lajevardi, Nazita. 2020. *Outsiders at Home: The Politics of American Islamophobia.* New York: Cambridge University Press.

Lajevardi, Nazita. 2021. "The Media Matters: Muslim American Portrayals and the Effects on Mass Attitudes." *Journal of Politics* (OnlineFirst).

Lajevardi, Nazita, Kassra A. R. Oskooii, Hannah Walker, and Aubrey Westfall. 2020. "The Paradox between Integration and Perceived Discrimination among U.S. Muslims." *Political Psychology* 14:587–606.

Margolis, Michele F. 2018. *From Politics to the Pews: How Partisanship and the Political Environment Shape Religious Identity.* Chicago: University of Chicago Press.

Medin, Douglas L. 1981. "Concepts and Conceptual Structure." *American Psychologist* 44:1469–81.

Nyhan, Brendan, and Jason Reifler. 2010. "When Corrections Fail: The Persistence of Political Misperceptions." *Political Behavior* 32:303–30.

Oakes, Penelope J., John C. Turner, and S. Alexander Haslam. 1991. "Perceiving People as Group Members: The Role of Fit in the Salience of Social Categorizations." *British Journal of Social Psychology* 30:125–44.

Ocampo, Angela X., Karam Dana, and Matt A. Barreto. 2018. "The American Muslim Voter: Community Belonging and Political Participation." *Social Science Research* 72:84–99.

Oskooii, Kassra A. R. 2016. "How Discrimination Impacts Sociopolitical Behavior." *Political Psychology* 37: 613–40.

Oskooii, Kassra A. R., Nazita Lajevardi, and Loren Collingwood. 2019. "Opinion Shift and Stability: The Information Environment and Long-Lasting Opposition to Trump's Muslim Ban." *Political Behavior* 12:1–37.

Pettigrew, Thomas F., and Linda R. Tropp. 2006. "A Meta-Analytic Test of Intergroup Contact Theory." *Journal of Personality and Social Psychology* 90:751–83.

Raghunathan, Suman. 2017. "Too Many Americans Think Patriotism Means Racism and Xenophobia." *The Nation*, September 11.

Salaita, Stephen George. 2005. "Ethnic Identity and Imperative Patriotism: Arab Americans Before and After 9/11." *College Literature* 32:146–68.

Shaheen, Jack G. 2014. *Reel Bad Arabs: How Hollywood Vilifies a People*, 3rd ed. Northampton, MA: Olive Branch Press.

Skipworth, Sue Ann, Andrew Garner, and Bryan J. Dettrey. 2010. "Limitations of the Contact Hypothesis: Heterogeneity in the Contact Effect on Attitudes toward Gay Rights." *Politics & Policy* 38:887–906.

Tajfel, Henri, and John Turner. 1979. "An Integrative Theory of Intergroup Conflict." In *The Social Psychology of Intergroup Relations*, edited by William G. Austin and Stephen Werchel, 33–47. Pacific Grove, CA: Brooks Cole.

Tehranian, John. 2007. "Selective Racialization: Middle-Eastern American Identity and the Faustian Pact with Whiteness." *Connecticut Law Review* 40:1201.

Tessler, Mark. 2003. "Arab and Muslim Political Attitudes: Stereotypes and Evidence from Survey Research." *International Studies Perspectives* 4:175–81.

Turner, John C., Penelope J. Oakes, Stephen A. Haslam, and Craig McGarty. 1994. "Self and Collective: Cognition and Social Context." *Personality and Social Psychology Bulletin* 20:454–63.

Zagefka, Hanna, Rupert Brown, Murielle Broquard, and Sibel Martin. 2007. "Predictors and Consequences of Negative Attitudes toward Immigrants in Belgium and Turkey: The Role of Acculturation Preferences and Economic Competition." *British Journal of Social Psychology* 46:153–69.

FIVE

Anti-Muslim Religious Communication in India and the United States

A Comparative and Interpretive Analysis

Laura Dudley Jenkins and Rina Verma Williams

This chapter is a transition point in the volume, using a comparative perspective to focus on forms of communication by political actors to rally non-Muslims against Muslim minority communities. Comparing India and the United States demonstrates that, despite starkly different demographic realities, Muslims and Islam are imagined and delegitimized in two of the world's largest secular democracies through similar approaches to vilifying Islamic law. We begin with a review of the literature on Islamophobic discourses and then explain how discourse and visual analyses allow us to interpret and compare these xenophobic narratives. Through longstanding anti-Muslim tropes in India and examples of contemporary anti-Muslim political communication in the US, we find that the more recent negative narratives about Muslim Americans repeat themes that scholars have observed in India for several decades.

President Donald Trump's (empirically debunked) campaign claim that thousands of Muslims in New Jersey cheered from rooftops after the 9/11 attacks (Kessler 2015; Fine and Khawaja 2005)[1] echoed eerily with long-

---

1. The claim was rated "4 Pinnochios" by the *Washington Post* and "Pants on Fire" by Politi-Fact (Carroll 2015).

standing, stubbornly persistent, and widely circulated rumors that Muslim Indians cheer for Pakistan during cricket matches—a virtually life-and-death issue in India (Varshney 2002; Chowdhry 2000). Such claims question the legitimacy of Muslims' loyalty, belonging, and even citizenship in their respective countries.

But compared to the US, India has a longer history of anti-Muslim political rhetoric, primarily from the Hindu right. The academic literature about this anti-Muslim communication reveals that attacks on Islamic law are a common political tactic and identifies three major themes in this anti-Muslim messaging in India: gender threat (i.e., Islamic law oppresses women), demographic threat (i.e., Islamic law enables and encourages Muslim population growth), and violent threat (i.e., Islamic law and its adherents are violent and barbaric). At the same time, anti-Muslim political communication in the US also vilifies Islamic law—and by extension the Muslim minority—as sexist, expansionist, and barbaric. In other words, we find that elites in India and the US use similar cues in characterizing religious minorities (namely, the threats they supposedly pose in terms of gender, demographics, and violence) for political purposes.

The parallels between the portrayals of Muslims and Islamic law in India and the US are particularly striking because the socioeconomic status of the Muslim minorities and legal status of Islamic law in both cases are so different. In India, Muslims are the largest religious minority (at about 14 percent of the population), after Hindus (who make up over 80 percent of the population). Muslim Indians have lived in the subcontinent for centuries. Since India's independence in 1947, Muslims have experienced discrimination and disadvantage on virtually every measure: employment, education and literacy, health, and housing, among many others. An Indian government study found that Muslims are often even more disadvantaged than India's Dalit (formerly "untouchable") communities (Sachar 2007). In the US, by contrast, Muslims are about 1 percent of the population in a country that is about 70 percent Christian. Unlike most Muslim Indians, Muslim Americans tend to be wealthy, educated, and from families that immigrated in recent generations (Wormald 2015).

India formally recognizes different religious laws for specified family legal matters in a system known as "personal laws." Marriage, divorce, inheritance, and adoption are governed by one's religion, although government administrators or judges implement the laws. This form of legal pluralism extends back to British colonial rule and continued in modified form after independence, but it remains a controversial practice. Each religious community practices their own personal laws, yet Islamic law has been the central focus in controversies over the personal laws system and a frequent target of Hindu nationalist political elites.

Even though the US does not formally recognize religious laws, the political tactic of attacking Islamic law exists in America as well. Since 2010, activists have mounted a state-level strategy of advocating and implementing "anti-Sharia" laws, or legal bans on the admissibility or use of foreign laws (directed at outlawing Islamic law). This has resulted in eight state bans and dozens of bills (often following model legislation from Islamophobic organizations) and the distribution of literature featuring misinformation and inflammatory images about Muslims and Islam.

After introducing key literature on Islamophobic discourses and our interpretive and comparative methods, we detail in the section "Different Contexts" the demographic and legal differences impacting Muslim minorities in India and the US. Specifying these different contexts is both analytically and empirically important. Analytically, we find that surprisingly similar negative communication occurs across these quite different national political contexts. Empirically, this section is an important corrective to the negative political communication about Muslim laws and demographics, which ranges from distorted to fabricated.

In the next section, "Similar Discourses," we highlight three common themes gleaned from the secondary literature on anti-Muslim politics in India and use discourse and visual analyses to examine these themes in examples of anti-Muslim political communication in the contemporary US. Our conclusion discusses our finding of similar communications in different contexts and calls for further research to measure the impact of such political communication on attitudes. It also encourages research on the efficacy of actions to counter the transnational Islamophobic networks and the messages they propagate.

Literature: Islamophobic Discourses in India and the US

Islamophobia is socially constructed fear or hatred of Muslims and Islam. The religious studies scholar and anthropologist Peter Gottschalk emphasizes that Islamophobia is a group phenomenon: Islamophobia is "unjustified social anxieties toward Islam and Muslim culture . . . a socially shared sensibility, not a psychological condition of an individual. As opposed to personal fears of spiders, snakes and heights, Islamophobia originates from and is sustained by a group" (2013, 170–71). Discourse and visual analyses shed light on *how* this fear and hatred is socially sustained and spread. Notable studies of visual Islamophobia include Gottschalk and Gabriel Greenberg's analysis of political cartoons (2008) and Jack Shaheen's book and documentary about portrayals of "Arabs" on film (equated with "Muslims" by many in the West) (Shaheen 2009; Jhally et al. 2006). After 9/11, scholars supplemented these critiques of popular media portrayals by examining communication by political or government leaders. For instance, Junaid Rana analyzed government communication, including an FBI press release and poster, to reveal how they created a "moral panic" and a generalized—and racialized—fear of Muslim Americans (2011, 57).

In India, anti-Muslim political communication has a longer history. Amrita Basu shows how the Hindu nationalist Bharatiya Janata Party came to power by playing on "antipathy toward the state, interlaced with anti-Muslim sentiment" (2015, 13). Anti-Muslim discourses in India, spread by a web of Hindu nationalist organizations and activists, have at least three major strands. First, right-wing and Hindu nationalist elites have long stressed the need to "protect" women from Muslim men (Banerjee 2005; Sehgal 2014). This gender threat has been a major theme of rumors provoking communal violence from partition in 1947 until now. Rumors of the threat that Muslims supposedly pose to women even precede partition (Jenkins 2019, 188–90). Second, demographic threat, especially the relative size and growth rates of the Hindu and Muslim communities, has been a popular political theme since India's independence. Independence occurred simultaneously with the partition of Pakistan from India, a policy driven, in part, by demographic fears that the Muslim minority would overtake the Hindu majority (Nussbaum 2007, 202–3; Appadurai 2006). Third, Hindu elites construct Islam as a "violent tradition" to, ironically, inspire violence against Muslims (Robinson 2005, 29).

Some of the most powerful anti-Muslim communication in India combines all three of these threat themes—gender, demographic, and violent—in a widely and systematically spread "love jihad" rumor that Muslim men seduce and forcibly convert non-Muslim women to have Muslim offspring (Rao 2011). This rumor has roots in similar stories extending back to the colonial era but has been repeatedly revived in Hindu nationalist elites' speeches and activists' social media campaigns from the mid-2000s to the present, often springing up around elections (Jenkins 2019, 180–215).

Though political Islamophobia in the US is pronounced in the post-9/11 era, Islamophobia is not new to America. Indeed, it has arguably been present in various forms since the nation's founding and periodically activated in contemporary politics during the OPEC oil embargo (1973–74), the 1979 Iranian revolution and hostage crisis (1979–81), and the 1991 Gulf War (Gottschalk 2013, 176). But following 9/11, America led a new phase of global Islamophobia with consequences that have reverberated throughout the world. Gottschalk argues that in the US, earlier "anti-Muslim expressions arose when people who genuinely knew no better drew from a common fund of inherited stereotypes." By contrast, "the new millennium has witnessed very willfully distorted information about Muslims and Islam" (2013, 175–78). Indeed, "a well-funded industry of political professionals has helped to promote Islamophobic ideas in the American political sphere" (Love 2017, 92–93).

Because India has been in this "willful distortion" phase of political Islamophobia for a longer period—when politicians and activists politicize and systematically spread Islamophobia—comparative and contextual analyses of India can shed light on this troubling development in the US. We find a comparison between India and the US to be both uncommon and uniquely productive. Both countries are large, diverse, established, constitutional secular democracies. But India has a long experience with political Islamophobia, and the US took this path after 9/11. Do the three prominent discourses in India's Islamophobia (gender threat, demographic threat, and violent threat) appear in the US as well?

This comparison is timely due to many Americans' and Indians' negative attitudes toward Muslims. In the US, a Pew survey used a "feeling thermometer" to measure respondents' views of various religious groups. In 2017, American respondents rated Muslims the lowest: 48 on a 1–100 scale, even below atheists at 50 (Pew only uses the "feeling thermometer" in its US surveys). In a different Pew survey, India had the highest percentage of respondents "very concerned" or "somewhat concerned" about the rise of Islamic extremism in their country (84 percent); in the US, 70 percent were very or somewhat concerned about this (Pew Research Center 2017, 2005).

These negative attitudes have coincided with the spate of state-level laws in the US prohibiting the use of Sharia. While these laws may seem to be a logical outcome of negative feelings about Muslims and Sharia, the relationship between this legal trend and public attitudes is more complex. Anti-Sharia laws (and the campaigns in support of them) also contribute to, rather than simply reflect, Islamophobic views. Instead of proving causal direction, our discourse analysis of anti-Muslim political communication sheds light on the reciprocal relationship between fears and policies.

Gottschalk and Greenberg describe this dynamic in their book, *Islamophobia*: "Like a vicious cyclone feeding off its own energy, these sentiments cumulatively feed policies that in turn produce reactions that reinforce the original sentiments" (2008, 6). Mitchell and Toner researched the diffusion of anti-Sharia initiatives in the US, providing a comprehensive table of such initiatives and observing that Southern and conservative states are more likely to support them. But they also note that there is still uncertainty about why some states consider or adopt these policies, suggesting that "it is likely due to the perceived threat of Islamic practice in the United States" (2016, 737–38, 721). Our discourse analysis sheds light on *how* such a perceived threat is generated. Because a study of all Islamophobic discourse is far too vast, we focus on narratives about Islamic law or Sharia.

Methods: Interpretive and Comparative Analysis

Our interpretive methods are distinct from the many positivist chapters in this volume. In this section we explain our approach, including its interpretive and comparative aspects and our choice of sources and examples.

Interpretive Analysis

Inspired by interpretive political scientist Cecelia Lynch, we identify "dominant interpretations," constructed by those in power, that shape "what kinds of actions leaders and their publics are supposed to take." By "tacking back and forth" between dominant and alternative interpretations, we challenge dominant claims. Finally, we question and reexamine not only the dominant narratives (which are foundational in the communication of societal norms and values) but also our own assumptions (Lynch 2014, 305, 304, 307). We acknowledge our normative assumptions that Islamophobia is bad, which we maintained throughout the project, while gaining a better grasp of its political pull. Using an "abductive" approach, we started this project not with a theory to prove or disprove but rather with a "puzzle, surprise or tension," namely, our observation that anti-Muslim arguments we had followed for years in the context of Indian politics (our primary field of study) seemed on the rise in US politics (Schwartz-Shea and Yanow 2012, 27).

Like David Howarth, we define discourse as "historically specific systems of meaning which form the identities of subjects and objects," paying particular attention to "the construction of antagonisms and the drawing of political frontiers between 'insiders' and 'outsiders.'" As discourse includes "a wide range of linguistic and non-linguistic material," we use both textual and visual analyses. We compare not to offer causal explanations or substantiate general laws of political behavior but rather "to further our understanding . . . of identity formation and hegemonic practice" in different times and places. We do this by problematizing the way certain discursive practices both "construct and normalize particular representations of issues" (2000, 9–11, 139, 135).

By interpreting political communication, we shift the focus of political inquiry from "more or less stable or structured outlooks" to the "argumentative practices that recharge, articulate and recirculate ideas" (Martin 2014, 93). This circulation of ideas about insiders and outsiders also involves communication in the form of visual images. By interpreting images and how texts are visually presented in addition to the words themselves, we consider the way communication that increasingly combines the "visual and the verbal" gets "multilayered messages across" (Howells and Negreiros 2012, 5). We do this by identifying "key themes" in the verbal and visual communication we examine (Rose 2014, 210–20). This necessitates in-depth analysis of a small number of examples to discuss not only what is written but also how the presentation of words and images communicates these themes and persuades the reader or viewer.

Comparative Analysis

Our comparisons of India and the US begin with demographic comparisons of Muslims in both countries, followed by comparisons of the legal and political status of Islamic law. We conclude with the discourse analyses of anti-Muslim political communications. Our demographic comparison reveals that their smaller numbers and relatively high socioeconomic status have not protected contemporary Muslim Americans from some timeworn themes from the Islamophobic playbook. These demographics also serve as a factual counterpoint to one of the Islamophobic discourses we examine—the purported demographic threat to majority religious communities. For readers who may not be familiar with the term, our legal analysis includes a primer on "Sharia" and how it is used in Indian and American legal contexts. Although both are secular democracies, India uses Muslim personal law in several civil legal areas, while the US does not (except in rare cases to adjudicate disputes involving civil contracts that refer to religious laws, and only if they comply with relevant US laws).

Through discourse analysis we identified three major Islamophobic themes in anti-Muslim political communication in India. To see whether and how these themes are currently used in the US, we examined materials about anti-Sharia legislation produced by three of its major backers (Jihad Watch, Breitbart News, and the American Public Policy Alliance) and chose three distinct types of political discourse for more detailed textual and visual analyses: a Jihad Watch pamphlet entitled "Islam 101," a Breitbart News article on anti-Sharia legislation, and the website of the American Public Policy Alliance, an organization that provides model anti-Sharia legislation and advocates for this legislation in US state legislatures. This set of materials features a range of types of anti-Muslim advocacy, including a blatantly anti-Muslim organization (Jihad Watch), a news site that amplifies racist messaging (Breitbart News), and an innocuous-sounding yet xenophobic organization with the professional veneer of a think tank (American Public Policy Alliance).[2] The Southern Poverty Law Center has called the American Public Policy Alliance an "anti-Muslim hate group" (2019c). Each example represents one type of negative religious communication that is politically disenfranchising for a scrutinized religious minority. Importantly, these examples include forms of religious communication that scholars may overlook because of their secular tenor. But as forms of xenophobic communication that the public may find credible due to their scholarly facade, these examples are important to assess.

Different Contexts: Demographic and Legal Analysis and Comparisons

Muslims in India and the US present starkly different demographic characteristics on multiple critical measures: percentage of population, how long they have been in the country, income and educational levels, and their own perceptions of how well they are doing. Their legal contexts are also distinct. India's legal system includes Muslim family law but the US's does not, yet similar discursive tropes and politicized arguments over Sharia appear in both countries.

Demographic Divergences

Muslims are India's largest religious minority at 14.23 percent but only make up an estimated 0.9 percent of the US population. Although Hindu

---

2. We focus on identifiable anti-Muslim political or media organizations. Although they have a web presence, they are distinct from anonymous Islamophobic messaging online or via social media, a form of communication that is outside the scope of this study but another trend worthy of further study (Jenkins 2019, 180–215).

nationalism "portrays Muslims as 'invaders' and 'foreign transplants'" (Chowdhry 2000, 103), Islam "is as old in India as in Turkey. Indian Islam is older than American Christianity and European Protestantism" (Ludden 1996, 5). Indian Muslims have among the lowest income and education levels in the country: only 12 percent of Indian Muslims have a secondary education, and "less than 20 percent of Muslims have a spending capacity equivalent to or higher than the national average of Rs. 1050" (Sachar 2007). And Muslims' own perceptions reflect the data: Gallup found that Muslims in India are the most likely of all religious groups in the country to view themselves as "suffering" at 32 percent, a much higher rate than that of Hindus at 23 percent (Gallup 2011).[3] The same Gallup study found that Indian Muslims are, on their present income, least likely to be living comfortably and most likely to be finding it very difficult in comparison to Hindus and all other religious groups (Gallup 2011).

In the US, conversely, Muslims constitute a tiny (if growing) fraction of the population: 0.4 percent in 2007, 0.9 percent in 2014, 1 percent in 2016, and an expected rise to 2 percent by 2050 (Wormald 2015). And a vast majority are recent immigrants: fully 64 percent of Muslims in America are immigrants, with only 17 percent being second generation and 18 percent being third generation or higher (Wormald 2015). American Muslims are also diverse in terms of race, including a significant Black Muslim population, ethnicity, and national origin (Calfano 2018). They are largely better off than their Indian counterparts in terms of income and education levels. Two-thirds of US Muslims (66 percent) live in households with incomes above $30,000, with 20 percent at $100,000 or more (Wormald 2015). And educationally, Muslims stand behind only Hindus, Jews, and Buddhists in terms of proportion of population with a graduate or postgraduate college degree: 23 percent of Muslims have a college degree, and 17 percent have a postgraduate degree. As in India, their socioeconomic status is reflected in their perceptions of their own status and standing. American Muslims were more likely than Muslims in any other Western country to say they are "thriving," and 46 percent report good/excellent financial status (see fig. 5.1).

Data collection on religious groups in the two countries converges and diverges in curious and notable ways. In both countries, nationwide cen-

---

3. "Gallup classifies respondents as 'thriving,' 'struggling,' or 'suffering' according to how they rate their current and future lives on a ladder scale with steps numbered from 0 to 10 based on the Cantril Self-Anchoring Striving Scale. People who rate their current life situation and their life in five years a '4' or less are considered suffering" (Gallup 2011).

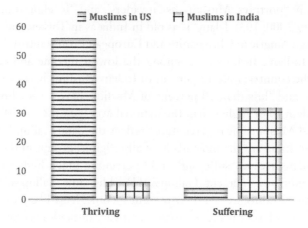

Fig. 5.1. Percent "Thriving" and "Suffering"
Note: Gallup classifies respondents as "thriving," "struggling," or "suffering" according to how they rate their current and future lives on a ladder scale with steps numbered from 0 to 10 based on the Cantril Self-Anchoring Striving Scale. People who rate their current life situation and their life in five years a "4" or less are considered suffering (Gallup 2011).

suses are conducted decennially. The first Indian census was completed under British colonial rule by 1872 and has been carried out every ten years since independence. Historically, the Indian government gathered religious data but did not release it. For the most recent 2011 census, however, religious data were released in 2015. But this appeared to be after it had leaked (which it regularly did in prior iterations too). After independence, the Indian government's rationale for not releasing religious data was assumed and understood by researchers to be related to the desire not to exacerbate "communal" or interreligious (and especially Hindu-Muslim or even anti-Muslim) tension. In the US, however, the US Census Bureau does not gather religious data at all. As a result, researchers are reliant on independent polling organizations such as the Pew Research Center to release their own estimates of religious proportions in the US. In contrast to the Indian government's open concerns about interreligious tensions rising in response to census data, it seems less immediately clear what the US government's rationale might be for not even gathering such data. The convergences and divergences between different countries with respect to the collection of data on religion present a seemingly fruitful path for further research.

Different Legal Contexts

Sharia can be defined as Islamic law, or "divinely revealed principles and values" (Esposito 2001, ix, 130, 152). Law in Islam includes both Sharia and Fiqh: "Shariah refers to God's divine law as contained in the Quran and the sayings and doings of Muhammad (hadith). *Fiqh* refers to the scholarly efforts of jurists (fuqaha) to elaborate the details of sharia through investigation and debate" (Esposito 2003, 148). We will use the terms "Islamic law," "Sharia" (sometimes spelled Shariah or other ways), or "Muslim personal law," depending on the context and case, but warn that the terms used by the people or organizations we are quoting are not always used appropriately or accurately.

The political debate in India is largely over what is known as "Muslim personal law," so that term will appear in the Indian examples and analyses. The term "Sharia" is used more often by the anti-Islamic law activists in the US and will appear in the examples and analyses of their discourse. These activists, as we will show below, do not venture into the complexities of Islamic jurisprudence, interpretations, histories, or contexts. A point-by-point rebuttal of their claims and an introduction to Islamic law are beyond the scope of this chapter, but to counter the portrayals generated by anti-Muslim activists' inaccurate, selective, and sensationalistic renderings of "Sharia," we recommend the work of Esposito (2001) and Ruthven (2012). Both provide nuanced academic introductions to Muslim law, including family law and women's rights.

Unlike the US, India routinely uses religious laws pertaining to family matters of different communities in a system known as "personal laws." Established by the British in 1772 to preserve religious neutrality and avert ethnic unrest, the personal laws were retained at independence in 1947 as a form of multiculturalism and to secure the rights of minority religious communities, especially Indian Muslims. Thus Islamic family law is formally recognized in India, though it applies only to Muslims and is administered through a unified, secular court system (Galanter and Krishnan 2000).

At independence, India's Constituent Assembly debated whether to retain the personal laws of different religious communities or to establish a secular, uniform code of family laws applicable to all Indians. Proponents of retaining the personal laws argued that they would give a sense of security to religious minorities and were consistent with an Indian secularism defined as "equidistance," or the equal treatment of all religions by the state (Williams and Jenkins 2015). Conversely, advocates of a uniform civil code held that unified laws are the basis for a common national identity and that the personal laws as a holdover of British colonial divide-and-rule policies would fragment nascent Indian national unity and prevent progressive legal reforms to advance women's rights. In the end, the Constituent Assembly adopted a compromise advocated by Jawaharlal Nehru, India's first prime minister. The Indian Constitution includes an article that calls on the state to "endeavor to secure for the citizens a uniform civil code throughout the territory of India" (Article 44) as a directive principle rather than a fundamental right; directive principles are unenforceable in a court of law. And the personal laws—including distinct sets of family laws for Muslims, Christians, and Hindus (a category that has legally encompassed Sikhs, Buddhists, and Jains)—were also retained, though without explicit constitutional protection (Williams 2013b, 715).

This compromise did not end controversy over personal laws in India. In fact, they have been a source of persistent political tension and anti-Muslim rhetoric, finally breaking into interreligious Hindu-Muslim violence in the 1980s (Williams 2006). In particular, right-wing and Hindu nationalist political elites argue that Indian Muslims' adherence to Islamic law signals anti-national inclinations and a refusal to integrate into the national mainstream. Hence, a focus on Islamic law to delegitimize the identity and belonging of Indian Muslims—especially Muslim men—is a central tactic of Islamophobic communication in independent India.

US civil law is not uniform either, but it varies geographically, by jurisdiction rather than by religion. Nevertheless, as in India, anti-Muslim activists proclaim an urgent need to protect women and the majority population from the purported threat posed by Islamic law. David Yerushalmi and Frank Gaffney spearheaded the US-based anti-Sharia campaign, which began in 2010 and led to a proliferation of state legislation to restrict judges from considering Sharia or foreign laws. Yerushalmi, a lawyer, proposed model legislation. Gaffney, a former Reagan Defense Department official who started the Center for Security Policy in 1988, took up the anti-Sharia cause over the last decade (Smith 2015, 210; Elliott 2011; Southern Poverty Law Center 2019a).

In a classic verbal dehumanization of a minority, Gaffney says of Muslims: "They essentially, like termites, hollow out the structure of the civil society and other institutions" (quoted in Shane, Rosenberg, and Lipton 2017). The Southern Poverty Law Center's "extremist file" on Frank Gaffney has numerous other examples of his anti-Muslim stances and warnings about "creeping Shariah" (Southern Poverty Law Center 2019b).

The website and reports of Gaffney's Center for Security Policy use the professionalized language of a policy think tank to dehumanize Muslim Americans—portraying them as a threat to US constitutional democracy. The Southern Poverty Law Center has named the Center for Security Policy a "Designated Hate Group," with an "anti-Muslim" ideology, describing its shift from a mainstream hawkish think tank to, over the last decade, the premier organization "demonizing Islam and Muslims under the guise of national security" (2019a).

In contrast to the picture painted by Yerushalmi, Gaffney, and the Center for Security Policy, American constitutional secularism prohibits courts from enforcing religious law such as Sharia. Like Jewish law and Catholic canon law, Islamic law may inspire language in contracts related to family law or financial transactions, and sometimes disputes over these contracts end up in court. The courts can "enforce agreements that are drafted with religious principles in mind, provided they meet the requirements of secular law such as contract law and family law" (Patel, Duss, and Toh 2013, 50n19; Jones v. Wolf 442 US. 595, 603 [1979]). Religious laws do not override US or state law. In a cheeky move to highlight this point, Representative Ellie Hill Smith introduced an amendment to Montana's anti-Sharia bill specifying that the ban should apply to both Sharia and the Law of Moses, including "the use of bears in retaliation for mocking the bald (II Kings 2:23–4)" (Loranger 2017).

Responding to a report by Gaffney's Center for Security Policy, which included the "Top 20" cases of Sharia supposedly being applied in US courts, New York University Law School issued a detailed response: In thirteen cases Sharia principles were ultimately rejected by the courts; of the remaining cases some did not involve Sharia at all, and of the ones that involved Sharia, how exactly the outcomes were unjust under US secular law was unclear. The NYU scholars examined the two cases most highlighted by the anti-Sharia activists. In one, a defense of marital rape had been ultimately overturned. (Notably, some US states still do not recognize sexual assault within marriage, so changing those state laws would more effectively protect women in those states—of all religious communities—from marital rape.) In the second case, the *prosecutors* called a murder an "honor killing," but this concept was never raised as a defense, and the murderer was found guilty. Moreover, honor killings are a cultural phenomenon not defensible through Islamic law; indeed, honor killings have been characterized as the "antithesis of Islamic morality," based on analysis of Islamic legal texts (Ali 2003). The NYU study concluded, "Undeterred by facts and spurred on by the network of anti-Muslim activists, lawmakers across the country have devoted significant public time and resources to addressing this nonexistent threat" (Patel, Duss, and Toh 2013, 6–7).

Various religious organizations raised similar concerns about xenophobic innuendos granted gravitas through new state laws and a proposed constitutional amendment. Oklahoma's "Save Our State" amendment, in the words of the American Jewish Committee's amicus brief against it (submitted in collaboration with Baptist, interfaith, and Islamic organizations, among other groups), "is devised to combat a problem that Oklahoma has never even encountered—and it does so in a manner that brands members of a tiny religious minority as pariahs" (American Jewish Committee et al. 2011, 6). That message, they argued, was "underscored by the campaign to pass the Save our State Amendment—a campaign that, again and again, focused on the need to combat a threat that Muslims and Islamic law supposedly posed to Oklahoma" (5–6).

The state-by-state legal campaign to ban Sharia law in American courts began with that Oklahoma "Save Our State" referendum in 2010. The effort resulted in a constitutional amendment that was struck down for discriminating between religions without justification (Smith 2015, 211). The model legislation subsequently morphed into a more general ban on "foreign" law, while the proponents continued to stress the supposed threat from Sharia. The American Public Policy Alliance spearheaded the campaign, promoting model legislation known as "American Laws for American Courts." Eight states passed bans on Sharia or "foreign law" in just a few years: Oklahoma (in 2010, but overturned), Idaho (2010), Louisiana (2010), Tennessee (2010), Arizona (2011), Kansas (2012), South Dakota (2012), and North Carolina (2013) (Smith 2015, 210; Mitchell and Toner 2016, 737–38). The Montana House voted in support of such a bill in March 2017 (Loranger 2017). In a 2018 report, the Southern Poverty Law Center counted a total of 201 anti-Sharia bills from 2010 to 2017 in forty-three states and found that in 2017 alone forty-three bills were introduced and two enacted, in Texas and Arkansas (Shanmugasundaram 2018).

Similar Discourses: Fomenting Fears around Gender, Population, and Violence

Three predominant themes together define how discourses around Islamic law have been deployed to mark Muslims as "other": gender, population growth, and violence. We analyze each of these themes in turn, outlining the Indian case followed by analysis of whether and how each theme appears in US political discourse around Islamic law.

Theme 1: Women as "Victims of Islam"

Constructing Muslim women as hapless victims of Islamic law—and hence of Muslim men and Islam itself—has long been a prevalent strategy of Islamophobia in India. Certain provisions of Islamic law receive enhanced attention in this regard: those relating to polygamy, divorce, and maintenance (alimony). Other provisions—such as those on marriage and property/inheritance rights—put Islamic law in a better light, as they are more gender progressive (especially as compared to Hindu law); as such, notably, they receive less attention from Islamophobic forces (Menon 2014, 482).

A major controversy over Muslim personal law in the 1980s provides a clear example of this theme in operation (Williams 2006, chap. 5; Pathak and Sunder Rajan 1989). In 1985, the Indian Supreme Court upheld an award of monthly maintenance (alimony) for a destitute and divorced Muslim woman, Shah Bano Begum.[4] The judgment was opposed by many conservative Indian Muslims, including religious leaders who argued that it contravened the provisions of Islamic family law as widely practiced in India. In response to protests and demonstrations against the judgment by parts of the Muslim community, the Indian government passed the Muslim Women (Protection of Rights on Divorce) Act (1986) to effectively overturn it (Jenkins 2000).

Political controversy over the judgment and the bill turned centrally on gender (Menon 2000). Hindu right politicians and public figures argued that Indian Muslim women should have the same legal rights as all other Indian women and thus supported the judgment and opposed the bill. Yet their arguments, rather than pointing out gender inequality in all religions' personal laws, advocated the abolishment of the personal laws altogether and Islamic law in particular. In other words, the Hindu right's arguments were more "anti-Muslim" than "pro-women" (Kishwar 1986). Even secular and left elites did not necessarily or overtly deny the underlying view that Islamic law oppressed Muslim women. They simply held that, either way, it was the prerogative only of Muslims to change their own laws.

Visual analysis of two typical images—a comic in the case of India and a web image in the case of the US—exemplifies the theme that Islamic law oppresses women. Globally, communication has become more visual (Howells and Negreiros 2012), and visual images are a prevalent form of communication that we social scientists neglect analyzing as a form of "text" at our own peril (Hansen 2011; Weber 2008). Methodologically, visual analysis entails detailed exegesis of an image, interweaving descrip-

---

4. *Mohd. Ahmed Khan v. Shah Bano Begum* 1985 SCR (3) 844.

tion with explanation. Because the relevant aspects of the images are described below, and to avoid further spreading hateful messages, we have intentionally elected not to reproduce the images. This follows increasingly standard practice in analysis of such images.[5]

The cartoon "Change for Better" ("Triple Talaq" 2016)[6] exemplifies at a glance the first theme of Muslim personal law in India: the oppression of women. The right half of the image shows a Muslim man and his wife. The man is dressed in green and wears the stereotypical markers of Muslim men in India: a beard and white skullcap. In case of any lingering doubt as to his religious identity, a green star and crescent hover above his head. He is depicted quite clearly as a caveman, barbaric and backward: hunched over, knuckles dragging, and carrying a club over his shoulder. On the club the words "triple talaq" (or "triple divorce") are inscribed, signifying a provision of Islamic law that allows a Muslim man to divorce his wife by repeating the word "talaq" ("I divorce thee") three times. Triple talaq is thus signified as a power—a threat—Muslim men hold over Muslim women. On his green kurta (long overshirt) are the words "Muslim Law Board." This is a reference to the All India Muslim Personal Law Board, a powerful organization consisting primarily of male Muslim religious leaders founded in 1973 to protect Islamic law in India from encroachments by the state (http://www.aimplboard.in). This imagery establishes the equation between Islamic law, Muslim men, and Islam itself.

The woman, presumably his wife, is standing behind him in a full burka—a form of veiling that is actually relatively uncommon in India (Shams 2016). She is held by the man with a rope around her neck, invoking a noose. She carries several burdens. In one hand a suitcase with the words "e-mail divorce" refers again to the idea of quick and easy divorce—for men—granted by Islamic law. Her other hand balances additional burdens on her head: a trunk labeled "polygamy" and a sack labeled "child bride." Under the personal laws in India, Muslim men are permitted to have up to four wives (the polygamy provision is analyzed in the next section). The reference to child marriage evokes historical opposition, by some Muslims, to being subjected to the Child Marriage Restraint Act (1929, amended

---

5. We do note that the images we analyze are fully cited by their source. On the ethics of image use and the power of images that misrepresent minorities, see Gross (1991).

6. For reasons of space and because it is one step removed from the argument, we have not analyzed the left half of the cartoon, which advocates a uniform civil code as a way to reform (the barbarism of) Islamic law. A Google reverse image search revealed that the cartoon was originally penned by political cartoonist Manoj Kureel, an advocate and supporter of the current Bharatiya Janata Party government in India, and shared on his Twitter feed on October 15, 2016. As of May 2020, Twitter had suspended his account.

1978), which set minimum ages of marriage in colonial India (Sinha 2000). The overall message of this cartoon is the burdening and victimization of Muslim women by barbaric Islamic law, Muslim men, and Islam itself.

Critics of personal laws in India focus on Muslim law, particularly laws that disfavor women rather than those that put Muslim women in a better position than women of other religious communities. Notably, *all* of India's personal laws, even after some reforms of Hindu and Christian laws, continue to be disadvantageous for women. One problem that results from attacks on Muslim law is that members of this minority feel besieged, making conservative Muslim leadership such as the All India Muslim Personal Law Board reluctant to advocate reforms (despite much Islamic jurisprudence that could be drawn upon to engage in pro-women reforms). Therefore, while Muslim majority Pakistan and Bangladesh previously ceased to recognize "instant divorce," India remained one of a few countries to continue to allow the practice of triple talaq, until the Indian Supreme Court in *Shayara Bano v. Union of India and Others* (2017) declared this practice unconstitutional. Notably, Muslim women pushed for this decision through their own organizations, such as the Bharatiya Muslim Mahila Andolan, and were not simply victims waiting to be "saved" from Muslim men or Islam by Hindu nationalists (Teater and Jenkins 2019). However, the verdict itself was seen as flawed in multiple ways—including advancing anti-Islamic law stereotypes—even by those who had advocated for the change (Schultz 2018; Safvi 2017). Rather than rejecting Islamic law, the Bharatiya Muslim Mahila Andolan drew on Islamic law to challenge "customary practices" and even started a "women qazi training institute" on Islamic learning and theology (Bharatiya Muslim Mahila Andolan 2016a, 2016b).

The theme of women as victims of Islam is also prevalent in US Islamophobic rhetoric and imagery about Sharia. The ease of divorce for men is one common theme. But other gendered issues have become entangled with the anti-Sharia legislative campaign. For example, legislation proposed in North Carolina combined anti-foreign and anti-Sharia law language with limits on abortions. At one point, it was combined with an anti-sex-selective abortion law, which was later separated out and passed separately in October 2013.

The gender threat discourse in conjunction with the anti-Sharia campaign is encapsulated in a Breitbart News story entitled "Montana Democrats Vote against Bill Banning Sharia Law, Call It 'Repugnant.'" The text discusses the passage of Montana House Bill 97 along party lines. It quotes a Democratic lawmaker critiquing the bill as "anti-Muslim bigotry" and a

Republican lawmaker defending it in the name of a "constitution [that] is constantly under assault" (Kew 2017). While the words of the article contain no mention of women, except for female legislators criticizing the bill, an image brings the gender threat discourse to the fore. A photo as large as the written article fills the space below the headline. The foreground features a woman in an all-white modest dress and hijab, kneeling and looking at the ground. Looming above her—and the viewer, as the photo is shot from below—is a man in a long brown tunic and pants, gloves, and a hood with eye slits, reminiscent of a medieval executioner, brandishing a long stick and seemingly preparing to beat her. In the background, an audience dominated by men and boys fills two levels of open balconies and the rooftop, topped by a black dome with a crescent spire against an ominous gray sky. With no caption to indicate time, place, or circumstance, the editor leaves the viewer to read the image as generic "Sharia" in action, in light of the headline about Sharia just above.[7] The editor juxtaposes the repugnant image (implied to be the potential future for American women if anti-Sharia bills are not passed) with the Democrats' declaration, featured in the headline, that the bill itself is repugnant to belittle their claim.

With words rather than images, the American Public Policy Alliance uses the gender threat trope to advocate on its website for "American Laws for American Courts" legislation: "To protect women and children, identified by international human rights organizations as the primary victims of discriminatory foreign laws . . . we are preserving *individual* liberties and freedoms which become eroded by the encroachment of foreign laws and foreign legal doctrines, such as Shariah" (American Public Policy Alliance, n.d.a). The overall appearance of the website—clean blue and white, few images, ad-free, and without the visual cacophony and informal, cheeky language of the blatantly Islamophobic Jihad Watch—suggests that the benign-sounding American Public Policy Alliance is just another Washington think tank.

Vague references to human rights organizations, such as the one in the above passage, are amplified in another section of the site that paints their xenophobic message as "civil rights," a rhetorical strategy known as catachresis (an exaggerated, mistaken, forced, or paradoxical comparison): "This movement is the civil rights struggle of the 21st century." This section goes on to warn: "We face a serious problem: a well-organized movement has emerged to support the imposition of discriminatory Shariah law

---

7. A reverse Google image search indicated that this image was originally published in the British tabloid *The Daily Mail*, in a story about Indonesia.

in America for Muslims (with some groups openly supporting Shariah's authority for all citizens including non-Muslims). . . . Shariah law denies Americans (especially Muslim American women and children) their civil rights" (American Public Policy Alliance, n.d.b).

Organizations spreading critiques of Sharia purport to be protecting women. But, in practice, prohibitions on recognizing Sharia (as in North Carolina) can hurt Muslim women in the US: "Lawyers specializing in Islamic law said such legislation could make it harder for Muslim women married in Islamic countries under Shariah law to obtain alimony and child support payments because husbands will be able to argue they were never married. Judges will be prohibited from recognizing those Shariah marriage contracts" (Sacirbey 2013). As in India, majority activists' attacks in the US on Islamic law in the name of protecting women are a way to mobilize patriarchal nationalism but are not an effective way to actually improve the status of women.

Theme 2: Fomenting Fears of Minority Population Growth

A second predominant tactic of "othering" Muslims by generating fear of Islamic law is through demographic arguments about population growth. A long-standing narrative of Islamophobic political discourse in India holds that provisions of Islamic law encourage the rapid population growth of Muslims and will ultimately enable Muslims to outnumber Hindus. This narrative dates back to the 1800s, supported by various mathematical analyses of census data. A new wave of "Muslims are taking over the country" hysteria routinely follows each decennial census. Such analyses have repeatedly been demonstrated to be mathematically inaccurate, and Hindus have never constituted less than an overwhelming majority in India (75 percent before independence and partition and over 80 percent of the population throughout the postcolonial period). Nonetheless, the "common sense" "wisdom" persists (Williams 2013a; Datta 1993), spread by the Hindu right and inadequately contested by left and secular forces.

Several provisions of Islamic law are cited as central to Muslims' ability to grow at disproportionate rates: polygamy, child marriage and easy divorce, and proselytization,[8] an Islamic law "package" that is seen as giving Muslims "fertile" ground for population growth through a combination of high birthrates and conversion efforts. Each of these aspects is easily shown

---

8. Proselytization is not part of Sharia, strictly speaking, but is portrayed as part of the overall package of what Islam mandates that allows and encourages its spread and growth. Hence, we include the analysis here.

to be factually inaccurate. Hindus are actually more polygamous than Muslims in India (Puniyani 2003), and easy divorce by custom is also more common among lower-caste Hindus than Muslims (Dommaraju 2016).

Islam is indeed the fastest-growing religion around the world. But there is no evidence that this is due to provisions of Islamic law. Two reasons account for Muslims' growth rate globally, factors that repeat themselves in India. One is the relative youth of the overall Muslim population: the median age of Muslims globally is twenty-three years, compared to thirty years for non-Muslims. Second, Muslim women have higher fertility rates—3.1 children on average per Muslim woman compared to 2.3 children for other groups—but, again, it is not at all clear that this is due to any provisions of Islamic law (Lipka 2017). In India, poverty and illiteracy are as likely as religion to explain high Muslim fertility rates (Chowdhry 2000; Sachar 2007). In the last census period, the actual rate of increase of the growth rate slowed for Muslims while it increased for Hindus (Daniyal 2017). Mainstream news outlets consistently publish articles debunking the myth of Muslim population growth (Rukmini and Singh 2017; Soz 2016; Shariff 2015).

Yet, in matters of identity politics, facts often do not matter as much as beliefs. As a result, the Hindu right in particular perpetuates the myth of Muslim overpopulation via Islamic law as a way to stoke fear and hatred of Muslims. Anthropologist Arjun Appadurai, pointing to examples in India as well as in the US and Europe, called a majority stoking fear of a minority the "fear of small numbers" (Appadurai 2006). The 2001 census found that the Muslim population in India increased almost 200 percent from 1961 to 2001 (India, n.d.), reinforcing the feeling of many Hindus of an exploding Muslim population in India (Shariff 2015). This was contradicted by a finding of the Sachar Committee, which found that the Muslim population in India would stabilize between 17 and 21 percent of the Indian population by 2100 (Sachar 2007).

It is also no coincidence, in our view, that the provisions of Islamic law that are cited as enabling disproportionate population growth are virtually identical with those that are cited as proof of Islam's and Islamic law's oppression of women. Polygamy, early marriage, and easy divorce serve as dual signifiers of both oppression of Muslim women and an aggressive population growth agenda of Islam. We will show shortly that the theme of violence also blends seamlessly into this mix.

The demographic threat theme is even more far-fetched in the US, and thus a bit less prevalent, but the American Public Policy Alliance website prominently features a report by Gaffney and his Center for Security

Policy that tries to make the case: "Although self-identified Muslims currently comprise less than one percent of the American population, immigration policies enacted over the previous two decades have encouraged an increasing influx of Muslim refugees into this country. All-too-often, they come from conflict zones where Shariah-adherence is the norm. State and local governments have virtually no input on where and how these refugees are settled. . . . Given the Center's continuing concern with these developments, this study was undertaken to document the steady expansion of Shariah influence in the American court system" (Center for Security Policy 2014, 8–9). In this passage, the term "self-identified Muslims" implies there may be crypto-Muslims undercover in the US and not captured by demographic data. The theme of Muslim demographic encroachment in US anti-Sharia publications features refugee and immigrant influxes leading to more Sharia, in contrast to the message in India that Muslim law supposedly leads to more rapid Muslim reproduction.

Jihad Watch's "Islam 101" pamphlet picks up on the demographic influx theme in a line of argument that appeared in the answer to a "FAQ" (namely, "If Islam is violent, why are so many Muslims peaceful?") in the "Islam 101" section of the Jihad Watch website (Davis, n.d.). The answer merges the demographic threat theme with the violent threat theme: "In any given social context, as Islam takes greater root—increasing numbers of followers, the construction of more mosques and 'cultural centers,' etc.—the greater the likelihood that some number of its adherents will take its violent precepts seriously. This is the problem that the West faces today" (Davis, n.d.). Once the influx "takes greater root" in America or the West, this metaphor implies, Muslims permanently change the demographic balance by holding their ground and growing. The passage also evokes images the reader may have noticed in their own communities, such as new mosques or cultural centers, and associates them with a threat to the "West."

Unlike India, where religious census data are among the most politically sensitive, the US does not count religion on its census, but it does count race. Islamophobia and its complex relationship with racism along with the way the US Census counts (or fails to count) the race, ethnicity, or national origin of many Muslim Americans are subjects beyond the scope of this chapter (see Kumar 2012; Chow 2017). But the demographic anxiety of some non-Muslims in the US is akin to, and in some cases interlinked with, racial anxieties over the Census Bureau's "minority-majority" forecasts (Gans 2017). Due to extremely small percentages, we posit that demographic arguments are harder to make in the US. But, as in India, the actual number of Muslims in the US is not an overriding factor in the majority's receptivity to demographic threat arguments. US states passing the Sharia bans actually have among the lowest percentages of Muslim residents, ranging from twentieth to thirty-sixth nationally in the number of adherents to Islam per 100,000 residents—from North Carolina with 273 Muslims per 100,000 residents to Arizona with 134 per 100,000 (Smith 2015, 212).

Theme 3: Spreading the Idea of Islam as Violent

Islamophobic narratives depicting Muslims and Islam as violent abound in India and manifest into particular forms. The first is sexual violence, which is closely tied to the first and second themes. The narrative here is that Muslim men snatch away (via seduction or forcibly, as in kidnapping) naive, innocent Hindu women to rape them and produce even more Muslim babies. There are multiple variations on this form—from the historical argument that because Hinduism bans widow remarriage, chaste Hindu widows could be lured into converting to Islam to marry a Muslim man as a way to satisfy sexual needs and desires, to the more recent mythologies of "love jihad," which suggest that Muslim men actually prowl around trying to find unprotected young Hindu women to grab them, rape them, or make them fall in love and, generally, to nefariously sexually abuse them and have Muslim babies.[9] "Islam and Muslims are portrayed in villainous terms as teaching and practicing violence, especially violence against women. . . . Rape and forced conversion of Hindu women are portrayed as central to the Islamic enterprise in India" (Chowdhry 2000, 107). And hence, remarkably, anti-Muslim activists deftly combine all three themes of gender, population growth, and violence.

Another manifestation of the theme of Muslim violence in India is the simple specter of the terrorist jihadist Muslim who willingly sacrifices his own life along with those of others in the quest to spread Islam. In the Indian discourse, these imagined Muslims are linked with, or have shadowy, nefarious ties to, Pakistan.

But we found that this theme of violent Muslims and Islam in the Indian context bears a striking difference both from the first two themes and from the US case: the theme of violence in the Indian case is not explicitly linked to Islamic law. To some extent the image of the sexually violent Muslim who

---

9. It is worth noting that the underbelly of this construction is the total elision of Hindu women's agency. In this narrative, consent is not possible and the idea of a Hindu woman falling in love with a Muslim man is written off as impossible on its face.

desires, kidnaps, and rapes Hindu women can be indirectly linked to (or placed in the same family as) the gendered and demographic themes out-lined above. Yet popular discourse or even the most Islamophobic Hindu right-wing narratives do not commonly link either the sexually violent or the jihadi terrorist stereotypes to any specific or even general provisions of Islamic law. We suggest this finding is related to the structure of the Islamic laws that are actually in practice in India. As previously noted, India only recognizes religious *family* laws, but secular, uniform *civil* (other than certain family laws) and *criminal* laws were codified under British colonial rule and have been in force since the 1860s (Williams 2006). Accordingly, discourses and images about violent Islamic criminal laws—such as stoning women or cutting off the hands of thieves—are rendered irrelevant in the Indian case.

In the US, however, "violent Islam" is a major theme within anti-Sharia discourse, as embedded within the examples discussed above—the gender threat photograph of flogging and the demographic threat "FAQ." Jihad Watch further develops this theme in "Islam 101": "It is apparent that any meaningful application of Sharia is going to look very different from any-thing resembling a free or open society in the Western sense. The stoning of adulterers, execution of apostates and blasphemers, repression of other religions, and a mandatory hostility toward non-Islamic nations punctuated by regular warfare will be the norm. It seems fair then to classify Islam and its Sharia code as a form of totalitarianism" (Davis, n.d.). The director of Jihad Watch, Robert Spencer, in another pamphlet that one can download or order in bulk (for $1 each), combines the fears of numbers and violence: "Blasphemy laws protecting Islam may not yet be adopted in the West, but Muslim mobs are ready to enforce them anyway" (Spencer 2013, 25). This pamphlet's cover features gender and violence, with two distressed nuns in the midst of the bombed-out rubble of a church, under the title "Islam: Religion of Bigots" in a font stylized to evoke the Arabic script against a green background.

The American Public Policy Alliance website's page on "Sharia Law" conjures a similar image with words: "Shariah mandates violent Jihad as religious obligation. Violent jihad's purpose against non-Muslims or for-mer Muslims is to establish Islam's rule worldwide" (American Public Policy Alliance, n.d.c). This verbal caricature of Islam appears on a site purportedly developed to further civil debates. For instance, the Center for Security Policy's downloadable report, under the American Public Policy Alliance's "Media Kit" tab, on the one hand states that "institutionalized, authoritative Shariah doctrine is comprehensive and by definition without limit in its ambitions and scope" and that "the threat of being charged under Shariah, whether officially or unofficially . . . carries with it the constant threat of being murdered." That characterization within the report is, on the other hand, in stark contrast to the report's purported objective: "to encourage an informed, serious, and civil public debate and engagement with the issue of Shariah in the United States of America. We hope that the debate that this study intends to encourage and inform will be met with a renewed commitment to keep the Constitution of the United States the Supreme Law of the Land" (Center for Security Policy 2014, 14). Like the American Public Policy Alliance, the Center for Security Policy has an innocuous name, a professional website, and links to reports with appendices and bibliographies, mimicking the sites of policy think tanks that provide legitimate research. These sites could easily fool students or state legislators researching Sharia or appear in casual online searches for information about Islamic law. Whether sensationalized or sober in tone or appearance, the discourses of Islamophobic organizations in the US associate Sharia with violent threats, often in combination with gender threats and demographic threats.

Conclusion

Neither democracy nor secularism—nor both in conjunction with each other—spells the end to Islamophobia. Indeed, our two case studies are both constitutional secular democracies. Islamophobic communications within secular democracies may differ from those used in other types of states. As anthropologist Talal Asad observed, "A secular state does not guarantee toleration; it puts into place different structures of ambition and fear" (2003, 8). To better understand the structures of ambition and fear generated by contemporary Islamophobic activists, we focused on three communicative discourses designed to resonate with secular and democratic ideas, namely, attacking Muslims as the harbingers of Sharia and doing so in the name of (1) maintaining women's rights, (2) preserving majority rule by the current religious majority, and (3) protecting citizens from violence. In practice, such rhetoric undermines women's rights, democracy, and peace.

In this chapter we examined and compared common anti-Muslim and anti-Sharia tropes in India and the US. We argue that attacking Islamic law to construct Muslims as "others" is a primary tactic of Islamophobia that is evident in both places and trace the parallels in the debates around such laws and the image of Muslims and Islam constructed by anti-Muslim communications. Together, three Islamophobic discourses—gender oppression, population growth, and violence—combine to create an image of Muslims, and of Islam, as barbarizing women in a violent quest to become numerically dominant. We argue it is no coincidence that all three themes appear in both cases—indeed, we suggest that the themes are deeply imbricated and inextricable from each other. Wherever they appear, we posit they are likely to appear in tandem with each other.

Some different emphases emerge when comparing the countries, which need additional research to document and analyze but which seem to emerge from the different legal and administrative contexts. Due to its actual experience with Islamic law, India's gender discourse seems to selectively emphasize aspects of Muslim family law that disadvantage women. In contrast, the US's inexperience with Sharia functions as a blank slate, so images of a woman being flogged or nuns in peril can be used to instill fear in people with no experience of Sharia in practice.

Different emphases occur in the second theme as well. Demographic threat messaging in the two contexts has historically emphasized rapid reproduction in India and refugees or immigrants in the US, although Indian politicians are increasingly criticizing and restricting Muslim immigrants too. These different emphases emerge in part from their different political histories and census policies. Muslims have lived in the area that is now India for centuries, whereas Muslims in the US are more likely to be recent arrivals. After partition, welcoming additional Muslims fueled India's national identity as a secular state in contrast with archrival Pakistan, although more recent policies in India are not welcoming at all. These include new documentation requirements to prove citizenship and denial of religious refugee status to Muslims from neighboring countries (Jenkins and Teater 2020). Unlike the US, India has counted religion from the time of colonial censuses; thus, the Muslim birthrate in India has long been a talking point of the Hindu right. In neither country did actual population numbers appear to be an effective antidote to quell alarming demographic innuendo.

The theme of violence does not resonate as much with Indians' experience of Muslim law, which is restricted to family and not criminal law. It is, however, a theme of US-based anti-Sharia activists, who use words and images to paint a dystopian future of macabre punishments. As with the gender theme, this difference stems from legal contexts. Unlike Americans, Indians are aware of Muslim personal law as part of their constitutional system of legal pluralism. Indian experience with Muslim family law, from colonial times to the present, shows it has not been a slippery slope to

Muslim criminal law. Further comparative study could examine in more detail, with additional primary documents from both countries, the degree of convergence of Islamophobic tactics and themes, despite the geographic distance and demographic divergence.

This chapter also raises new questions conducive to other forms of research, including public opinion and network analyses. What is the impact of these xenophobic tactics on attitudes, including Muslims' own sense of belonging or insecurity as well as the broader society's support for the religious freedom of minorities? Further comparative work about Muslim minorities' identities could build on Calfano's innovative book on the attitudes and identities of Muslims in the context of American politics (2018). More work on how anti-Muslim minority messages impact support for religious freedom is important because this support may increasingly depend on whose freedom is involved. A Pew study of Pentecostals in ten countries suggests that many people are more supportive of religious freedom for their own religious group and less supportive of the religious freedom of other religious groups; India had the biggest gap, but the US also showed a large disparity in willingness to support the religious freedoms of others (Pew Research Center 2006). Discourses and images in current circulation, such as the ones examined in our study, are likely to make this gap even bigger.

Further research is also needed to trace the degree to which these common communication tactics, and even specific phrases, arguments, and images, are independently emerging or the result of the transnational influence of growing Islamophobic networks and organizations. Recent research suggests that these messages (and messengers) are linked regionally within South Asia, between Sri Lanka and Myanmar, for instance (Gravers 2015; Holt 2016). To what extent are these messages and organizations developing global networks including both Asian countries and the US? Finally, our study points to a need for further research into the efficacy of counter-narratives and counter-imagery to combat such Islamophobic attacks.

Once they reached national-level office, Indian prime minister Narendra Modi and US president Donald Trump each toned down, to varying degrees, some of their own anti-Muslim rhetoric, but they have repeatedly failed to censure the xenophobic discourse of their associates. In some cases, they promoted it. For instance, in March 2017 Prime Minister Modi named Yogi Adityanath to be chief minister of India's largest state, Uttar Pradesh. Adityanath is a prominent proponent of the false rumor, circulating in India for at least a decade, that Muslim men are systematically conspiring to seduce, convert, and impregnate Hindu girls, a so-called love jihad. Once Adityanath became chief minister, he advocated for and promoted the formation of vigilante groups of men to harass and attack couples and minority men (Pandey 2017; Jenkins 2019). Amit Shah, the minister of home affairs and president of the ruling Bharatiya Janata Party, has repeatedly referred to Muslim migrants as termites, the same metaphor used by Frank Gaffney (quoted above) in the US context. This language works in tandem with efforts to deport Rohingya refugees and to challenge the citizenship of thousands of Muslims in the state of Assam (Ghoshal 2019; "Show Me Your Papers" 2019).

Meanwhile, in the US, a phrase from Trump's "Executive Order: Protecting the Nation from Foreign Terrorist Entry into the United States" of January 27, 2017, shows the influence of anti-Sharia activism spreading from state policy to national policy: "The United States cannot, and should not, admit those who do not support the Constitution, or those who would place violent ideologies over American law" (Trump 2017a). The revised executive order of March 6, 2017, includes a "transparency" section stating that the secretary of homeland security will issue reports every 180 days on the numbers of foreign nationals in the US who have been charged with terrorism, who have been "radicalized," and who have engaged in acts of "gender-based violence against women" (Trump 2017b, section 11). Anti-Muslim political communication emphasizing women, population, and violence continues. And taken together, these examples of political actors engaging in harmful communication about a religious minority group point to the need for scholars to be attuned to the many forms of religious communication from political elites and the substantial consequences it poses to targeted minorities.

REFERENCES

Ali, Keica. 2003. "Honor Killings, Illicit Sex, and Islamic Law." Feminist Sexual Ethics Project. Accessed May 28, 2017. www.Brandeis.edu/projects/fse/muslim/honor.html

American Jewish Committee et al. 2011. Brief of Amici Curiae filed in *Muneer Awad v. Paul Ziriax et al.* ACLU (website). Accessed April 30, 2017. www.aclu.org/legal-document/awad-v-ziriax-amicus-brief-american-jewish-committee-et-al

American Public Policy Alliance. n.d.a. "American Laws for American Courts." American Public Policy Alliance (website). Accessed March 11, 2019. http://publicpolicyalliance.org/legislation/american-laws-for-american-courts/

American Public Policy Alliance. n.d.b. "Civil Rights: This Movement Is the Civil Rights Struggle of the 21st Century." American Public Policy Alliance (website). Accessed March 11, 2019. http://publicpolicyalliance.org/civil-rights/

American Public Policy Alliance. n.d.c. "Shariah Law." American Public Policy Alliance (website). Accessed March 11, 2019. http://publicpolicyalliance.org/issues -2/shariah-law/

Appadurai, Arjun. 2006. *Fear of Small Numbers: An Essay on the Geography of Anger.* Durham, NC: Duke University Press.

Asad, Talal. 2003. *Formations of the Secular: Christianity, Islam, Modernity.* Stanford: Stanford University Press.

Banerjee, Sikata. 2005. *Make Me a Man! Masculinity, Hinduism, and Nationalism in India.* New York: State University of New York Press.

Basu, Amrita. 2015. *Violent Conjunctures in Democratic India.* New York: Cambridge University Press.

Bharatiya Muslim Mahila Andolan. 2016a. "Muslim Family Law—Draft Sent to the P.M." Bharatiya Muslim Mahila Andolan (website). Accessed March 7, 2019. https://bmmaindia.com/2016/01/01/muslim-family-law-draft-sent-to-the-pm -2/

Bharatiya Muslim Mahila Andolan. 2016b. "Woman Qazi Training Institute: Darul Uloom Niswaan." Bharatiya Muslim Mahila Andolan (website). Accessed March 7, 2019. https://bmmaindia.com/2016/02/10/women-qazi-training-ins titute-darul-uloom-niswaan/

Calfano, Brian. 2018. *Muslims, Identity, and American Politics.* New York: Routledge.

Center for Security Policy. 2014. *Shariah in American Courts: The Expanding Incursion of Islamic Law in the U.S. Legal System.* Washington, DC: Center for Security Policy Press. Accessed November 11, 2020. https://www.centerforsecurit ypolicy.org/wp-content/uploads/2014/12/Shariah_in_American_Courts1.pdf

Carroll, Lauren. 2015. "Fact-checking Trump's Claim that Thousands in New Jersey Cheered When World Trade Center Tumbled." Politifact, November 22. Accessed November 11, 2020. https://www.politifact.com/factchecks/2015/nov /22/donald-trump/fact-checking-trumps-claim-thousands-new-jersey-ch/

Chow, Kat. 2017. "For Some Americans of MENA Descent, Checking a Census Box Is Complicated." NPR Codeswitch, March 11. Accessed May 31, 2017. http://www.npr.org/sections/codeswitch/2017/03/11/519548276/for-some-ar ab-americans-checking-a-census-box-is-complicated

Chowdhry, Geeta. 2000. "Communalism, Nationalism and Gender: Bharatiya Janata Party (BJP) and the Hindu Right in India." In *Women, States, and Nationalism: At Home in the Nation?,* edited by Sita Ranchod-Nilsson and Mary Ann Tétreault, 98–118. New York: Routledge.

Daniyal, Shoaib. 2017. "5 Charts That Puncture the Bogey of Muslim Population Growth in India." *Dawn,* February 10. Accessed May 12, 2017. https://www.da wn.com/news/1203166

Danjoux, Ilan. 2014. "Don't Judge a Cartoon by Its Image: Interpretive Approaches to the Study of Political Cartoons." In *Interpretation and Method: Empirical Research Methods and the Interpretive Turn,* edited by Dvora Yanow and Peregrine Schwartz-Shea, 353–67. Armonk, NY: M. E. Sharpe.

Datta, Pradip Kumar. 1993. "'Dying Hindus': Production of Hindu Communal Common Sense in Early 20th Century Bengal." *Economic and Political Weekly* 28:1305–19.

Davis, Gregory M. n.d. "Islam 101." Jihad Watch. Accessed May 15, 2017. https://www.jihadwatch.org/islam-101

Dommaraju, Premchand. 2016. "Divorce and Separation in India." *Population and Development Review* 42:195–223.

Elliott, Andrea. 2011. "The Man behind the Anti-Shariah Movement." *New York Times*, July 30, A1.

Esposito, John L. 2001. *Women in Muslim Family Law*. Syracuse, NY: Syracuse University Press.

Esposito, John L. 2003. *The Oxford Dictionary of Islam*. New York: Oxford University Press.

Fine, Gary Alan, and Irfan Khawaja. 2005. "Celebrating Arabs and Grateful Terrorists: Rumor and the Politics of Plausibility." In *Rumor Mills: The Social Impact of Rumor and Legend*, edited by Gary Alan Fine, Veronique Campion-Vincent, and Chip Heath, 189–206. New Brunswick, NJ: Aldine Transaction.

Galanter, Marc, and Jayanth Krishnan. 2000. "Personal Law and Human Rights in India and Israel." *Israel Law Review* 34:101–33.

Gallup. 2011. "Muslims in India: Confident in Democracy Despite Economic and Educational Challenges." Gallup (website). Accessed May 27, 2017. https://news.gallup.com/poll/157079/muslims-india-confident-democracy-despite-economic-educational-challenges.aspx

Gans, Herbert J. 2017. "The Census and Right-Wing Hysteria. *New York Times*, May 11. Accessed May 12, 2017. www.nytimes.com/2017/05/11/opinion/sunday/the-census-and-right-wing-hysteria.html?ref=opinion

Ghoshal, Devjyot. 2019. "Amit Shah Vows to Throw Illegal Immigrants into the Bay of Bengal." Reuters, April 12. Accessed September 26, 2019. https://www.reuters.com/article/india-election-speech/amit-shah-vows-to-throw-illegal-immigrants-into-bay-of-bengal-idUSKCN1RO1YD

Gottschalk, Peter. 2013. *American Heretics: Catholics, Jews, Muslims and the History of Religious Intolerance*. New York: Palgrave Macmillan.

Gottschalk, Peter, and Gabriel Greenberg. 2008. *Islamophobia: Making Muslims the Enemy*. Lanham, MD: Rowman and Littlefield.

Government of India. n.d. *Census of India Website: Office of the Registrar General & Census Commissioner, India*. Ministry of Home Affairs. Office of the Registrar General & Census Commissioner. Accessed May 26, 2017. https://censusindia.gov.in/

Gravers, Mikael. 2015. "Anti-Muslim Buddhist Nationalism in Burma and Sri Lanka: Religious Violence and Globalized Imaginaries of Endangered Identities." *Contemporary Buddhism* 16:1–27.

Gross, Larry. 1991. "The Ethics of (Mis)representation." In *Image Ethics: The Moral Rights of Subjects in Photographs, Film and Television*, edited by Larry Gross, John Stuart Katz, and Jay Ruby, 188–202. New York: Oxford University Press.

Hansen, Lene. 2011. "Theorizing the Image for Security Studies: Visual Securitization and the Muhammad Cartoon Crisis." *European Journal of International Relations* 17:51–74.

Holt, John. 2016. *Buddhist Extremists and Muslim Minorities: Religious Conflict in Contemporary Sri Lanka*. New York: Oxford University Press.

Howarth, David. 2000. *Discourse*. Buckingham, UK: Open University Press.

Howells, Richard, and Joaquim Negreiros. 2012. *Visual Culture*. New York: Polity.

Jenkins, Laura Dudley. 2000. "Shah Bano: Muslim Women's Rights." *Teaching Human Rights Online*. Accessed November 10, 2020. https://homepages.uc.ed u/~thro/shahbano/allshahbano.htm

Jenkins, Laura Dudley. 2019. *Religious Freedom and Mass Conversion in India*. Philadelphia: University of Pennsylvania Press.

Jenkins, Laura Dudley, and Kristina M. Teater. 2020. "Hindu Perspectives on the Right to Religious Freedom." In *Routledge Handbook of Freedom of Religion or Belief*, edited by Silvo Ferrari, Mark Hill, Arif Jamal, and Rossella Bottoni. London: Routledge.

Jhally, Sut, Jeremy Earp, Andrew Killoy, Mary Patierno, Simon Shaheen, and Jack G. Shaheen. 2006. *Reel Bad Arabs: How Hollywood Vilifies a People*. Northampton, MA: Media Education Foundation. www.Mediaed.org

Kessler, Glenn. 2015. "Trump's Outrageous Claim that 'Thousands' of New Jersey Muslims Celebrated the 9/11 Attacks." *New York Times*, November 22. Accessed November 11, 2020. https://www.washingtonpost.com/news/fact-checker/wp /2015/11/22/donald-trumps-outrageous-claim-that-thousands-of-new-jersey -muslims-celebrated-the-911-attacks/

Kew, Ben. 2017. "Montana Democrats Vote against Bill Banning Sharia Law, Call It 'Repugnant.'" *Breitbart*, March 31. Accessed April 20, 2017. http://www.bre itbart.com/big-government/2017/03/31/montana-democrats-vote-against-bill -banning-sharia-law-call-it-repugnant/

Kishwar, Madhu. 1986. "Pro Women or Anti Muslim? The Shahbano Controversy." *Manushi: A Journal about Women in Society* 32:275–90.

Kumar, Deepa. 2012. *Islamophobia and the Politics of Empire*. Chicago: Haymarket Books.

Lipka, Michael. 2017. "Muslims and Islam: Key Findings in the U.S. and around the World." Pew Research Center, February 27. Accessed May 12, 2017. http:// www.pewresearch.org/fact-tank/2017/02/27/muslims-and-islam-key-findings -in-the-u-s-and-around-the-world/

Loranger, Erin. 2017. "House Advances Bill That Would Prohibit Sharia Law." *Billings Gazette*, March 20. Accessed May 31, 2017. http://billingsgazette.com /news/government-and-politics/house-advances-bill-that-would-prohibit-shar ia-law/article_4648cf03-89e8-5a65-8be6-325bd21f91a8.html

Love, Erik. 2017. *Islamophobia and Racism in America*. New York: New York University Press.

Ludden, David E. 1996. "Introduction. Ayodhya: A Window on the World." In *Contesting the Nation: Religion, Community, and the Politics of Democracy in India*, edited by David E. Ludden, 3–15. Philadelphia: University of Pennsylvania Press.

Lynch, Cecilia. 2014. "Critical Interpretation and Interwar Peace Movements: Challenging Dominant Narratives." In *Interpretation and Method: Empirical Research Methods and the Interpretive Turn*, edited by Dvora Yanow and Peregrine Schwartz-Shea, 300–308. Armonk, NY: M. E. Sharpe.

Martin, James. 2014. *Politics and Rhetoric: A Critical Introduction*. New York: Routledge.

Menon, Nivedita. 2000. "State, Community and the Debate on the Uniform Civil Code in India." In *Beyond Rights Talk and Culture Talk: Comparative Essays on the Politics of Rights and Culture,* edited by Mahmood Mamdani, 75–95. New York: St. Martin's Press.

Menon, Nivedita. 2014. "A Uniform Civil Code in India: The State of the Debate in 2014." *Feminist Studies* 40:480–86.

Mitchell, Joshua L., and Brendan Toner. 2016. "Exploring the Foundations of US State-Level Anti-Sharia Initiatives." *Politics and Religion* 9:720–43.

Nussbaum, Martha. 2007. *The Clash Within: Democracy, Religious Violence, and India's Future.* Cambridge, MA: Harvard University Press.

Pandey, Alok. 2017. "UP Chief Minister Delivers Early on a Promise: Anti-Romeo Squads in Action." *NDTV,* March 22. Accessed March 25, 2017. http://www.nd tv.com/india-news/on-yogi-adityanaths-orders-up-police-begin-work-on-anti -romeo-squads-1672069

Patel, Faiza, Matthew Duss, and Amos Toh. 2013. "Foreign Law Bans: Legal Uncertainties and Practical Problems." Brennan Center for Justice, New York School of Law. Accessed November 11, 2020. https://www.brennancenter.org /our-work/research-reports/foreign-law-bans-legal-uncertainties-and-practic al-problems

Pathak, Zakia, and Rajeswari Sunder Rajan. 1989. "Shahbano." *Signs* 14:558–82.

Pew Research Center. 2005. "How Non-Muslim Public View Muslims." Pew Research Center Global Attitudes & Trends, July 14. Accessed May 1, 2017. http://www.pewglobal.org/2005/07/14/ii-how-non-muslim-publics-view-mus lims/

Pew Research Center. 2006. "Spirit and Power." Pew Research Center Religion & Public Life, October 5. Accessed October 7, 2016. http://www.pewforum.org /2006/10/05/spirit-and-power/

Pew Research Center. 2017. "American Express Increasingly Warm Feelings toward Religious Groups." Pew Research Center Religion & Public Life, February 15. Accessed May 1, 2017. http://www.pewforum.org/2017/02/15/americans-expr ess-increasingly-warm-feelings-toward-religious-groups/

Puniyani, Ram. 2003. *Communal Politics: Facts versus Myths.* Thousand Oaks, CA: Sage.

Rana, Junaid. 2011. *Terrifying Muslims: Race and Labor in the South Asian Diaspora.* Durham, NC: Duke University Press.

Rao, Mohan. 2011. "Love Jihad and Demographic Fears." *Indian Journal of Gender Studies* 18:425–30.

Robinson, Rowena. 2005. *Tremors of Violence: Muslim Survivors of Ethnic Strife in Western India.* New Delhi: Sage.

Rose, Gillian. 2014. *Visual Methodologies: An Introduction to Researching with Visual Materials.* London: Sage.

Ruthven, Malise. 2012. *Islam: A Very Short Introduction.* New York: Oxford University Press.

S., Rukmini, and Vijaita Singh. 2017. "Muslim Population Growth Slows." *The Hindu,* February 13. Accessed May 12, 2017. http://www.thehindu.com/news /national/Muslim-population-growth-slows/article10336665.ece

Sachar, Rajindar. 2007. *Report on Social, Economic, and Educational Status of the Mus-*

lim Community of India. Government of India. Prime Minister's High Level Committee. November. Delhi: Akalank Publications.

Sacirbey, Omar. 2013. "Anti-Sharia Bill Passed in North Carolina without Governor Pat McCrory's Signature." *Huffington Post*, August 27. Accessed May 31, 2017. http://www.huffingtonpost.com/2013/08/27/anti-sharia-bill-north-carol ina-gov-pat-mccrory_n_3823796.html

Safvi, Rana. 2017. "I'm a Muslim Woman and This Triple Talaq Bill Is Not What I Fought For." *Daily O*, December 29. Accessed March 12, 2019. https://www.da ilyo.in/voices/triple-talaq-bill-muslim-women-bjp-uniform-civil-code-parliam ent-supreme-court/story/1/21436.html

Schultz, Kai. 2018. "India Criminalizes Instant 'Talaq' Divorces for Muslim Men." *New York Times*, September 20. Accessed March 12, 2019. https://www.nytimes .com/2018/09/20/world/asia/india-talaq-muslim-divorce.html

Schwartz-Shea, Peregrine, and Dvora Yanow. 2012. *Interpretive Research Design: Concepts and Processes*. New York: Routledge.

Sehgal, Meera. 2014. "Defending the Nation: Militarism, Women's Empowerment, and the Hindu Right." In *Border Politics: Social Movements, Collective Identities, and Globalization*, edited by Nancy A. Naples and Jennifer Bickham Mendez, 60–94. New York: New York University Press.

Shaheen, Jack G. 2009. *Reel Bad Arabs: How Hollywood Vilifies and People*. Northampton, MA: Olive Branch Press.

Shane, Scott, Matthew Rosenberg, and Eric Lipton. 2017. "Trump Pushes Dark View of Islam to Center for U.S. Policy-Making." *New York Times*, February 1. Accessed May 28, 2017. https://www.nytimes.com/2017/02/01/us/politics/don ald-trump-islam.html?_r=0

Shanmugasundaram, Swathi. 2018. "Anti-Sharia Law Bills in the United States." Southern Poverty Law Center. Accessed March 7, 2019. https://www.splcenter .org/hatewatch/2018/02/05/anti-sharia-law-bills-united-states

Shariff, Abusaleh. 2015. "Myth of Muslim Population Growth." *Indian Express*, September 2. Accessed May 12, 2017. http://indianexpress.com/article/opinion /columns/myth-of-muslim-growth/

"Show Me Your Papers: India's Hunt for 'Illegal Immigrants' Is Aimed at Muslims. Many Are in Fact Citizens." 2019. *The Economist*, July 11. Accessed September 26, 2019. https://www.economist.com/leaders/2019/07/11/indias-hunt-for-ille gal-immigrants-is-aimed-at-muslims

Sinha, Mrinalini. 2000. "Refashioning Mother India: Feminism and Nationalism in Late-Colonial India." *Feminist Studies* 26:623–44.

Smith, David T. 2015. *Religious Persecution and Political Order in the United States*. New York: Cambridge University Press.

Southern Poverty Law Center. 2019a. "Center for Security Policy." Southern Poverty Law Center (website). Accessed March 7, 2019. https://www.splcenter.org /fighting-hate/extremist-files/group/center-security-policy

Southern Poverty Law Center. 2019b. "Frank Gaffney, Jr." Southern Poverty Law Center (website). Accessed March 7, 2019. https://www.splcenter.org/fighting -hate/extremist-files/individual/frank-gaffney-jr

Southern Poverty Law Center. 2019c. "Tracking Anti-Muslim Legislation across the U.S." Southern Poverty Law Center (website). Accessed March 8, 2019.

https://www.splcenter.org/data-projects/tracking-anti-muslim-legislation-acro
ss-us#

Soz, Salman Anees. 2016. "RSS Claims about Rapid Growth of the Muslim Population Are Simply False." *The Wire*, July 9. Accessed May 12, 2017. https://thewire
.in/64570/rss-claims-rapid-growth-muslim-population-simply-false/

Spencer, Robert. 2013. *Islam: Religion of Bigots*. Sherman Park, CA: David Horowitz
Freedom Center. Accessed March 11, 2019. https://www.frontpagemag.com
/fpm/199833/islam-religion-bigots-frontpagemagcom

Teater, Kristina M., and Laura Dudley Jenkins. 2019. "Religious Regulation in
India." *Encyclopedia of Politics and Religion*. New York: Oxford University Press.

"Triple Talaq and the War of the Mullahs: Let Not Shahbano Case Be Repeated."
2016. *Uday India*, November 17. Accessed March 12, 2019. https://udayindia
.in/2016/11/17/triple-talaq-and-the-war-of-the-mullahs-let-not-shahbano-ca
se-be-repeated/

Trump, Donald. 2017a. "Executive Order Protecting the Nation from Foreign Terrorist Entry into the United States." The White House (website), January 27.
Accessed May 25, 2017. https://www.whitehouse.gov/the-press-office/2017/01
/27/executive-order-protecting-nation-foreign-terrorist-entry-united-states

Trump, Donald. 2017b. "Executive Order Protecting the Nation from Foreign
Terrorist Entry into the United States." The White House (website), March 6.
Accessed May 25, 2017. https://www.whitehouse.gov/the-press-office/2017/03
/06/executive-order-protecting-nation-foreign-terrorist-entry-united-states

Varshney, Ashutosh. 2002. *Ethnic Conflict and Civic Life: Hindus and Muslims in India*.
New Haven, CT: Yale University Press.

Weber, Cynthia. 2008. "Popular Visual Language as Global Communication:
The Remediation of United Airlines Flight 93." *Review of International Studies*
34:137–53.

Williams, Rina Verma. 2006. *Postcolonial Politics and Personal Laws: Colonial Legal
Legacies and the Indian State*. New Delhi: Oxford University Press.

Williams, Rina Verma 2013a. "Failure to Launch: Women and Hindu Nationalist
Politics in Colonial India." *Politics, Religion & Ideology* 14 (4): 541–56.

Williams, Rina Verma. 2013b. "The More Things Change: Debating Gender and
Religion in India's Hindu Laws, 1920–2006." *Gender and History* 25:711–24.

Williams, Rina Verma, and Laura Dudley Jenkins. 2015. "Secular Anxieties and
Transnational Engagements in India." In *Multiple Secularities beyond the West:
Religion and Modernity in the Global Age*, edited by Marian Burchardt, Monika
Wohlrab-Sahr, and Matthias Middell, 19–38. Boston, MA: DeGruyter.

Wormald, Benjamin. 2015. "Religious Landscape Study." Pew Research Center
Religion & Public Life, May 11. Accessed November 11, 2020. https://www.pe
wforum.org/religious-landscape-study/

SIX

The Consequences of Denominational Typicality on Individual Political Attitudes

Michael W. Wagner and Amanda Friesen

This chapter focuses on a religious communication microfoundation—self-perceived typicality with one's religious group. As discussed in regard to the "Santorum" experiment featured in chapter 3, identity group prototypicality may be critical for effectively communicating religious views and ideas among intended audiences. This is because religious communication is often a context-dependent phenomenon that requires a sense of identity for the religious that enables them to participate in their faith community. But when it comes to politics, do individual-level perceptions of group prototypicality and context impact the communication of attitudes? In a nation with constitutionally enshrined rights to the free exercise of religion and the prevention of a government-established religion, it is at least intellectually imaginable that Americans might separate their political preferences from their sacred ones. What is theoretically possible, though, is often quite different from what is empirically demonstrable. There is robust evidence that Americans' political and religious views are inter-related (Smidt et al. 2010; Djupe and Gilbert 2009; Friesen and Wagner 2012; Putnam and Campbell 2010; Smidt, Kellstedt, and Guth 2009; Layman 2001; Wald and Calhoun-Brown 2018; Campbell 2007; Kellstedt and Green 1993).

After the behavioral revolution in political science, a dominant explanation for how Americans approached faith and politics rested on denominational differences (Carmines and Layman 1997; Sundquist 1983). For example, the New Deal coalition's strong Roman Catholic contingent did ecclesiastical and political battle with mainline Protestants for much of the twentieth century, thereby explaining both religious and political cleavages. However, more recent explanations about the comingling of faith and politics begin with exhortations about preferences on "culture war" issues (Hunter 1991) and generally end with the sorting of American Christians into categories like "religious traditionalist" and "religious modernist." These categories exist across denominational affiliation and account for the "great divide" between partisans in the contemporary era (Layman 2001). The traditionalist-modernist divide, while the dominant one in current politics and religion research, is not without its critics (Djupe and Gilbert 2006; Leege et al. 2002; Friesen and Wagner 2012). As McTague and Layman (2009, 356) note, some believe "our framework may be too narrow while another school of thought suggests that it may be too broad."

While simultaneous claims of broadness and narrowness may imply that the religious traditionalism/modernism perspective's porridge is, thus, "just right," we argue that one's perceived contextual place (i.e., social identity) in a religious denomination continues to play a crucial, independent role in the shaping of political attitudes. In this chapter, we show how one's self-reported sense of feeling like a prototypical member of a denomination is connected to political attitudes. While large-scale, replicated survey measures are crucial to contribute to this line of inquiry, we spent time listening and interacting with people of faith in their environments and local networks to shed light on what it means for individuals to "belong." Thus, we rely on a series of focus group conversations conducted in eight adult Sunday school classes (across seven Christian denominations) in three large American cities. Rather than relying on survey measures or personal interviews, we realized that facilitating focus groups allowed us to observe and record rich conversations between members of already intact small groups. This is important because network composition is critical to understanding political expression and participation (Van Duyn 2018). The conversations we facilitated revealed how parishioners in both homogeneous and heterogenous networks communicate with each other and view themselves within their religious communities.

While some important denominational differences emerged in our analysis, those calling themselves prototypical Christian congregants also generally expressed political views that align with conservative issue preferences that Republicans favor, especially on social issues. Even so, our interviews also revealed that what it means to be a "typical" member of a faith community varies widely across the American theological spectrum. Our results suggest that to comprehensively understand the ways in which Americans view the relationship between religion and politics, it is necessary to understand who thinks of themselves as prototypical members of their faith, what they think a typical member of their church is in the first place, and how they talk about these positions with their peers. More generally, our results align with recent work suggesting that the context that exists within a relevant social network can affect the expression of political attitudes (Van Duyn 2018).

Measuring Faith and Politics: The State of the Art

Most analyses of political attitudes and associations that incorporate the role of religion examine some combination of the "Three Bs": believing, behaving, and belonging. While religious belief and religious affiliation have much in common, religious affiliation, or belonging, is considered the most important component in the relationship between politics and religion (Kleppner 1970; Berelson, Lazarsfeld, and McPhee 1954). Smidt, Kellstedt, and Guth's (2009) thorough review of the "Three Bs" perspective concludes that belonging is often operationalized broadly, as group affiliation or religious tradition with its obligatory geographic, ethnic, denominational, or doctrinal ties. At the beginning of the twentieth century, religious affiliation was a strong correlate to partisanship. The New Deal coalition, which brought Catholics and religious minorities into the Democratic fold, competed for political power with non-Southern white Protestants aligned with the Republican Party (Carmines and Layman 1997). The civil rights movement brought Black Protestants to the Democratic Party just as Southern whites began identifying with the GOP (Carmines and Stimson 1989).

And, while "belonging" matters, its importance overlaps with religious differences within specific denominations (Smidt, Kellstedt, and Guth 2009). This segues into "believing," which also is a central feature of the contemporary relationship between religion and politics (Stark and Glock 1968; Hunter 1991; Jelen 1991). Sociologists of religion have spent the last several decades presenting evidence consistent with the "restructuring hypothesis": differences in belief among members of the *same denomination* have more important political consequences than differences *between denominations* (Hunter 1991; Wuthnow 1988; Layman 2001). This perspective posits that modern politics crosses denominational lines and is better explained by beliefs that religious traditionalists across denominations hold dear as compared to beliefs that religious modernists—across those same denominations—believe themselves. Doctrinal orthodoxy is the most often used measure to conceptualize believing. It typically combines different measures of beliefs about the veracity of the Bible and the nature of the afterlife into an index (Layman 2001; Jelen 1989; Wilcox 1990; Kellstedt and Green 1993). Despite their virtues, measures of believing rarely tap into particular beliefs held by specific denominations (but see Mockabee, Monson, and Grant 2001). For example, evangelical Christians believe in a traditional definition of marriage, but evangelical Baptists and Evangelical Free Christians have divergent doctrinal perspectives on whether people should try to turn their religious beliefs into official public policy (Friesen and Wagner 2012).

The third major measure examining how religion and politics mix is "behaving." Two discrete kinds of behavior have earned scholarly attention: private devotionalism (i.e., praying at home) and ritual activity (i.e., taking communion) (Leege, Wald, and Kellstedt 1993). Some scholars also include one's self-reported importance of religion in one's everyday life to measure behaving. Some evidence indicates that belief is not as important as behaving and, especially, belonging (Putnam and Campbell 2010). Merging American National Election Studies measures of believing, behaving, and belonging, Layman's (2001) measure of religious traditionalism shows with impressive precision how systematic differences in religious traditionalism across denominations account for change in the American party system. From the 1970s to the late 1990s, religious traditionalists became more likely to identify as Republicans while religious modernists moved toward identification as Democrats (Carmines and Wagner 2006).

The emphasis on this "great divide" generally measured these concepts from the point of view of a religious traditionalist, that is, with questions about being born-again or literal translations of the Bible. In 2008, the American National Election Studies added questions as to whether one has tried to be a good Christian and, when trying to be one, whether it is more important to avoid sin or to help others. Mockabee, Wald, and Leege (2012) show marked differences between evangelical Protestants (56 percent avoiding sin) and mainline Protestants and Roman Catholics (43 percent and 36 percent avoiding sin, respectively). The authors' measures of "communitarian" and "individual piety" predict party identification and attitudes about moral issues, while the communitarian measure also is negatively correlated with conservative positions on economic issues.

Some critics of the "Three Bs" approach contend that the measures are tarnished with conceptual and measurement errors that hide relevant variation within and across individuals, congregations, and religious communities (Djupe and Gilbert 2006, 2009; Jelen 1992; Verba, Schlozman, and Brady 1995; Guth et al. 1997). Perhaps in response, Smidt, Kellstedt, and Guth (2009) suggest that scholars should examine each "B" independently from each other. We suggest this is especially important when thinking about the expression of issue preferences when religious networks intersect with the opportunity for political discussion.

We believe that the cases where individuals express a preference about religion's role in society that is "against type" (from a religious traditionalist/modernism perspective) may be explained by something outside religiosity/religious traditionalism scales: how typical one considers oneself within her or his denominational context. Denominational faith statements vary widely with respect to how, and indeed whether, the ideas and beliefs encountered in church should manifest in government (Friesen and Wagner 2012). When individuals express views demonstrating a lack of ideological constraint on a religious traditionalism scale, their particular denomination's view on religion's role in society should help explain the disconnect. This is because typical classifications of religious affiliation by denomination pertain to differences in religious beliefs (e.g., the literal truth of the Bible, perspectives on the end of days, etc.) rather than the role that religious beliefs should play in a democratic society with the constitutional separation between church and state. This disconnect can have enormous consequences for how individuals choose to engage in democratic deliberation, or even simple political discussion, with those around them. Van Duyn's (2018) pathbreaking exploration of a group of rural Texas liberal women revealed that those who live in rural areas, and do not fit in politically with their neighbors, can go as far as to form secret societies to find a safe harbor where they can talk politics without fear of social repercussions. While homogeneous networked enclaves encourage participation and facilitate the development of more confident and extreme attitudes, the networked silence Van Duyn describes is one in which individuals who disagree with the dominant voices in a network can form alternative networks to express themselves.

Behaviors such as those exhibited by these Texans may be found more among those who do not consider themselves to be typical members of their faith. van Knippenberg and Hogg (2003) argue that prototypical group members are stronger group identifiers and behave in ways that are more group oriented. Hogg and Reid (2006, 11) explain, "Self-categorization causes our thoughts, feelings, perceptions, and behavior to conform to our prototype of the in-group." Extrapolating these ideas to one's denominational affiliation, we argue that those who consider themselves prototypical denomination members are more likely to adopt and express public policy preferences consistent with their idea of what the typical member of their church believes (compared to other denomination members who consider themselves less prototypical). As a point of comparison outside religion, this is a dynamic similar to non-Christian Americans who desire to be considered prototypical Americans showing more patriotism than non-Christians less interested in prototypicality (Jacobs and Theiss-Morse 2013).

If we think of a church's official position on an issue as a norm to inculcate to parishioners, prototypical congregants should be more likely to express preference for said position. But here is where differences in religious motivation manifest. For example, those who view religion as what it can do for them are extrinsically motivated and answer affirmatively to statements like "What religion offers me most is comfort in times of trouble and sorrow," while intrinsically motivated individuals are more likely to say, "My whole approach to life is based upon my religion" (Gorsuch and McPherson 1989, 352). People even join churches for explicitly political reasons. When people do switch faiths, it is usually to bring one's religious affiliation in line with one's political views (Putnam and Campbell 2010; Patrikios 2008).

Our goal in this analysis is to understand whether people's self-reported sense of typicality in their denomination predicts their issue preferences, how people talked about their preferences, and their location on a contemporary scale measuring religious traditionalism. For most Christian denominations, we expect that increased self-perceived typicality increases the probability of holding political views consistent with the church's teachings. Using current measures, this means an individual alignment with positions that are more religiously traditionalist in nature. That said, the denomination in question matters. For a denomination like the United Church of Christ, which has less of an official doctrine, we do not expect a positive link between self-perceived typicality and issue positions. We provide evidence for these claims below and suggest scholars should not be too quick to abandon notions of belonging and its importance in shaping the attitudes of the faithful.

Methods

When exploring a new concept or seeking to understand established large-scale survey findings, qualitative data collection can provide detailed explanations and valuable insight beyond a closed-ended survey response

(Smidt, Kellstedt, and Guth 2009; Brady, Collier, and Seawright 2004; Creswell 2003, 2008; Saint-Germain, Bassford, and Montano 1993; Walsh 2012). To this end, we conducted a series of focus groups in 2011 and 2012 in three large cities in different regions of the US. Using the Association of Religion Data Archives (www.arda.com), we selected the top two or three most populous denominations for each city and then randomly selected congregations from a denominational website (e.g., the United Methodist Church at www.umc.org). We sent an email invitation explaining the project to the lead pastor or a pastor in charge of small groups, Sunday school classes, or other church life categories. If there was no response within a week, we made a follow-up telephone call to inquire about participation before moving on to the next randomly selected church. In the South, we wished to contact an evangelical nondenominational church and used the Yellow Pages to find one. After numerous nonresponses and declinations of participation from churches selected in this manner, we drew upon local informants—with whom we had contact for the larger project—to find a church willing to participate. In total, we spoke to four groups in the Northwest (Catholic, Presbyterian USA, and two Evangelical Lutheran Church in America [ELCA] groups), two groups in the South (evangelical nondenominational and United Methodist), and two groups in the Northeast (Episcopalian and United Church of Christ).

Within already formed adult small groups or Sunday school classes, participants met either during their regularly scheduled time (during a weekly Bible study or Sunday school) or at a prearranged time convenient for the authors and group members. All groups met at their place of worship. Before the focus group discussion began, participants completed a questionnaire involving demographic, religious, and political questions. Facilitated by one of the authors using a semi-structured protocol of open-ended questions, each group met for about an hour, and the discussion was digitally recorded and transcribed verbatim.

Table 6.1 displays the descriptive statistics of the religiosity variables included on the focus group questionnaire, such as whether one was born-again, how important one views religion in everyday decision-making, biblical views, and our newly developed typicality inquiry:

> On a scale of 1 to 10, where would you place yourself in regard to how "typical" you are of a member of your religious affiliation? (e.g., If you are Catholic, a rating of 10 would indicate you believe and act like most Catholics. A score of 1 would indicate that you consider yourself very different from other Catholics.)

TABLE 6.1. Religiosity Descriptives for Focus Group Participants

	Typicality	Born Again	Biblical Views	Religious Importance	N
Catholics	M = 8.4 SD = 2.3	40% Yes 60% No	Inspired: 100%	M = 3.6 SD = .55	5
Mainline Protestants	M = 5.6 SD = 2.1	21% Yes 67% No 12% Don't Know	Fables: 33% Inspired: 67% Actual: 0%	M = 3.33 SD = .85	33
Evangelical Protestants	M = 6.2 SD = 2.2	90% Yes 10% No	Fables: 0% Inspired: 30% Actual: 70%	M = 4 SD = 0	10

Because of the small sample sizes, meaningful conclusions cannot be drawn from correlations. However, the descriptive statistics demonstrate that our groups are fairly representative of how these denominational groups are theologically defined (e.g., nearly all of the evangelicals considered themselves born-again). More useful than analysis of statistics on these small samples is an examination of how individuals categorize themselves and how this corresponds to their discussion content.

Our opening prompt was "Tell us about your church," followed by "What does your church believe?" and "What is the role of religion in society?" Answers to these questions provide insight on typicality because they enable the examination of individual perceptions of their church (denomination) and its central beliefs. We classified our participants as prototypical if they scored 7 or above on the scale. With the exception of the Catholic focus group, there was a great deal of variance in how prototypical each of our focus group participants considered themselves to be in their church. Below, we discuss how self-professed prototypical and atypical members of each denomination describe their church and the role they prefer religion to play in society. We have created pseudonyms for the participants, which are indicated below with some of their direct quotes.

Congregationalists

While all of our Congregationalist participants identified as Democrats, the prototypical members of the northeastern United Church of Christ focus group independently mentioned how they came to the church after a long process of searching out faith communities that would fit their pre-existing political and social beliefs. One participant said her reason for membership was "definitely the progressive aspect of (name of) Church." Another participant mentioned that her search process involved trying to discern various churches' politics virtually.

> I looked on a few different websites in order to look for a church, and how things are presented on the website was a key factor for me in coming here. Really I decided I would become a member here before I actually showed up.

A participant who considered himself to be an atypical member of the same church explained that his life in the church was not due to a long search but because of a strong rejection of his former faith and a member of his social network attended the Congregational church. Still, when it comes to politics, his views were very typical of the other Congregationalists, helping to explain his comfort in expressing his political views.

> I'm a friend of (another participant), I started coming when she started working here. I was raised Catholic, and I have a very negative view of the Catholic Church. What keeps me coming here is what I consider to be the sincerity. I mean, religion is supposed to be about openness, about acceptance, about kindness, about tolerance, about helping one another, and the people here are not hypocrites. They live the Christian message in my view. . . . But also I mean yes, specific issues like marriage equality. I mean I happen to come from a family, we've always had gay friends in my family. And to think that people who call themselves Christians condemn gay people to me is madness. What this congregation would be without some of its gay members, I mean we would be so impoverished.

Putnam and Campbell (2010) show that those who switch faiths systematically pick a new faith that fits their political views. In our sample, the intentional search for a church home that shared their political views was also a hallmark of feeling like a typical Congregationalist; and though the atypical member agreed with the church's political leanings, his negative past church experiences may have made him reluctant to feel as though he was a typical part of any Christian group. Further, the less intentional, more relational way in which he came to attend the Congregationalist church also may help to account for his perceptions of atypicality. Even so, perhaps because his political views were typical of his fellow parishioners, he appeared comfortable talking politics in a group where he otherwise did not feel like a typical member.

Episcopalians

The Episcopalian participants who expressed feelings of typicality were those who saw a connection between the religious traditions associated with the church and the traditions of social activism within the particular parish. One woman, before describing how she appreciated the connection between her church's progressive role in her city's piece of the Occupy Wall Street movement, discussed how she appreciates the nature of liturgy and worship in her church.

> There's a reason for everything, I mean, some people might think it's fussy, but I like that everything is thought through and grounded in some kind of uh, theological or historical you know, reason. So it's more, for me it's more than just the aesthetics. I mean, yes it's wonderful that it's pretty and well done, and there's a reason why each piece is where it is.

While most self-professed typical Episcopalians in the group agreed, another participant who reported feeling atypical only stressed the religious tradition of the church, while longing for less socially liberal politics of what she described as the past.

> Tradition means a lot, it means a lot to me. I think that's what church is about. That is what church is about. It is about tradition. Religion in general, I mean, if you're Hindu, if you're Buddhist, it's about the tradition. It's about keeping it going. I like being part of the apostolic tradition. I don't do revision history. But now, it has become so Laura Ingraham nasty ugly attacking. I guess I'm just more comfortable with the country club Republican(s). And they were just run out of office.

The atypical Episcopalian also identified as politically independent (compared to the other participants, who identified as Democrats). Perhaps for this atypical individual, when thinking of denominational typicality, political leanings and social activism were her point of reference for "belonging."

Methodists

As was the case with Episcopalians, typical Methodists highlighted the traditions of their church (denomination), tying the beliefs of their particular faith to the work of improving life in their own community. One Methodist who considered herself to be typical said,

> Our church's beliefs are pretty traditional for the United Methodist Church uh, individual members have a variety of beliefs but as the church itself goes, I think the church believes that we followed the ministry and the leadership of Jesus as the son of God, that the Bible is the revealed book of God as a guide to how we should live our lives and interact in community with others, when I say community I mean not just local community but the world community as well, that we have a responsibility to give from our many blessings uh, to others in our community and to help them find their own way and stand on their own two feet.

The Methodists who felt atypical were far more likely to embrace the "messiness" of faith, praising the church's diversity of viewpoints. One woman said,

> There are (adult Sunday school) classes that are different and you can kind of choose like, I feel like our side of the class is pretty liberal and I like that, I like to be able to—we can think out loud, say whatever we want to say or need to say and uh, it's acceptable and not only that but encouraged, so we really like that. The middle is messier.

Another self-professed atypical member of the Methodist focus group said,

> I think the reason we stay here (in the United Methodist Church) is because it draws people from all over the county and all over the community rather than being just in one, our neighborhood, where it's pretty single-minded.

Unlike the atypical Episcopalians, the atypical Methodists were more likely to express comfort in ambiguity and note that they were less concerned with doctrine. And unlike the social network Van Duyn (2018) chronicled in Texas, the Methodist social network embraced ambiguity and difference, leaving people more comfortable to publicly disagree in their political expressions. The typical members of our Methodist focus group were more likely to highlight specific doctrinal elements of their faith and connect them to promoting social good. However, another way in which the Methodists were different from other politically relevant social networks was that they were both more ideologically moderate and more religiously traditionalist than their atypical counterparts.

ELCA Lutherans

While typical ELCA Lutherans we spoke with exhibited high degrees of religious traditionalism versus those who identified as atypical Lutherans, there was considerable diversity with respect to ideology and partisanship among the typical identifiers. Some religiously traditional typical identifiers were strong conservatives and Republicans, while others were strong liberals and members of the Democratic Party. For a typical Lutheran Republican, religion's role in society is about "respect" and "connecting" faith to life while being "open-minded," as "(name redacted) and I are on different ends of the political spectrum, but we respect each other here." A typical Lutheran Democrat made a similar point, noting that there are a variety of ways to "follow the example [of Jesus]. And following the example is the part that drew me to the whole thing."

A self-described atypical Lutheran preferred to keep connections between faith and politics separate, noting that he liked the church because "the Christ that we raise up and gather around is the Christ that was forever pushing the boundaries and you know, reaching out to walk with you know, all kinds of citizens and folk, acceptable and unacceptable," but that he talks politics "at work." Though on opposite sides of the partisan spectrum, typical Lutherans saw clear connections between their political views and their understanding of the purpose of the church, while atypical Lutherans saw politics and religion as separate realms (see also Van Duyn 2018).

Presbyterians

In general, the Presbyterians we met with who identified as typical Presbyterian were more conservative ideologically and exhibited higher levels of measures associated with religious traditionalism. For example, typical Presbyterians were more likely to identify as being "born-again" than atypical congregants. An atypical Presbyterian did not think religion was as important to his daily decision-making as the typical Presbyterians, nor were his views about the Bible as traditional as typical Presbyterians. However, there was considerable diversity in the economic views and the religious views of typical Presbyterians in our focus group sample. The exchange below between three men who all rated themselves as an 8 or above on the typicality measure highlights how typicality becomes murky when thinking about politics in a mainline church.

> JAKE: Interesting question. Um, my take is that the Democrats tend to take care of people more than Republicans do. And can say you know, they're more in favor of social programs, so you can say from a church perspective or from a faith perspective, it's taking care of the people who can't take care of themselves, so I would make that connection with the Democrat side.
>
> RYAN: Yeah, I would tend to agree with that. But this, very generally speaking, is how those things go. It's sort of in my observation, too.
>
> LEE: Yeah, sometimes in taking care of, I think that the government has gradually served the, uh, role of the church and some of the social organizations, so when they come in and you know, we'll take care of the single parents, and so there are all these programs without expectations, without values. But whereas before you have, well let's go back to the 1900s, you have thriving social groups, and I've said this to this group before, [inaudible] all these social welfare groups have protective orders and now the government, social security and other things have come in to take that.

Lee identified as an independent on our survey and considers himself socially liberal and economically conservative, whereas the other two, who identify as Democrats, both rank their social and economic ideologies as "liberal." Elsewhere in the conversation, the group members discussed how the tension of trying to talk about political differences leads them to circle back to bedrock theological beliefs they know will be shared. This suggests that the presence of a bedrock belief system that applied to all—in this case, the theological beliefs of the group—can be enough to foster cohesion in networks even when other belief systems—such as political ideology—are the subject of disagreement.

Evangelicals

In the American South, the evangelical focus group we met with generally identified themselves as conservative, Republican, and born-again.
However, there was considerable diversity with respect to how typical a
member of the evangelical community each participant claimed to be. One
typical evangelical explained what he believed the church was about: "The
gift that Christ gave us that died on the cross is a free gift, no works can
take you into the presence of God or out of the presence of God, it's all
by the gift of Christ himself." Another said that "you can't separate" God
from anything in day-to-day life and that one major purpose of the church
was to foster individuals' relationship with God. The only evangelical who
identified himself as atypical was much more comfortable with ambiguity
in the teachings of the church.

> When our church says we believe the Bible word for word, what we
> mean within the context of what the literary style is. So you know,
> there's a sophistication there that says, hey if it's poetry, I'm gonna
> interpret it literally as poetry. If it's history, I'm gonna interpret it
> literally as history, and it looked like within politics and within the
> media, you get portrayed as when you say you believe if word for
> word, well you're either anti-intellectual, you're anti-science or
> you're against these, which shows a very, very naive understanding
> of interpretation. . . . And so we could have a debate within our own
> church about well, okay creation, is it twenty-four hours as it is now,
> is it a literary device, is it ages in a period, is it theistic evolution?
> And then have a debate, well what should be taught in school.

Prototypical evangelicals expressed a desire to seek and share the "truth"
but were less comfortable with a deliberative process to find it. Indeed,
the feelings of typicality in the evangelical church we visited lined up
with Republican Party identification, while the atypical participant was a
Democrat.

Roman Catholics

We met with the Roman Catholic focus group in the Northwest. All but
one participant in the conversation felt as though she or he was a typical

Catholic, which they tended to indicate was built around the social justice mission of the Catholic faith. One "typical" man said, "I like it because [the church] seems like it's where the rubber meets the road." When one of the authors said, "What do you mean?" another man answered,

> This is it. This is, if you were in church this morning you would've seen there are people who don't even have houses who come here. You know, people who don't have a place to rest at night, come here. I think that one of the reasons why I started going here is I was, I just thought you know as I get better and better at helping people, this is the place to be. This is where I'll learn it.

The Catholic participant who identified as atypical also believed in the central importance of the church's social justice mission but made a direct connection between it and the crucifixion of Jesus Christ: "The response to the crucifixion is to do it more, and to find ways to relieve the suffering of those who are still being treated, are not given opportunities that they deserve as human beings." Interestingly, the atypical Catholic scored higher on measures of religious traditionalism than most of the typical Catholics in this group and was more conservative on economic political issues and with respect to his general ideology than his fellow parishioners.

Discussion and Conclusion

Religious context clearly matters for individual-level communication: people who felt comfortable expressing their political views tended to be surrounded by people with whom they had something in common: a bedrock set of principles. This suggests that the notion of religious belonging may pack more punch than some scholars have assumed. Social scientists of religion have been debating the issues of how and why people of faith connect politics and religion for decades, with many settling along the lines that orthodoxy and commitment (believing and behaving) matter more than the old standard of affiliation (belonging). Our study suggests we ought not abandon denomination but should think more deeply about variance in "belonging."

Thoughtful engagement with belonging might shed light upon the mixed results found in research exploring the effects of heterogenous and homogeneous communication networks on political participation. For example, understanding how belonging can vary as a social identity might help explain why cross-cutting discussion in heterogeneous discussion networks can both mobilize and demobilize political participation (Mutz 2002; Huckfeldt, Johnson, and Sprague 2004). A focus on belonging can also help scholars unpack why homogeneous discussion networks can produce greater attitude extremity (Sunstein 2001) in some cases while mobilizing discussion in others (Karpowitz and Mendelberg 2014).

Joining scholars who emphasize the institutional influence of clergy and social networks (Djupe and Gilbert 2009), we suggest that individual orientations toward the institution and others in one's faith community also may be at play. From our focus group members, we learn that typical members of liberal mainline Protestant congregations (i.e., Congregationalists, Episcopalians, and some Lutherans) tend to connect their affiliation and church with political and social attitudes, whereas the atypical members were drawn to the respective churches for more theological reasons. In the Roman Catholic group, the typical members chose their particular parish because of its efforts to translate church teachings into tangible social justice. It is important to note that these groups were in predominantly white congregations, where political viewpoint and partisan diversity are more present than they would be in places like historically African American churches and denominations (Calhoun-Brown 1998; McClerking and McDaniel 2005; Shelton and Cobb 2017).

Typical members of the ELCA group, atypical Methodists, and some typical Presbyterians embraced the diversity of opinion within their church walls—reflecting the theological and political variance among congregants in churches in the theological middle. That is, typicality within these denominations may be murkier than for those on the theological extremes, whose members tend to be more homogenous in political and religious beliefs. The only atypical evangelical in that focus group embraced ambiguity and a reasonable debate about church teachings. These were not shared by the more typical group members, who indicated more staunch attitudes about the settled nature of church doctrine. If atypicality is related to an individual's incongruity with other church members' political attitudes or to a difference in the acceptance or perception of diverse opinions, the consequences could be a reduction in political participation or the avoidance of political discussion (Djupe and Gilbert 2009).

Finally, simply adding another variable to the mix is not helpful unless it can explain beyond the commonly replicated religiosity measures. Our focus groups, while clearly not representative, hinted that typicality in an adult population may be more related to political congruency and the perception or acceptance of conflict within one's faith community, at least with some mainline Christian denominations (but see Margolis 2018). Partisan elites seek to exploit these relationships. For example, several journalists and partisan operatives have pointed out that evangelical Christians are strong supporters of President Donald Trump, despite Trump's multiple divorces, payoffs to adult film stars with whom he had engaged in sex while married to the First Lady, lack of familiarity with the Bible, and so forth. The contemporary media ecology tends to reinforce connections people make between social identities such as their faith and their partisan identity (Mason 2018; Wagner et al. 2014). This appears to be especially true when it comes to the expression of political views or the decision to stop talking politics with someone altogether (Wells et al. 2017). When considered in religious networks, individuals who participate in small groups may have more politicized social networks, be receptive to clergy cues, and connect their religion and politics (Djupe and Gilbert 2009).

Indeed, recent work on rising rates of secularization points to political conflict and/or polarization in churches as contributing to those who leave and could otherwise disengage from other parts of civic life (Djupe, Neiheisel, and Sokhey 2018). Our findings suggest that political divides rooted in denominational affiliations have not been displaced by the rise of the differences in religious traditionalism and modernism among people of faith across denominations, contributing to a more comprehensive explanation of the role that religion plays in the American political system—a role that appears to cement polarized partisan identities for many while excluding others from a political system that does not represent them.

REFERENCES

Berelson, Bernard R., Paul R. Lazarsfeld, and William N. McPhee. 1954. *Voting: A Study of Opinion Formation in a Presidential Campaign*. Chicago: University of Chicago Press.

Brady, Henry E., David Collier, and Jason Seawright. 2004. "Refocusing the Discussion of Methodology." In *Rethinking Social Inquiry: Diverse Tools, Shared Standards*, edited by Henry E. Brady and David Collier, 15–32. Lanham, MD: Rowman and Littlefield.

Calhoun-Brown, Allison. 1998. "The Politics of Black Evangelicals: What Hinders Diversity in the Christian Right?" *American Politics Quarterly* 26:81–109.

Campbell, David E., ed. 2007. *A Matter of Faith: Religion in the 2004 Presidential Election*. Washington, DC: Brookings Institution Press.

Carmines, Edward G., and Geoffrey C. Layman. 1997. "Issue Evolution in Postwar American Politics: Old Certainties and Fresh Tensions." In *Present Discontents: American Politics in the Very Late Twentieth Century*, edited by Byron E. Shafer, 89–134. Chatham, NJ: Chatham House.

Carmines, Edward G., and James A. Stimson. 1989. *Issue Evolution: Race and the Transformation of American Politics*. Princeton: Princeton University Press.

Carmines, Edward G., and Michael W. Wagner. 2006. "Political Issues and Partisan Alignments: Assessing the Issue Evolution Perspective." *Annual Review of Political Science* 9:67–91.

Creswell, John W. 2003. *Research Design: Qualitative, Quantitative, and Mixed Methods Approaches*. Thousand Oaks, CA: Sage.

Creswell, John W. 2008. *Educational Research: Planning, Conducting, and Evaluating Quantitative and Qualitative Research*. 3rd ed. Upper Saddle River, NJ: Pearson Education.

Djupe, Paul A., and Christopher P. Gilbert. 2006. "The Resourceful Believer: Generating Civic Skills in Church." *Journal of Politics* 68:116–27.

Djupe, Paul A., and Christopher P. Gilbert. 2009. *The Political Influence of Churches*. New York: Cambridge University Press.

Djupe, Paul A., Jacob R. Neiheisel, and Anand E. Sokhey. 2018. "Reconsidering the Role of Politics in Leaving Religion: The Importance of Affiliation." *American Journal of Political Science* 62 (1): 161–75.

Ellis, Christopher, and James A. Stimson. 2011. "Pathways to Conservative Identification: The Politics of Ideological Contradiction in the United States." In *Facing the Challenge of Democracy: Explorations in the Analysis of Public Opinion and Political Participation*, edited by Paul M. Sniderman and Benjamin Highton, 120–50. Princeton: Princeton University Press.

Friesen, Amanda, and Michael W. Wagner. 2012. "Beyond the 'Three Bs': How American Christians Approach Faith and Politics." *Politics and Religion* 5:224–52.

Gorsuch, Richard L., and Susan E. McPherson. 1989. "Intrinsic/Extrinsic Measurement: I/E-Revised and Single-Item Scales." *Journal for the Scientific Study of Religion* 28 (3): 348–54.

Guth, James L., John C. Green, Corwin E. Smidt, and Lyman A. Kellstedt. 1997. *The Bully Pulpit: The Politics of Protestant Clergy*. Lawrence: University Press of Kansas.

Hogg, Michael A., and Scott A. Reid. 2006. "Social Identity, Self-Categorization, and the Communication of Group Norms." *Communication Theory* 16 (1): 7–30.

Huckfeldt, Robert, Paul E. Johnson, and John Sprague. 2004. *Political Disagreement: The Survival of Diverse Opinions within Communication Networks*. New York: Cambridge University Press.

Hunter, James Davison. 1991. *Culture Wars: The Struggle to Define America*. New York: Basic Books.

Jacobs, Carly M., and Elizabeth Theiss-Morse. 2013. "Belonging in a 'Christian Nation': The Explicit and Implicit Associations between Religion and National Group Membership." *Politics and Religion* 6 (2): 373–401.

Jelen, Ted G. 1989. "Biblical Literalism and Inerrancy: Does the Difference Make a Difference?" *Sociological Analysis* 49: 421–29.

Jelen, Ted G. 1991. *The Political Mobilization of Religious Beliefs*. New York: Praeger.

Jelen, Ted G. 1992. "Political Christianity: A Contextual Analysis." *American Journal of Political Science* 36:692–714.

Karpowitz, Christopher F., and Tali Mendelberg. 2014. *The Silent Sex: Gender, Deliberation, and Institutions*. Princeton: Princeton University Press.

Kellstedt, Lyman A., and John C. Green. 1993. "Knowing God's Many People: Denominational Preference and Political Behavior." In *Rediscovering the Religious Factor in American Politics*, edited by David C. Leege and Lyman A. Kellstedt. Armonk, NY: M. E. Sharpe.

Kleppner, Paul. 1970. *The Cross of Culture: A Social Analysis of Midwestern Politics, 1850–1900*. New York: Free Press.

Lane, Robert E. 1962. *Political Ideology: Why the American Common Man Believes What He Does*. New York: Free Press.

Layman, Geoffrey C. 2001. *The Great Divide: Religious and Cultural Conflict in American Party Politics*. New York: Columbia University Press.

Leege, David C., Kenneth D. Wald, and Lyman A. Kellstedt. 1993. "The Public Dimension of Private Devotionalism." In *Rediscovering the Religious Factor in American Politics*, edited by David C. Leege and Lyman A. Kellstedt. Armonk, NY: M. E. Sharpe.

Leege, David C., Kenneth D. Wald, Brian S. Krueger, and Paul D. Mueller. 2002. *The Politics of Cultural Differences: Social Change and Voter Mobilization Strategies in the Post-New Deal Period*. Princeton: Princeton University Press.

Margolis, Michele F. 2018. *From Politics to the Pews: How Partisanship and the Political Environment Shape Religious Identity*. Chicago: University of Chicago Press.

Mason, Lilliana. 2018. *Uncivil Agreement: How Politics Became Our Identity*. Chicago: University of Chicago Press.

McClerking, Harwood K., and Eric L. McDaniel. 2005. "Belonging and Doing: Political Churches and Black Political Participation." *Political Psychology* 26 (5): 721–34.

McTague, John M., and Geoffrey Layman. 2009. "Religion, Parties, and Voting Behavior: A Political Explanation of Religious Influence." In *The Oxford Handbook of Religion and American Politics*, edited by Corwin E. Smidt, Lyman A. Kellstedt, and James L. Guth, 330–70. Oxford: Oxford University Press.

Mockabee, Stephen T., Joseph Quin Monson, and J. Tobin Grant. 2001. "Measuring Religious Commitment among Catholics and Protestants: A New Approach." *Journal for the Scientific Study of Religion* 40:675–90.

Mockabee, Stephen T., Kenneth D. Wald, and David C. Leege. 2012. "In Search of the Religious Left: Re-examining Religiosity." In *Improving Public Opinion Surveys: Interdisciplinary Innovation and the American National Studies*, edited by John Aldrich and Kathleen McGraw, 278–98. Princeton: Princeton University Press.

Mutz, Diana C. 2002. "The Consequences of Cross-Cutting Networks for Political Participation." *American Journal of Political Science* 46 (4): 838–55.

Patrikios, Stratos. 2008. "American Republican Religion? Disentangling the Causal Link between Religion and Politics in the US." *Political Behavior* 30 (3): 367–89.

Putnam, Robert D., and David E. Campbell. 2010. *American Grace: How Religion Divides and Unites Us*. New York: Simon & Schuster.

Saint-Germain, Michelle A., Tamsen L. Bassford, and Gail Montano. 1993. "Surveys and Focus Groups in Health Research. *Qualitative Health Research* 3:341–67.

Shelton, Jason E., and Ryon J. Cobb. 2017. "Black Reltrad: Measuring Religious Diversity and Commonality among African Americans." *Journal for the Scientific Study of Religion* 56 (4) :737–64.

Smidt, Corwin E., Kevin R. den Dulk, Bryan T. Froehle, James M. Penning, Stephen V. Monsma, and Douglas L. Koopman. 2010. *The Disappearing God Gap? Religion in the 2008 Presidential Election.* Oxford: Oxford University Press.

Smidt, Corwin E., Lyman A. Kellstedt, and James L. Guth. 2009. "The Role of Religion in American Politics: Explanatory Theories and Associated Analytical and Measurement Issues." In *The Oxford Handbook of Religion and American Politics*, edited by Corwin E. Smidt, Lyman A. Kellstedt, and James L. Guth, 3–42. Oxford: Oxford University Press.

Smith, Buster G., and Byron Johnson. 2010. "The Liberalization of Young Evangelicals: A Research Note." *Journal for the Scientific Study of Religion* 49 (2): 351–60.

Smith, Tom W. 1990. "Classifying Protestant Denominations." *Review of Religious Research* 31 (3): 225–45.

Steensland, Brian, Jerry Z. Park, Mark D. Rengerus, Lynn D. Robinson, W. Bradford Wilcox, and Robert D. Woodberry. 2000. "The Measure of American Religion: Toward Improving the State of the Art." *Social Forces* 79 (1): 291–324.

Sundquist, James L. 1983. *Dynamics of the Party System: Alignment and Realignment of Political Parties in the United States.* Washington, DC: The Brookings Institution.

Sunstein, Cass. 2001. *Republic.com.* Princeton: Princeton University Press.

Van Duyn, Emily. 2018. "Hidden Democracy: Political Dissent in Rural America." *Journal of Communication* 68 (5): 965–87.

Van Knippenberg, Daan, and Michael A. Hogg. 2003. "A Social Identity Model of Leadership Effectiveness in Organizations." *Research in Organizational Behavior* 25 (1): 243–95.

Verba, Sidney, Kay Lehman Schlozman, and Henry E. Brady. 1995. *Voice and Equality: Civic Voluntarism in American Politics.* Cambridge, MA: Harvard University Press.

Wagner, Michael W., Chris Wells, Lewis A. Friedland, Katherine J. Cramer, and Dhavan V. Shah. 2014. "Cultural Worldviews and Contentious Politics: Evaluative Asymmetry in High-Information Environments." *Good Society* 23 (2): 126–44.

Wald, Kenneth D., and Allison Calhoun-Brown. 2018. *Religion and Politics in the United States.* 8th ed. Lanham, MD: Rowman & Littlefield.

Walsh, Katherine Cramer. 2012. "Putting Inequality in Its Place: Rural Consciousness and the Power of Perspective." *American Political Science Review* 106 (3): 517–32.

Wells, Chris, Katherine J. Cramer, Michael W. Wagner, German Alvarez, Lewis A. Friedland, Dhavan V. Shah, Leticia Bode, Stephanie Edgerly, Itay Gaby, and Charles Franklin. 2017. "When We Stop Talking Politics: The Maintenance and Closing of Conversation in Contentious Times." *Journal of Communication* 67 (1): 131–57.

Wilcox, Clyde. 1990. "Religion and Politics among White Evangelicals: The Impact of Religious Variables on Political Attitudes." *Review of Religious Research* 32:27–42.

Wuthnow, Robert. 1988. *The Restructuring of American Religions: Society and Faith since World War II.* Princeton: Princeton University Press.

SEVEN

#Evangelical

How Twitter Discusses American Religion

Ryan Burge

We saw in the previous chapter that a sense of group prototypicality among religious identifiers is crucial for spurring the communication of their political views. But this is not the only aspect of group typicality important in religious communication. Part of determining prototypicality involves settling the question of just what qualities an identity group is perceived to have. There are at least two paths to making this determination: (1) focusing on ingroup member perceptions (as we saw with the Santorum experiment from chapter 3) or (2) honing in on what outgroups, including the wider public, perceive as a group's defining characteristics.

From the standpoint of politics and religious communication, there may be no more important group label than "evangelical." For many observers of American religion, the most consequential development in the last fifty years has been the rise and continued influence of the Religious Right (Armstrong 2010). These conservative Christians are typically referred to collectively as "evangelicals" by both the scholarly community and the popular press. For instance, books with titles such as *American Evangelicals: Embattled and Thriving* (C. Smith 1998) and *Faith in the Halls of Power: How Evangelicals Joined the American Elite* (Lindsay 2007) are widely cited among those who study this phenomenon scholastically. Popular magazines like *Newsweek* run cover stories with titles such as "Evangelical Christians

Helped Elect Donald Trump, but Their Time as a Major Political Force Is Coming to an End" (Burleigh 2018). Perhaps the most famous example is *Time* magazine's declaration of 1976 as the "Year of the Evangelical" (Wald and Calhoun-Brown 2006, 206). Despite the word's constant usage, does anyone know what "evangelical" really means?

The term has become ubiquitous in American political discourse, yet there is a surprising amount of uncertainty that surrounds the definition of "evangelical." Even famous members of the evangelical community like Billy Graham struggled to succinctly define the term. Yet, while scholars and theologians have debated the proper parameters to qualify someone as an evangelical, the public frequently uses the term in everyday conversation. Does the way the average American talks about evangelicals match up with the way scholars understand the term? Are scholars defining the word in a way that would be completely foreign to the average American? To answer these questions, I scraped nearly 180,000 tweets that contained the word "evangelical" over a span of twenty months from the popular social media platform Twitter. The results indicate that the public is increasingly understanding the term to be linked with the world of modern American politics and less with the spiritual world.

How Do Evangelicals Define the Term?

It is prudent to carefully consider how those who identify as evangelicals describe the term (again, referencing the prototypicality argument from previous chapters). In fact, if one queries "What is an evangelical" on Google, the first site returned is from the National Association of Evangelicals (NAE), a collection of diverse groups that identify as theologically conservative Christians. Membership covers a variety of institutions from a number of different parts of society including schools, religious denominations, and churches throughout the US ("About NAE" 2018). The NAE's page entitled "What Is an Evangelical?" begins by noting that the word "evangelical" comes from the Greek word *euangelion*, which can be translated as "good news" or "gospel." This situates that definition clearly in a theological context, with a particular emphasis on the story of Jesus, which is contained in the four Gospels of the New Testament ("What Is an Evangelical?" 2018). Religious commentators note that the term was first used as a descriptor by Martin Luther when he instigated what became the Protestant Reformation in the early sixteenth century (Merritt 2015). The lineage of the current usage of "evangelical" can most likely be traced to the Great Awakening, a series of revivals led by pastors like George Whit-field and Jonathan Edwards in the 1800s. These orators preached a mes-sage that emphasized having a transformational "born-again" experience that would leave the participant fundamentally changed and equipped to live a life trying to emulate Jesus (Kidd 2009).

But the components of evangelical theology go beyond just having a born-again experience. If one browses further on the NAE's website, read-ers find the "Statement of Faith," which contains seven statements about the organization's belief structure. This document begins by describing the Bible as "the only infallible, authoritative Word of God." In addition, it affirms a belief in a Trinitarian God, as well as a belief in the literal life, death, and resurrection of Jesus Christ, which conferred salvation to all those who believe in its power ("Statement of Faith" 2017).

It is crucial to note what is included as part of the NAE's description of "evangelical" and what is missing. Nowhere on any of the three above reference pages is any mention of political ideology or partisanship made. Likewise, there is no mention of racial qualifications for being an evangeli-cal. In fact, the "Statement of Faith" indicates, "We believe in the spiritual unity of believers in our Lord Jesus Christ" (2017). However, other articles on the association's website do acknowledge that evangelicalism is deeply intertwined with both racial and political concerns. For example, in "Evan-gelical: What's in a Name?" Mark Noll, a professor at Wheaton College, notes that evangelicalism is "now often used simply for the most active sup-porters of Donald Trump." In addition, Noll notes that recent scholarship on evangelicals has placed a great deal of emphasis on adherents who are white and has given much less attention to evangelicals of color. Noll goes on to describe evangelicalism becoming more globalized and diverse and therefore even more difficult to define in any meaningful way (Noll 2018).

Other evangelical academics and leaders also struggle with finding a way to conceptualize the term. For instance, the Christian historian George Marsden writes, "During the 1950s and 1960s the simplest, though very loose, definition of an evangelical in the broad sense was 'anyone who likes Billy Graham'" (1990, 6). Marsden indicates that this period in American history was dominated by Reverend Graham and his organization, the Billy Graham Evangelistic Association. However, he goes on to note that "no one leader or set of spokesperson can begin to speak for the whole move-ment" (6). What may be the most interesting addendum to Marsden's defi-nition is that Billy Graham himself was once asked to define the term, and his response was, "Actually, that's a question I'd like to ask somebody, too." Graham eventually painted a picture where his adherents stood between extreme fundamentalists on one end and extreme liberals on the other, with evangelicals at the midpoint between these two groups (Mattingly 2013).

While Graham was asked this question in a 1987 interview, more contemporary evangelical leaders have also struggled with their own precise definition. For instance, Rick Warren, the pastor of Saddleback, an evangelical megachurch in Southern California, as well as the author of *The Purpose Driven Life*, could not come to a succinct description himself. Instead, Warren said, "I know what the word 'evangelical' is supposed to mean. . . . I mean, I know what the word 'evangelical' used to mean" (Mattingly 2013). Warren acknowledged that in recent years the term had been fused with a specific brand of conservative Republican politics. The best-selling author noted that in almost every one of his media interviews he was consistently asked questions about the political hot topics of the day, especially gay marriage (Mattingly 2013).

Despite the vagueness of many of these evangelical elites' responses, the vast majority of evangelical organizations tend to accept a definition from historian David Bebbington. The so-called Bebbington quadrilateral contends that evangelicalism contains four core beliefs: biblicism, a high regard for the Bible; crucicentrism, an emphasis on the salvific impact of Jesus's death on the cross; conversionism, an understanding that every person needs to have a born-again experience; and activism, a belief that faith should inform and impact public life (Bebbington 1988). This definition has been updated and operationalized by LifeWay Research, a polling firm affiliated with the Southern Baptist Convention. Under LifeWay's definition an individual must agree with the following four questions to be consider an evangelical:

1. The Bible is the highest authority for what I believe.
2. It is very important for me personally to encourage non-Christians to trust Jesus Christ as their Savior.
3. Jesus Christ's death on the cross is the only sacrifice that could remove the penalty of my sin.
4. Only those who trust in Jesus Christ alone as their Savior receive God's free gift of salvation.

According to a 2015 LifeWay survey, 24 percent of respondents agreed with each of those statements and were therefore categorized as an evangelical Christian (Smietana 2015).

Another prominent evangelical research firm, the Barna Research

Group, uses a two-stage classification scheme to first identity someone as "born-again" and then to further filter this group into those who are both "born-again" and "evangelical." For Barna, the criteria to define an evangelical Christian include a series of seven questions that includes "believing that Jesus Christ lived a sinless life while on earth," "believing in the existence of Satan," and "believing that the Bible is accurate in all that it teaches" (Hackett and Lindsay 2008, 504). Using this strict set of questions, the Barna group indicates that just 7 percent of American adults should be classified as "born-again evangelicals" (Barna 1994).

   Broadly speaking, it seems that evangelicals themselves struggle to arrive at a consistent and coherent definition of what the term really means. It would appear that when prominent evangelical leaders are asked to define it, they revert to Supreme Court justice Potter Stewart's famous maxim when asked to decide a difficult case on obscenity, "I don't know how to define it, but I know it when I see it" (Lattman 2007). Evangelical research firms have struggled between codifying a definition that is too open (and therefore overrepresenting the evangelical share of the population) and creating a criteria that is too strict (and excluding many people who would consider themselves to be evangelical). At the same time, as evangelicals wrestle with how to understand the term's meaning, academics employ a number of systems to create a meaningful typology of the amorphous concept.

How Do Academics Define the Term?

While pastors like Graham and Warren struggled to define the term "evangelical," social scientists were wrestling with the same problem. Samuel Stouffer made the earliest attempt at creating religious classification in 1955. Stouffer was interested in measuring how key concepts like political tolerance were distributed among different religious groups. He created a sorting scheme based on geography to divide Protestants into northern and southern groups. For Stouffer, Protestants in New England were more theologically moderate than their southern counterparts, and his typology did reveal important differences between the groups (Stouffer 1955). While many of Stouffer's findings were expanded through subsequent scholarship, his most enduring contribution may be his belief that Protestant Christianity contains both moderate and conservative factions.

   Following Stouffer, Tom Smith generated a tripartite typology that separated all religious groups into three categories (i.e., fundamentalist-moderate-liberal). For Smith, the fundamentalist category was a way to acknowledge the northern/southern divide first espoused by Stouffer but also to create a category for traditions that fell in the middle of the theological spectrum. Obviously, many groups that would today be considered evangelical, like Pentecostals and Southern Baptists, were considered "fundamentalists" in Smith's "FUND" scheme (T. Smith 1990). Following the work by both Stouffer and Smith, a subsequent wave of scholarship argued that while these schemes were clearly a move in a positive direction, they were overly reductive in that they forced completely disparate groups like Episcopalians and Jews into the same FUND category, when those groups had little in common (Green et al. 1996).

The largest step forward in defining evangelicals and other religious groups came in 2000 through the creation of the "RELTRAD" (i.e., "religious tradition") classification scheme. This approach expanded from Smith's three categories to create seven different religious groups. RELTRAD cleaves Protestants into three distinct groups: evangelical, mainline, and black Protestant, as well as creating categories for Jewish, Catholic, other religions, and those with no religious affiliation. RELTRAD uses the religious affiliation of respondents to sort them in one of these seven categories. Those who were categorized as evangelical include respondents affiliated with the Southern Baptist Convention, the Free Methodist Church, and those from Pentecostal traditions (Steensland et al. 2000).

For nearly the last two decades, when a social scientist created an evangelical category for their survey analysis, it was more than likely done so using the basic structure of RELTRAD. In fact, according to Google Scholar, the classification has been employed over thirteen hundred times in the past eighteen years. In subsequent years the RELTRAD authors revisited their typology several times, noting places where it needs refinement and extension (Woodberry et al. 2012; Steensland, Woodberry, and Park 2018). One of the practical benefits of RELTRAD is its widely circulated coding syntax creating the seven categories (and amended for errors) (Stetzer and Burge 2016).

But in the last few years, a number of scholars reassessed RELTRAD's measurement validity (Shelton 2018). For instance, Lehman and Sherkat (2018) contend that a better way to think about Protestant traditions is as a continuum with exclusivism on one end and universalism on the other. In addition, a number of scholars have backed away from using respondent religious affiliation to classify evangelicals, instead opting for a self-classification process. Now, a number of surveys ask respondents if they consider themselves "a born-again or evangelical Christian," and some recent empirical work has found that this approach is able to generate a sample of respondents that looks very similar to RELTRAD's affiliation approach to classifying evangelicals (Burge and Lewis 2018; Smith et al. 2018).

The Measurement Validity of "Evangelical"

Despite the dozens of articles written over the last six decades, academics have not coalesced around a singular approach to demarcating an evangelical Christian. A recent article by Hackett et al. (2018) may provide the best advice on the matter for researchers: "Choose the Method for Aggregating Religious Identities That Is Most Appropriate for Your Research." The authors note that some schemes (such as RELTRAD) are more suited toward measuring political outcomes (Hackett et al. 2018), which is a subtle acknowledgment that a good deal of work by religion scholars is measuring political behavior and public opinion. This, of course, runs counter to the vast majority of writing on this topic that emphasizes theological positions as the primary dimension on which evangelicalism should be defined. There is clearly a disconnect between the justification for creating religious categories and how researchers employ said categories.

Scholars have largely ignored the perspective of what may be the most important group in determining what constitutes an evangelical: the American public. One important part of defining concepts in social science is measurement validity—"the degree to which the measurement process measures the variable that it claims to measure" (Gravetter and Forzano 2011, 78). More specifically, social scientists need to be concerned with "face validity," which is the need for scientists to measure a concept congruent with how a neutral observer would understand the phenomenon (Nevo 1985). However, one wonders if the varied approaches that theologians and social scientists use to measure evangelicals are out of step with how the general public understands the term.

It seems possible, perhaps even likely, that the union between conservative Christians and the Republican Party in the US in recent years impacts how the average observer understands the concept of evangelical Protestantism. Using data scraped from the social media website Twitter, I consider a number of questions surrounding the concept of evangelicalism. For instance, do Twitter users see the term "evangelical" as largely associated with religious ideas, or do they believe that "evangelical" has largely become a political term? Has this association between evangelicals and Republicans grown during Donald Trump's presidency? In addition, is "evangelical" a term used by conservative Christians themselves, or is it a term that is more readily employed by those outside the bounds of the evangelical subculture?

The examples from Twitter of nonevangelical political and cultural elites provide at least tacit evidence that the general public sees evangelicalism through a Trumpian political lens. Though these are politically liberal figures, their impressions of evangelicalism and its linkage to Trump may influence how others view and react (see figs. 7.1, 7.2, 7.3). To get a much broader sense of how evangelicalism is perceived, I leverage a dataset of nearly 180,000 tweets collected over an eighteen-month period in 2017 and 2018; my analysis sheds light on how social media understands the term "evangelical."

Fig. 7.1. Tweet Example 1

Fig. 7.2. Tweet Example 2

Fig. 7.3. Tweet Example 3

Tweet Data

Data were compiled by scraping publicly available Twitter accounts containing the word "evangelical" using the "rtweet" package, which is written for use with the R statistical software program (Kearney 2018). This package utilizes the REST API, which is offered free of charge by Twitter. However, there are limitations on the number of tweets that can be collected. For instance, the API limits users searching for keywords to a maximum of 18,000 tweets or approximately ten days of Twitter history. Whenever one of those thresholds is met, no more tweets can be collected. If one wants to do a longitudinal analysis that traces the history of a term, that is not possible using the REST API and can only be accomplished by contracting with Twitter to gain archival access. To get around these limitations, I initiated a query on random dates over the last twenty months using "evangelical" in the search. Data were scraped and saved as a means to build up a large enough observation pool to assess trends over time.

In total, five blocks of tweets were collected. The first scrape began on February 23 and ran continuously until April 1, 2017, for a total of 63,310 tweets. The second scrape occurred between December 12 and December 17, 2017, for a total of 67,508 tweets. There were three separate scraping periods in 2018: April 16 through April 24 for 17,990 tweets; August 29 for 12,294 tweets; and December 5 through 14 yielding 17,980 tweets. In total, 179,534 tweets were collected from 115,551 Twitter users (452 tweets had a malformed date field and were excluded). Along with the tweet text, metadata including screen name and tweet time were included.

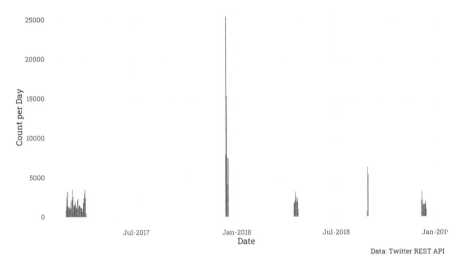

Fig. 7.4. Timeline of Evangelical Tweet Gathering

Frequency of Evangelical Tweets

One way to get a sense of the nature and structure of Twitter data is to consider the daily volume of tweets. While a substantial number of tweets were collected for this project, they represent a small fraction of the entire volume of tweets sent daily. According to the research firm Omnicore, approximately 500 million tweets are sent every day ("Twitter by the Numbers" 2018), and recent public earnings reports indicate that 326 million users access the site each month (Grothaus 2018). To get a sense of how my scraped data are distributed, figure 7.4 displays the number of tweets scraped per day that contained the word "evangelical" during the five aforementioned collection periods.

The average number of tweets containing the word "evangelical" over the 68 separate scrape days was 2,680 per day, which represents .000005 percent of all Twitter activity on a given day. Most notable from this graph is the sizeable spike that occurs in December 2017. The date with the highest frequency of evangelical tweets occurred on December 13, when a total of 25,316 tweets were scraped. The next day, December 14, included another 15,297 tweets. The reason for this frequency increase involves the aftermath of a special election in Alabama to choose who would take over Jeff Sessions's then-vacated US Senate seat. Roy Moore, the evangelical Republican in the race, had been accused of inappropriate contact with young women decades prior (Bump 2017). But despite these accusations, Moore received strong support from white evangelicals, with 80 percent casting their ballot for the former judge (J. Weber 2017). This resulted in a significant amount of Twitter activity concerning evangelicals and their political preferences. In fact, the four days with the most volume of evangelical tweets in this dataset were all in December 2017.

Content of Evangelical Tweets

There are a variety of approaches to empirically analyzing text data, with content analysis clearly favored by social scientists (Berelson 1952). This approach relies on the researcher reading and coding data to identify common terms and themes (R. Weber 1990). For decades this work was done by hand, a time-consuming process susceptible to analyst errors (Kracauer 1952). In recent years, computational ability has progressed, allowing researchers to count words and phrases in a systematic way and with greater reliability (Fan 1988). For instance, this corpus contains nearly 180,000 tweets, which consist of over 4.5 million words. Here, I employ the tidytext package written for R to conduct both unigram (single word) and bigram (two-word combination) counts for each of the five waves of tweets (Silge and Robinson 2016).

The goal will be to understand just how much of the language surrounding evangelicals is religious in nature and how much contains references to political events and figures. Obviously, this approach has its drawbacks, most notably that it cannot capture the context and nuance from these tweets. It also cannot analyze the images or memes that are attached to many tweets. However, in most cases, these word counts result in clear and straightforward interpretation.

Figure 7.5 visualizes the words that were most frequently used in "evangelical" tweets collected between February 23 and April 1, 2017. Note that for this and the forthcoming analysis, "stop words," which are common (including "the," "but," and "how"), have been removed (Wilbur and Sirotkin 1992). In the visualization, those words that could commonly be linked to the political arena are highlighted in red, with the nonpolitical terms in gray. Note that just five of the top twenty-five words can be closely linked to politics. The name of the forty-fifth president appears fourth on this list, just after "Christian," "Christians," and "Church." Also interesting is that the vice president's last name appears, occurring 501 times. Of course, there are a number of clearly religious terms, as well, including "God," "Bible," "Jesus," and "pastor."

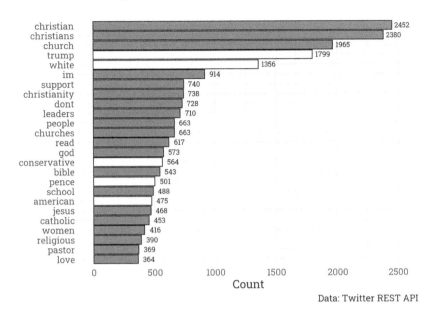

Data: Twitter REST API

Fig. 7.5. Most Frequent Words in February and March 2017

However, an analysis of bigrams in figure 7.6 reveals an additional level of nuance. While the total number of phrases that are explicitly political is fairly low, there are a number of bigrams related to Betsy DeVos's appointment as secretary of education. DeVos faced criticism from the political left that she favored charter schools and made financial contributions to a number of private Christian schools (Reitman 2017). Terms that allude to this controversy include "evangelical school" and "evangelical college." In addition, the term "Cyrus Prophecy" occurs 174 times. The term references a *Guardian* article describing the view of some evangelicals that Trump's electoral victory fulfilled biblical prophecy (Gordon 2017).

The second set of tweets were scraped in the aftermath of the Alabama special election that was previously described. The bigrams displayed in figure 7.7 show a much greater frequency of political terms intermingled with tweets that reference evangelicals. For instance, the most mentioned term, "white evangelicals," is a reference to news reports indicating that the group strongly supported Moore despite a variety of allegations against him of sexual misconduct with underaged girls (Goodstein 2017). Note that in the top twenty-five bigrams from this time period, twelve of them were related to the Alabama Senate election, either directly or indirectly. Another term, "death threats," appeared nearly 900 times in this five-day

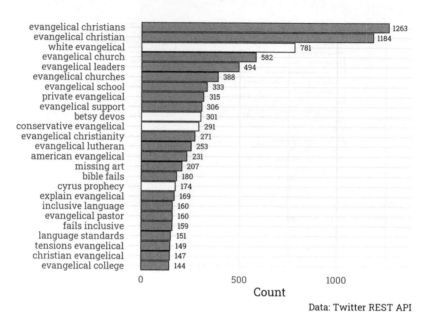

Data: Twitter REST API

Fig. 7.6. Most Frequent Bigrams in February and March 2017

time period. This is due to the widespread sharing of a profile of prominent evangelical Jen Hatmaker, who had publicly denounced Trump and
had reportedly received numerous death threats in the days and weeks that
followed (Stanley 2017).

In April 2018, the number of political unigrams and bigrams continued to rise. "Trump" is the word mentioned most frequently in evangelical tweets, occurring 3,754 times. Two stories appear frequently in the
bigrams list in figure 7.8: a report that describes an extramarital affair that
adult film actress Stormy Daniels had with Trump before he was president
(Tatum and Lee 2018) and new polling data showing evangelical support
for Trump had reached an all-time high (Burton 2018). In total, of the top
twenty-five two-word combinations, at least fifteen are related to politics
in some way.

Tweets scraped from both August and December 2018 tell a story of
a social media landscape that consistently links evangelicals with politics
generally or with President Trump specifically. For instance, the batch collected in December 2018 (see fig. 7.9) contains a flurry of tweets regarding
the funeral service of former president George H. W. Bush. As part of the
Episcopal ceremony, the congregation was led in a recitation of the Apos-
tle's Creed. During this portion of the proceedings, the television cameras

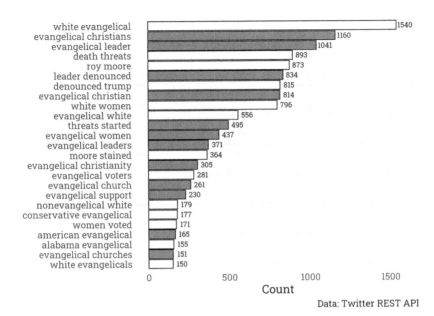

Fig. 7.7. Most Frequent Bigrams in December 2017

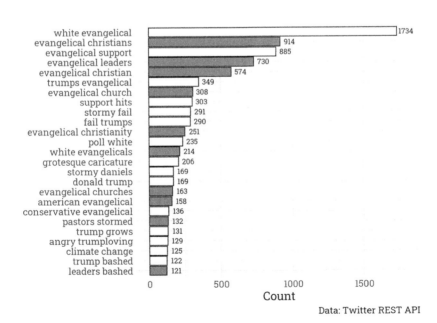

Fig. 7.8. Most Frequent Bigrams in April 2018

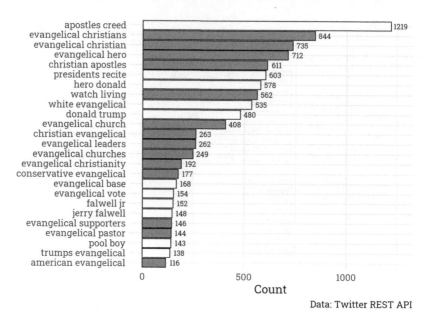

apostles creed — 1219
evangelical christians — 844
evangelical christian — 735
evangelical hero — 712
christian apostles — 611
presidents recite — 603
hero donald — 578
watch living — 562
white evangelical — 535
donald trump — 480
evangelical church — 408
christian evangelical — 263
evangelical leaders — 262
evangelical churches — 249
evangelical christianity — 192
conservative evangelical — 177
evangelical base — 168
evangelical vote — 154
falwell jr — 152
jerry falwell — 148
evangelical supporters — 146
evangelical pastor — 144
pool boy — 143
trumps evangelical — 138
american evangelical — 116

Count

Data: Twitter REST API

Fig. 7.9. Most Frequent Bigrams in December 2018

panned to a view of all the living former presidents as well as President Trump. While the rest of the congregation recited the creed, President Trump did not. He was roundly criticized, with many taking to Twitter to use this as proof that Trump is not a real evangelical (Dudar 2018). The other story that dominated evangelical tweets concerned prominent Trump supporter Jerry Falwell Jr., who was sued by a man whom he met in Miami, Florida (Roston 2018). Although the story had originally been published in May 2018, it was picked up by a number of influential Twitter users, allowing it to be retweeted several hundred times.

When taking a step back and looking at the full analysis from each of these time periods, there is a clear sense that, at least on Twitter, the term "evangelical" has a significant link to the political world. Figure 7.10 indicates the frequency of five popular political words as well as five popular religious words from the dataset. Consider this: among the 4.6 million words the dataset contains, the word "Trump" appears 29,054 times, while the word "Jesus" appears 6,710 times. "God" shows up 6,601 times, and "Bible" is mentioned 4,304 times. While both evangelical leaders and academics who study evangelicals consistently point to a group definition focused on theology, it would appear that the tweeting public perceives

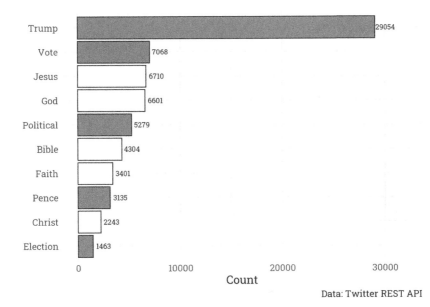

Fig. 7.10. Frequency of Key Political and Religious Terms

"evangelical" to be fused with the Trump presidency. Overall, this suggests a clear political tone to the communication environment surrounding this religious identity group.

Was this fusion the case from the beginning of Trump's term in office, or has the perception of a relationship between evangelicals and Trump grown over the past two years? Figure 7.11 displays the percentage of evangelical tweets each hour that also contain the word "Trump." Note that there is a great deal of variation in the concentration of evangelical Trump tweets in this sample. For instance, in spring 2017 there were many hours when Trump's name appeared in less than 10 percent of tweets that referenced evangelicals. However, there were also hours when "Trump" appeared in 80 percent of tweets also containing the word "evangelical." The red line in figure 7.11 indicates the trend over the twenty-month time period (which is clearly a positive one). This indicates that Twitter users were more likely to include the words "Trump" and "evangelical" in the same tweet in December 2018 than in March 2017—doubled from 15 percent in spring 2017 to 30 percent at the end of 2018. This finding supports the notion that the Trump presidency has had a measurable impact on the way the general public understands the term "evangelical," with

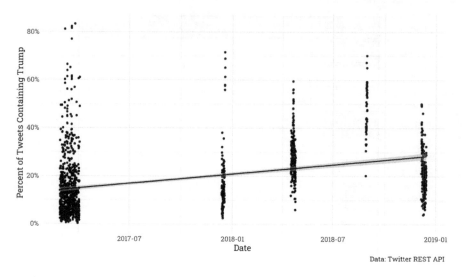

Data: Twitter REST API

Fig. 7.11. Trump Is Becoming More Linked with Evangelicals on Twitter

more social media discourse assuming the term is aligned more closely with politics than religion.

Who Is Driving the Use of the Term?

One of the difficulties with Twitter data is how little is known about each account user. Beyond what they provide in the description, no data are available to identify users as belonging to a certain racial, political, or religious group. Because of this limitation, it is not possible to know if evangelical Twitter users are more likely to use the term "evangelical" than those who do not identify with the religious group. However, a possible alternative is to look at what websites are linked in tweets that contain the word "evangelical." To assess this, I parsed the shortened URL embedded in these tweets from the text and visited each website. Figure 7.12 displays by full name all websites that appeared at least fifty times in the entire dataset of tweets.

Note that the websites that drive the most traffic around evangelicals are some of the most prominent media outlets in the US: the *New York Times*, *Politico*, and the *Washington Post*. For each of these three cases, it was not one specific story that went viral that drove view counts but, instead, a number of stories on topics like new polling numbers and special elections

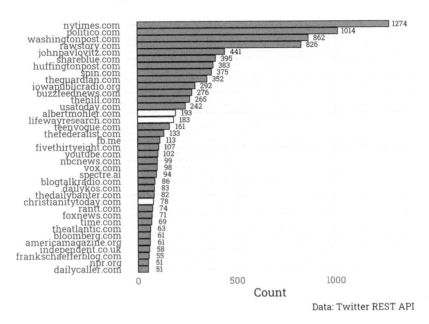

Fig. 7.12. Which Websites Drive Traffic about Evangelicals?

around the country. Of the websites on the list, just three—albertmohler. com, lifewayresearch.com, and christianitytoday.com—may be considered websites run by evangelicals that target a specifically evangelical audience. In total, these three sites received a combined 454 tweets, which is roughly a third as many as those the *New York Times* received alone. An important caveat is that the general readership of a site like the *Washington Post* is obviously larger than that of *Christianity Today*, which explains some of the disparity in the numbers. However, these results indicate something that may be important: Twitter users are generally interested in the political leanings of evangelicals, and this is evident by the fact that major news outlets generate a lot of social media traction by discussing this topic.

Discussion

Obviously, these results should give significant pause to both those who study the evangelical movement from a scholarly perspective and evangelicals themselves. As previously noted, the most widely accepted classification typology of American religion, RELTRAD, does not use political affiliation as its primary motivating criteria. Instead, users utilize a number of theological positions to subdivide Protestants into mainline and evangelical categories. However, the authors do manage to note that African American Protestants should be placed in a separate category because "the social experience of African Americans has subtly shaped their theological doctrines and has more explicitly influenced the social and economic implications they draw from them" (Steensland et al. 2000, 294). This subtle nod to the exclusion of African Americans from many parts of social and political life during slavery and segregation tacitly acknowledges that political partisanship and voting behavior should affect how scholars sort religious traditions. Going forward, the academic community needs to consider if political partisanship should play a role in constructing the criteria for religious classification more broadly. If not, academics' perception might fall further out of step with that of the general public.

For evangelicals themselves, these findings are sobering affirmation that the general public sees evangelicals not as a group of committed Christians trying to emulate Jesus but, instead, as a political movement that has become a key part of Trump's political base. Consider this: the word "love" appears in this dataset 2,620 times, while the words "hypocrisy," "hypocrite," and "hypocritical" appear a combined 2,730 times. As David French, a prominent evangelical and politically conservative commentator, noted in the aftermath of the 2016 election, "We have no one to truly blame but ourselves" (2016). If the goal of evangelical Christianity is to convert nonbelievers to the faith, then that task will seem nearly impossible when trying to convince someone who identifies as a Democrat to join the evangelical fold. There's an old saying attributed to a variety of sources: "When you mix politics and religion, you get politics." That certainly seems to be the case here, and in terms of what evangelicals are able to communicate from whatever religious perspectives they hold, it appears that the public has determined that the "evangelical" label is inherently a political one.

REFERENCES

"About NAE." 2018. National Association of Evangelicals. https://www.nae.net/about-nae/
Armstrong, Karen. 2010. *The Case for God.* Reprint ed. New York: Anchor.
Barna, G. 1994. *Virtual America: What Every Church Leader Needs to Know about Ministering in an Age of Spiritual and Technological Revolution.* Ventura, CA: Regal Books.
Bebbington, David W. 1988. *Evangelicalism in Modern Britain: A History from the 1730s to the 1980s.* London: Routledge.

Berelson, Bernard. 1952. *Content Analysis in Communication Research.* New York: Free Press.

Bump, Phillip. 2017. "Timeline: The Accusations against Roy Moore." *Washington Post*, November 16. https://www.washingtonpost.com/news/politics/wp/2017/11/16/timeline-the-accusations-against-roy-moore/

Burge, Ryan P., and Andrew R. Lewis. 2018. "Measuring Evangelicals: Practical Considerations for Social Scientists." *Politics and Religion* 4:745–59.

Burleight, Nina. 2018. "Evangelicals Helped Elect Trump, but Their Time as a Major Political Force Is Coming to an End." *Newsweek*, December 13. https://www.newsweek.com/2018/12/21/evangelicals-republicans-trump-millenials-1255745.html

Burton, Tara Isabella. 2018. "Poll: White Evangelical Support for Trump Is at an All-Time High." Vox, April 20. https://www.vox.com/identities/2018/4/20/17261726/poll-prri-white-evangelical-support-for-trump-is-at-an-all-time-high

Dudar, Hasan. 2018. "Trumps Criticized for Not Reciting Apostles' Creed at Bush Funeral." *USA Today*, December 6. https://www.usatoday.com/story/news/politics/2018/12/06/donald-trump-apostles-creed-george-h-w-bush-funeral/2224478002/

Fan, David P. 1988. *Predictions of Public Opinion from the Mass Media: Computer Content Analysis and Mathematical Modeling.* Westport, CT: Greenwood.

French, David. 2016. "Evangelicals, Our Problem Is Spiritual, Not Political." *National Review*, October 11. http://www.nationalreview.com/article/440968/evangelicals-spiritual-crisis-moral-failures-led-donald-trump

Goodstein, Laurie. 2017. "Has Support for Moore Stained Evangelicals? Some Are Worried." *New York Times*, December 14. https://www.nytimes.com/2017/12/14/us/alabama-evangelical-christians-moore.html

Gordon, James S. 2017. "Does the 'Cyrus Prophecy' Help Explain Evangelical Support for Donald Trump?" *The Guardian*, March 23. https://www.theguardian.com/commentisfree/2017/mar/23/cyrus-prophecy-evangelical-support-donald-trump

Gravetter, Frederick J., and Lori-Ann B. Forzano. 2011. *Research Methods for the Behavioral Sciences.* New York: Cengage Learning.

Green, John C., James L. Guth, Corwin E. Smidt, and Lyman A. Kellstedt. 1996. *Religion and the Culture Wars: Dispatches from the Front.* Lanham, MD: Rowman and Littlefield.

Grothaus, Michael. 2018. "Twitter's Q3 Earnings by the Numbers." Fast Company, October 25. https://www.fastcompany.com/90256723/twitters-q3-earnings-by-the-numbers

Hackett, Conrad, and D. Michael Lindsay. 2008. "Measuring Evangelicalism: Consequences of Different Operationalization Strategies." *Journal for the Scientific Study of Religion* 47:499–514.

Hackett, Conrad, Philip Schwadel, Gregory A. Smith, Elizabeth Podrebarac Sciupac, and Claire Gecewicz. 2018. "Choose the Method for Aggregating Religious Identities That Is Most Appropriate for Your Research." *Journal for the Scientific Study of Religion* 57:807–16.

Kearney, Michael W. 2018. "Rtweet: Collecting Twitter Data." Comprehensive R Archive Network. https://cran.r-project.org/package=rtweet

Kidd, Thomas S. 2009. *The Great Awakening: The Roots of Evangelical Christianity in Colonial America*. New Haven: Yale University Press.

Kracauer, Siegfried. 1952. "The Challenge of Qualitative Content Analysis." *Public Opinion Quarterly* 16:631–42.

Lattman, Peter. 2007. "The Origins of Justice Stewart's 'I Know It When I See It.'" *WSJ* (blog), September 27. https://blogs.wsj.com/law/2007/09/27/the-origins -of-justice-stewarts-i-know-it-when-i-see-it/

Lehman, Derek, and Darren E. Sherkat. 2018. "Specificity and Conceptual Clarity in the Measurement of Religious Identification." *Journal for the Scientific Study of Religion* 57:827–29.

Lindsay, D. Michael. 2007. *Faith in the Halls of Power: How Evangelicals Joined the American Elite*. New York: Oxford University Press.

Marsden, George. 1990. *Understanding Fundamentalism and Evangelicalism*. Grand Rapids, MI: Eerdmans.

Mattingly, Terry. 2013. "Defining Evangelical, or Not, in 2013." Uexpress, January 11. http://www.uexpress.com/on-religion/2013/1/11/defining-evangelical-or -not-in-2013

Merritt, Jonathan. 2015. "What Is an 'Evangelical'?" *The Atlantic*, December 7. https://www.theatlantic.com/politics/archive/2015/12/evangelical-christian/41 8236/

Nevo, Baruch. 1985. "Face Validity Revisited." *Journal of Educational Measurement* 22:287–93.

Noll, Mark A. 2018. "Evangelical: What's in a Name?" National Association of Evangelicals (website), January 23. https://www.nae.net/evangelical-whats -name/

Reitman, Janet. 2017. "Trump Education Secretary Betsy DeVos: A Win for the Christian Right." *Rolling Stone*, March 8. https://www.rollingstone.com/politics /politics-features/betsy-devos-holy-war-126026/

Roston, Aram. 2018. "Jerry Falwell Jr. and a Young Pool Attendant Launched a Business That Sparked a Bitter Dispute." BuzzFeed News, May 21. https:// www.buzzfeednews.com/article/aramroston/jerry-falwell-jr-michael-cohen-po ol-attendant-lawsuit

Shelton, Jason E. 2018. "Is RELTRAD Still the Gold Standard?" *Journal for the Scientific Study of Religion* 57:817–26.

Silge, Julia, and David Robinson. 2016. "Tidytext: Text Mining and Analysis Using Tidy Data Principles in R." *JOSS* 1 (3): 37.

Smietana, Bob. 2015. "What Is an Evangelical? Four Questions Offer New Definition." *Christianity Today*, November 19. http://www.christianitytoday.com/glea nings/2015/november/what-is-evangelical-new-definition-nae-lifeway-resear ch.html

Smith, C. S. 1998. *American Evangelicalism: Embattled and Thriving*. Chicago: University of Chicago Press.

Smith, Gregory A., Elizabeth Podrebarac Sciupac, Claire Gecewicz, and Conrad Hackett. 2018. "Comparing the RELTRAD and Born-Again/Evangelical Self-Identification Approaches to Measuring American Protestantism." *Journal for the Scientific Study of Religion* 57:830–47.

Smith, T. W. 1990. "Classifying Protestant Denominations." *Review of Religious Research* 31:225–45.

Stanley, Tiffany. 2017. "This Evangelical Leader Denounced Trump. Then the Death Threats Started." *POLITICO Magazine*, December 17. http://politi.co /2CsSLIx

"Statement of Faith." 2017. National Association of Evangelicals (website). https:// www.nae.net/statement-of-faith/

Steensland, Brian, Jerry Z. Park, Mark D. Regnerus, Lynn D. Robinson, W. Bradford Wilcox, and Robert D. Woodberry. 2000. "The Measure of American Religion: Toward Improving the State of the Art." *Social Forces* 79:291–318.

Steensland, Brian, Robert D. Woodberry, and Jerry Z. Park. 2018. "Structure, Placement, and the Quest for Unidimensional Purity in Typologies of American Denominations." *Journal for the Scientific Study of Religion* 57:800–806.

Stetzer, Ed, and Ryan P. Burge. 2016. "Reltrad Coding Problems and a New Repository." *Politics and Religion* 9:187–90.

Stouffer, Samuel A. 1955. *Communism, Conformity, and Civil Liberties: A Cross-Section of the Nation Speaks Its Mind.* Garden City, NY: Doubleday.

Tatum, Sophie, and M. J. Lee. 2018. "Stormy Daniels Is Cooperating with Federal Investigators." CNN, April 13. https://www.cnn.com/2018/04/10/politics/stor my-daniels-michael-avenatti-fbi/index.html

"Twitter by the Numbers: Stats, Demographics & Fun Facts." 2018. Omnicore, October 2. https://www.omnicoreagency.com/twitter-statistics/

Wald, Kenneth D., and Allyson Calhoun-Brown. 2006. *Religion and Politics in the United States.* Lanham, MD: Rowman Littlefield.

Weber, Jeremy. 2017. "Roy Moore Was 'a Bridge Too Far' for Alabama Evangelicals." *Christianity Today*, December 13. https://www.christianitytoday.com/news /2017/december/roy-moore-loss-alabama-evangelicals-senate-election-mohl er.html

Weber, Robert Philip. 1990. *Basic Content Analysis.* Vol. 49. Thousand Oaks, CA: Sage.

"What Is an Evangelical?" 2018. National Association of Evangelicals (website). https://www.nae.net/what-is-an-evangelical/

Wilbur, W. John, and Karl Sirotkin. 1992. "The Automatic Identification of Stop Words." *Journal of Information Science* 18:45–55.

Woodberry, Robert D., Jerry Z. Park, Lyman A. Kellstedt, Mark D. Regnerus, and Brian Steensland. 2012. "The Measure of American Religious Traditions: Theoretical and Measurement Considerations." *Social Forces* 91:65–73.

EIGHT

Mobilizing Prayer as a Political Resource

The Tactics of Religious-Political Movements

Kimberly H. Conger and J. Tobin Grant

In chapter 6, Wagner and Friesen discussed how religious beliefs, behavior, and belonging shape how religious people participate in politics. In chapter 7, Burge lamented that much of this research treats religion and politics as distinct, especially with regard to evangelicals. At its core, religion deals with the supernatural and the sacred. Politics is a secular pursuit with a focus on collective action aimed at influencing government and civil society. This separation is useful (or even necessary) for some research questions, but it may devalue how religious people view politics. For many, particularly religious activists, religion and politics are intertwined.

Beliefs about the supernatural are part of the socially constructed reality of religious people—and this reality must be effectively communicated in order to carry influence. The line where religion stops and the secular starts is not always distinct—family, politics, economics, and other parts of society exist in a cosmos that includes supernatural actors (Berger 1969). Depending on the religion, these supernatural actors may be passive or active in the lives—including the political lives—of citizens. God (or any other supernatural actor) may be viewed as doing much more than proscribe behavior. God may guide the decision-making of leaders, change future events, or even bring about political outcomes through divine means.

In this chapter, we examine how this aspect of religion shapes political strategy as it is communicated publicly. Specifically, how does the super-

natural reality created by religion carry over into politics? We focus specifically on one part of religion—prayer. Utilizing two types of data, religious-
political groups' websites and a survey of these groups' leaders, we examine
how these groups use prayer as a political resource.

Prayer is the quintessential religious act. Religions differ in their ontologies and teleologies of prayer, but few (if any) religions exist that do not
include prayer. It is through prayer that humans communicate with the
supernatural (Giordan 2012; Stark and Finke 2000). In America, a majority
of adults pray. In the 2014 General Social Survey, 58 percent of Americans
said they pray every day. Another 16 percent pray at least once a week.
Prayer is ubiquitous in American religion.

Despite the universality of prayer in religion, it remains understudied in social science (Giordan 2012). And, in political science specifically, prayer is rarely included in studies of religion and politics. When
it is included, it is treated as a distinctly religious act that may impact an
individual's political behavior. Perhaps this is because, for the most part,
prayer does not have the impact on politics like other aspects of religion
such as church attendance or religious tradition. Loveland et al. (2005),
for example, find that those who pray are more likely to join some types
of organizations, but they are not more likely to join political groups. In
many studies of prayer and politics, the frequency of prayer is viewed as
a proxy for private religious devotion (vis-à-vis communal acts such as
attending a worship service). There is nothing wrong with this approach,
but it ignores the meaning of prayer in the lives of those who practice it
(Ammerman 2014; Poloma and Pendleton 1991; Wuthnow 2011). For
those who pray, there is the belief that prayer "works." The 2007 Pew
Religious Landscape Survey found that 90 percent of adults who pray say
they have received a "definite answer to a specific prayer request."[1] Prayer
is viewed as an efficacious way to bring about results, change events, and
shape the future.

Political science need not concern itself with the efficacy of prayer. All
that we must acknowledge is that many view prayer as efficacious. It is
how religious people communicate with a supernatural actor who has the
power to shape events, including political outcomes. Prayer, we argue, can
be a political act in which a person literally calls for supernatural action to
shape political outcomes, which is, itself, an act of religious communication (albeit with a clear political dimension). Indeed, religious people who

---

1. Looking more broadly, 72 percent of Americans pray regularly and believe that at least
some of their prayers are answered: 81 percent who pray a few times a month or more often,
and only 10 percent said that their prayers are never answered.

believe in the power of prayer are unlikely to put such a powerful communicative tool aside when they enter politics.

Religious-Political Movements

Political movements and religious movements are both types of social movements; they each mobilize resources to achieve a collective outcome (McCarthy and Zald 1987; Sherkat 2006). The difference between a religious movement and a political movement is the goal of the collective action. A political movement seeks a collective outcome from the state or government; a religious movement seeks collective benefits from supernatural compensators (Sherkat 2006).

Under this conceptualization, the difference between a religious movement and a political movement is not the type of resource being mobilized. For example, a political movement may collect money to be used in an electoral campaign. A religious movement might collect money to fund a new ministry. Each movement mobilizes the same type of resource (money), but a political movement does so to influence government and a religious movement does so to seek God's favor.

The resources mobilized may be "political" or "religious." That is, a religious movement may marshal resources typically associated with political movements, and political movements may mobilize religious goods and services. For example, a religious movement may call upon people to vote as an act of religious obedience. The Church of Jesus Christ of Latter-day Saints (aka Mormons) usually remains (officially) silent on politics, but it sometimes takes clear positions on policy issues framed as referendums (a topic explored from the standpoint of religious elite cues on policy issues in chapter 9). When it does, members follow the lead of the church, as happened in 2008 in California's Proposition 8 on same-sex marriage (Campbell, Green, and Monson 2014). Voting—a political act—became an act of religious commitment. Likewise, a political movement may ask for prayer or include readings from scripture at a political rally. The type of resource is not the defining feature of a movement. It is the ends, not the means, that distinguish religious and political movements.

But some movements are not completely one or the other. A religious interest group is a religious-political movement (Grant, Kim, and Velez 2014). This is a unique kind of hybrid organization that espouses the logics of both religious movements and political movements. This kind of movement seeks to influence politics and seeks God's favor and frequently does not distinguish one from the other. In some cases, they may seek a political goal in order to receive supernatural benefits, for example, advocating for social justice out of devotion to God. In other cases, they may mobilize the faithful to seek God's favor so that they can achieve a preferred political outcome. Religious-political movements, therefore, are able to transform religious resources into political resources by making prayer into a political tactic.

Religious movements transition into religious-political movements when their goals include obtaining collective goods from the state. For religious firms (i.e., churches, congregations, and denominations), these goods may include deregulation (religious freedom) or rent seeking (tax breaks or grants). For other movements, they may be policy outcomes. Whatever the goal, success requires resources. But unlike their secular counterparts, religious-political groups value religious goods and services. Prayers are one such service. And prayer, at least among those who believe in it, is beneficial, if not necessary, for the success of religious-political movements.

Prayer as Political Resource

What is prayer? It is an essential aspect of religion given the link it creates between humanity and the supernatural. Giordan (2012, 78) defines prayer as "the dialogical act between humanity and divinity, and such a dialogical act can take the most diverse forms: from sacrifice to magic, from festivities to rituals, from different forms of recitation to mysticism." Prayers may be simple or may involve scripts, postures, garments, or actions. Prayers can be used as petition, thanksgiving, mediation, confession, intercession, and adoration (Meadow and Kahoe 1984). Prayer is also sociological (Giordan 2012). Even when offered privately, prayers use words, genres, and gestures that are located in a social context. It is in a religious community that one learns how to pray. What words should be used? Should one kneel? Stand? Raise one's hands? Must a head covering be worn? Should prayers be recited or improvised? To whom should prayers be given? The answers to these and many other questions about prayer are taught by others. Prayer is, therefore, one way that religious groups reinforce their identity among adherents and supporters.

But another important reason why groups mobilize prayer is that they believe it works. It is a direct communication action strategy to achieve collective political outcomes via supernatural means. Prayer is a way to achieve a political end. An example is how the evangelical organization

World Vision, one of the largest international humanitarian aid and development organizations, uses prayer in this manner. Its website includes a prayer asking God to help candidates and political leaders act to address poverty and justice.

> Father God, we are grateful that You love each of us no matter our status or abilities. Thank You that You walk with children and families struggling against poverty and injustice, calling us to do the same. We ask that candidates running for election would speak out about poverty and listen to the voices of the vulnerable. Give our leaders wisdom to create solutions that empower people living in poverty to survive and thrive. Help us to answer Your call to act justly, love mercy, and walk humbly with You.

While this prayer includes the identity building found in other prayers, its focus is on petitioning God to act in the political process. It is more than a call for those praying to act; the prayer is asking God to have candidates speak out on their issues and for their leaders to find solutions to poverty. Another example is the American Life League, a grassroots Catholic movement that works to end abortion and euthanasia. On its website the group reprinted an article, "Five Things You Can Do Right Now to End Abortion." The first thing on the list is to pray:

> You can pray anytime, anywhere. Consider spiritually adopting a preborn baby as an activity with the whole family. Stuck at home? Spend an hour in prayer, praying for the mothers, fathers, babies, clinic workers, and sidewalk counselors who will be at your local abortion clinic today. Put out a small fetal model to remind you to pray daily for preborn babies.
>
> Resolve to pray every day for an end to abortion and for the strengthening of the family. Pause reading this post right now and pray to end abortion. Your prayer could be as simple as:
>
>> Lord, Creator and Author of all life, protect the lives of all preborn babies who are in danger of abortion today. Help our country repent and turn back to You. Amen.

This prayer is a means of achieving one of the American Life League's goals: the complete end to abortion in America. Through prayer, the group works to help those considering abortion, assists those protesting in front of abortion clinics, and aids those working in the clinics. The primary purpose of prayer is as a tool to achieve the social and political outcomes of the movement.

Some groups even organize events centered around prayer. For example, the Family Research Council organizes the prayer event "Call 2 Fall" on the Sunday before Independence Day. The stated purpose of the event is for churches and families to pray to God for repentance so that God will "heal our land." The Family Research Council says the Call 2 Fall event comes "straight from the Bible":

> If my people, who are called by my name, will humble themselves and pray and seek my face and turn from their wicked ways, then will I hear from heaven and will forgive their sin and will heal their land. (2 Chronicles 7:14)

Churches and families are asked to agree to the following:

> I will answer God's call to fall on my knees in humility and seek His face in repentance so that He might forgive my sins and heal our land.

Prayer is a way for this political group to effect change via a quid quo pro with God—if enough people pray, then God heals America. Other groups organize events to pray for specific issues. In 2013, the Muslim Public Affairs Council joined with other groups to organize a "global qiyam" to pray for Syria. They asked for supporters to organize their local *qiyam* (a night service in which people stand and pray) on the same Friday. Supporters were also encouraged to follow the event on social media. Prayer events like this bring together a movement's members around the prayer act.

Even if a religious-political organization lacks actual faith in the efficacy of prayer, like hybrid organizations that rely on religious entities and religious persons for resources, calls for prayer demonstrate a religious commitment in the political realm. Hybrid organizations seek to credibly combine the logic and decision-making processes of organizations from different realms. Instead of compromising between two realms, or simply giving lip service to one, hybrid organizations seek to "selectively couple" their activities and resources (Pache and Santos 2012). This means that the organizations choose strategies that effectively represent one realm within the other. Instead of completely mirroring either, they choose the resources and strategies that both help them succeed and reinforce their identities in both realms. Thus, religious interest groups seek religious resources that can be effectively deployed in politics, often through acts of communication. They remain true to their identity as religious groups but in ways that translate into politics. The groups do not compromise their religious beliefs to be involved in politics, nor do they compromise their political stances to be seen as religious.

Because many religious organizations are not active in politics and often see involvement in the political process as distracting (at best) and corrupt (at worst), political groups can use prayer to put a gilded edge on otherwise unseemly politics. By framing action in terms of prayer, political actors are able to make political goals more tolerable; the framing helps put a political goal in terms acceptable to a religious audience. Sharp finds that elites may use references to prayer for several reasons. One is to justify actions that would otherwise be viewed negatively (Sharp 2013). An actor may discuss how he prayed about a decision, particularly one that would otherwise be viewed negatively. For example, when the New Jersey Family Policy Council merged with the national Family Policy Alliance (the policy wing of Focus on the Family), the council said its decision came "after much prayer and reflection." Rhetorically, mentioning prayer signals that the New Jersey Family Policy Council board sought divine wisdom and that its decision may be the will of God. Prayer, in this case, adds a religious rationale for an action.

Another purpose of prayer is to demonstrate investment to show the importance of an issue. When a group calls on supporters to pray, they are able to focus attention on an issue as a religious cause, even if the goal is political. In prayer, a person thinks about and often vocalizes support for a cause. As a result, people who pray for a cause may be more psychologically invested in the group's success and may give other resources to the effort. Prayers, particularly public prayers, are ways to affirm and to pronounce the values of the religious group. T'ruah is an organization of rabbis and cantors from across several streams of Judaism who are working for human rights. The T'ruah website includes resources for rabbis, including prayers that can be read at services. For example, a 2014 prayer on the Black Lives Matter movement is a prayer of protest and a prayer fully supporting the movement:

> We call to you in defiance of
> of [sic] a national system that betrays our noble ideals,
> where tanks and blood fill our streets,

where every Black man, woman, and child is
twenty times likelier to be killed by police.
We shout to the Heavens with one, unified voice:
Black. Lives. Matter.

The prayer, which is lengthy and poetic, states that those praying are
responsible to act, and they ask for God to move them to action. Another
example is a public prayer on the website of the Baptist Joint Committee
on Public Affairs, an organization that promotes religious liberty and the
historical Baptist promotion of the separation of church and state. The
prayer celebrates religious liberty and calls for a "change of heart" among
those who want to use government to promote their beliefs:

> We celebrate our freedom to stand before you on our own foot-
> ing uncompelled and uncoerced, freely chosen, freely choosing the
> mode, content and object of our worship.
>   We give you thanks for religious liberty.
>   Our prayers this day are for those who know not this most
> basic form of human dignity—to be their own arbiter of belief and
> practice.
>   We know there are powers still which have not discovered the
> beauty of diversity and—out of fear—compel those under their
> influence by threat or by overbearing culture to a single, static reli-
> gious experience.
>   We pray for a change of heart and for a change of policy among
> those.

Both of these prayers affirm the values held by the organization and ask
God to work to promote these same values. Prayers such as these are aimed
as much toward those who are praying as they are toward God. They proclaim what the values should be of those who are praying and ask God to
move them to stronger belief and action. Using these prayers, groups are
able to shape the religious and political identities of their members.

Prayer can be used to communicate concern and compassion for others.
Groups can ask for prayer for those who need help, even if that direct aid is
not provided. A political group can demonstrate compassion by asking for
prayer, for example, for victims of a natural disaster, when the group will
not provide other assistance. In 2017, the National Council of Churches
responded to the devastation caused by Hurricane Irma by stating that it

joins in prayer and solidarity with the people of Florida who were nearly universally affected by Hurricane Irma over the weekend of September 9–10, 2017. . . . We hold our sisters and brothers in the Caribbean in prayer as they cope with Hurricane Irma and its aftermath.

In the same statement, the National Council of Churches called for congressional action and for members to support their denominational relief agencies. But the council itself does not provide direct relief. Prayer was its only way to demonstrate support for those affected by the storm.

Calls for prayer may have other benefits for movements. Sincere or not, prayer has side effects. For an individual, prayer (particularly prayers for guidance and gratitude) is beneficial as a coping mechanism (Bade and Cook 2008). For interest groups, prayer can bring other side benefits. People who sign up for emails to pray for a group can also receive other information from interest groups. In the case of Call 2 Fall, those who agree to participate or to organize a local event are asked to provide their contact information. The form includes a checkbox (already checked) for Family Research Council emails "on the latest pro-family take on Washington's hottest issues." The same tactic is used by other groups. Bread for the World is a Christian organization working to end hunger in the US and in other countries. Its website shows that the group sees prayer as necessary for achieving an end to hunger.

We believe it is possible to end hunger. But not without God. When we pray, God listens. Jesus teaches us to pray, "Give us this day our daily bread" for ourselves and others. . . . Will you join us in this movement to pray faithfully for an end to hunger and poverty? Whenever you pray "give us this day our daily bread," you can include people who are hungry in our country and around the world.

Bread for the World then asks those who agree to pray to also provide their contact information so that they can "email you with actions you can take to help end hunger." Prayer is necessary. And if someone is willing to pray that God will support the movement, they may also appreciate learning about how else to support the movement.

One twist on this is when groups ask supporters to write prayers or to send their own list of needs that need prayer. Food for the Poor, an ecumenical Christian organization that provides resources to the poor in Latin

America and the Caribbean, states on its website that they "pray daily for the poor who are still suffering, our donors, and each other." They ask that supporters send them prayer requests so that the organization can pray for them. These requests can be submitted through a form on the website. Of course, this would also mean sending the group the person's contact information. J Street, a progressive Jewish organization that describes itself as "the political home for pro-Israel pro-peace Americans," asked supporters to write pro-peace prayers that they wanted President Obama to place in the Western Wall during his visit in 2013 to Israel. J Street said it would deliver all of the prayers to the American consulate in Jerusalem "so for the rest of his trip [President Obama] knows the American Jewish community has his back while pursuing peace in the region." The prayer submission form also included spaces for contact information and checkboxes to sign up for more information from J Street.

In sum, religious-political movements are not merely political organizations with religious motivations. They are movements that mobilize religious resources to achieve collective goods from both God and the government. Therefore, prayer should be seen as a political communication strategy, a resource to be mobilized. Even if prayer lacks efficacy, it is a way for groups with political goals to selectively couple them with religious goals. In the following analysis, we demonstrate that prayer is critical in religiously motivated political activity by examining how religious interest organizations think and talk about prayer both in their strategic planning and in their public statements.

Data and Analysis

We examined 362 religious-political interest groups by building on previous catalogs of religious interest groups. Luke Ebersol (1951) undertook the first major account of church lobbying and featured "16 groups with permanent Washington offices" (Hertzke 2009, 303). In the 1970s, 40 groups were active in Washington, and by 1994, when Weber and Jones published the institutional profiles of US religious interest groups, the number had increased to 120 (Lugo et al. 2011; Weber and Jones 1994). Recognizing the rapid increase of religious advocacy groups over the past four decades, the Pew Research Center's Forum on Religion & Public Life released a study spearheaded by Allen D. Hertzke examining the nature of these organizations operating in Washington, DC. Utilizing a broad definition of "advocacy"—that is, as efforts to shape public policy on religion-related issues in the US and abroad—the Pew Forum identified 216 "religion-related advocacy groups" based on a specific set of criteria (Lugo et al. 2011, 63). In addition to meeting this broad definition of advocacy of religion-specific matters, groups that were included in the initial study possessed a physical office in the nation's capital with at least one paid employee (Lugo et al. 2011). While the bulk of the 216 groups were those advocating on behalf of specific religious denominations, the criteria also allowed for the inclusion of interreligious and secular groups that engaged in similar efforts.

While building on the efforts of the Pew Forum's research, our list includes about 69 percent more groups than those compiled by the Pew Forum (Lugo et al. 2011). Most of the additional groups were identified because we did not require that the group have an office in Washington, DC; the groups merely had to have a national presence. This includes religious groups that mobilize on a small set of issues that directly affect their organization and other groups that may not need to have a full-time, paid staff located in the capital to lobby. Some are small operations that focus on organizing grassroots events using the internet. Together, the list includes a wide, broad collection of interest groups that are mobilized to impact national politics through a religious framework.

We report results from two datasets taken from these religious interest groups. First, we did searches of each group's website. We collected the total number of webpages and the number of webpages that include references to "pray" or "prayer." Together, this gives us measures of the group's web presence and the use of prayer on the websites. Second, we surveyed leaders from the national and state religious interest groups included in our list. The survey yielded responses from 137 organizational leaders. Each leader was given a list of dozens of activities and was asked to indicate which ones they had done. Most of these activities were ones that any interest group might do, but five included prayer.

Prayer in Interest Group Communications

Our first examination of religious interest groups looks at their use of prayer mobilization on their website. Groups range in their web presence from just a few to thousands of pages that are updated daily. For larger websites, the information often mirrors what is found in other forms of communication. Press releases, email appeals, reports, and other information are made available on their websites. Many have pages that ask readers to provide their names and contact information so that they can receive more information from the group. We used the Google search engine to identify pages from each website. Using the "site:" command, one can search for the presence of specific terms on a website. We searched for "pray" and "prayer" and recorded the number of pages with these terms and the total number of pages for each website. We used the size of the groups' website (in pages) as a measure of strategy of web use to inform and mobilize resources.

We also gathered data on how many of these pages refer to "pray" or "prayer." The number of pages that mention prayer is a measure of more than just direct appeals for people to pray. We view it as a gauge of the importance of prayer as a topic in a group's web mobilization strategy. Groups often ask readers to pray for specific topics or even to submit prayer requests that the group will pray for (many do so and also ask for email and other contact information). Some groups provide information on prayer events that people may attend.

We estimate a model of mentions of prayer on political-religious organization websites. This model has two dependent variables that are modeled simultaneously. The first is an indicator for whether prayer is ever mentioned on a website. Most of the websites have pages that mention prayer, but 18 percent of the groups never mentioned prayer. The second dependent variable is the log of the number of prayer pages; this is observed only for groups that mention prayer at least once. We use the log of the number of pages for two reasons. The first is to normalize the distributions. The log-normal model fits the assumptions of the linear regression model. Second, the log provides an easier substantive interpretation. Our interest is not the number of webpages per se. The log-normal model changes the interpretation so that the coefficients indicate the change in the percentage of pages, and when the independent variable is also a log, the coefficient is the change in the percentage of the dependent variable, given a 1 percent change in the independent variable.

We estimate a Heckman selection model that includes a probit for selection (1 = prayer mentioned; 0 = no prayer) and then linear regression for the log of prayer pages. For the selection portion of the model, our hypothesis is that the existence of prayer on the website should be driven by resources. The larger the website, the more likely it is that prayer will be included on the website.[2]

---

2. This is measured in thousands rather than the log of the number of pages. Substantively, the choice of functional form makes little difference in the substantive interpretation. By using the number rather than the log, we are able to better satisfy the assumption of the

TABLE 8.1. Prayer on Interest Group Websites

Independent Variable	Selection		Outcome	
Pages (in thousands)	0.26	(.05)*		
Pages w/o prayer(log 10)			0.66	(.04)*
Washington office			0.35	(.17)*
Lobbying			0.10	(.18)
Catholic			0.32	(.23)
Evangelical			0.54	(.19)*
Jewish			−0.54	(.25)*
Represents individuals			0.35	(.17)*
Represents religious bodies			0.50	(.25)*
No religious mission/name			−0.97	(.24)*
Constant	0.42	(.10)*	−0.19	(.32)*
Athrho		−1.12 (.22)*		
ln(sigma)		0.37 (.05)*		
N		350		

Note: * $p < .05$. Heckman selection model. Selection accounts for 66 observations that were otherwise missing. Outcome is the log of the number of pages that mention prayer. LR test of independence of equations, $p < .01$.

For the outcome portion of the model, we use two variables to measure the group's resources. The first is the resources the group has used on the website. To keep this distinct from the prayer pages, we use the log of the number of webpages that do not mention prayer. The second is whether the group has a Washington, DC, office. These are groups that have a national presence and have the resources to keep a permanent presence in the capital. The effects of both measures of resources are positive. The larger the group's web presence, the more pages it has that mention prayer. This effect is 0.66, which means that as the number of non-prayer pages increases by 1 percent, the number of prayer pages increases by 0.66 percent. This means that groups do not devote resources to prayer at the same rate that they do to other tactics. Still, as resources increase, the number of prayer pages increases. Groups that are able to have a Washington office have 42 percent more prayer pages than groups that are not.[3]

Prayer, as a political resource, will be mobilized more by groups that have access to that resource. We test this hypothesis by including two mea-

---

Heckman model to include at least one variable in the selection equation that is not in the outcome equation. The log of total pages is highly correlated with the log of pages without prayer, but the correlation between the number of total pages and the log of non-prayer pages is only 0.50.

3. This is the exponent of the coefficient; exp(0.35) = 1.42.

sures of the group's connection to denominations and other religious bodies. Following Hertzke's classification, we coded the type of group including groups that represent religious bodies. We also include an indicator for another type of group—groups that represent individuals (i.e., membership organizations). The baseline category includes groups that represent institutions, permanent coalitions, think tanks, and other groups that do not fit the other classifications. We find that groups representing religious bodies have 65 percent more prayer pages than other groups. We include a second measure of a group's connection to religion. We coded whether each group was explicitly religious in either its name or its mission statement. Groups without an explicit religious mission are still religious, but they do not identify with religion in their main purpose. Examples of this include many pro-life groups and relief organizations. These groups have 63 percent fewer prayer pages than groups that are explicit about their connection to religion.

These strong effects exist while controlling for other determinants of prayer on websites. We compare three traditions to other groups: evangelical, Catholic, and Jewish. Evangelicals have 72 percent more prayer pages. Jewish groups, however, have 42 percent fewer pages. We also included a measure for whether or not a group conducts lobbying, but we found no differences between groups that lobby and those that do not.

Religious Interest Groups and Prayer Advocacy

Prayer as a political communication strategy is more than mentioning the importance of prayer or asking for prayer on the organization's website. Because of the nature of prayer as both a direct and an instrumental strategy to change public policy, the approach taken to prayer by religious interest group leadership is an important element in understanding how religious interest groups create political strategies. These leaders' approach to utilizing prayer both in their own efforts and in their attempts to mobilize and leverage grassroots activities can provide a picture of where prayer fits into the arsenal of policy influence strategies and how hybrid religious political organizations choose to link prayer to political activity.

Because religious interest group leaders push the direction of their groups' goals and strategies, these leaders' perspective on the role of prayer in their organization and in advocacy efforts is an important clue to understanding prayer as a political tool. To observe the role of prayer in the decision-making of these organizations, we asked a sample of religious interest group leaders from our religious-political organization list how their groups approach and use prayer in their political advocacy. These data are part of a larger data collection on the strategy, decision-making, and coalition behavior of religious interest groups. Both national- and state-level group leaderships were contacted. While every available resource was utilized to build a representative sample, these data are not based on a random sample of the population of religious interest groups in the country. Our results should thus be taken with this caveat in mind.

Here, we concentrate not on a model of decision-making but on the proportion of respondents who answered a battery of questions about the types of strategies employed by their groups in the attempt to influence public policy. This battery asked respondents to list all the activities their group had participated in within the last two years, including lobbying, campaign donations, policy research, and grassroots mobilization, among others. A total of 137 respondents from all religious traditions and from national- and state-level religious interest groups participated. Most important were responses that allowed religious interest group leaders to gauge their groups' utilization of prayer. These included praying with organizational leadership, offering training or encouragement for members to engage their own religious bodies in prayer, contacting members and supporters and asking about a specific policy issue, and organizing prayer events for a specific policy issue.

On average, respondents listed that their organizations had engaged in 1.4 of the prayer activities in the past two years. Table 8.2 reports that while over 64 percent of the respondents listed at least one of the prayer

TABLE 8.2. Prayer Occurrence among Religious Interest Groups

Mean number of prayer activities reported	1.39
	Percentage
Organizational leadership prays	51.82
Offer member training for prayer	26.28
Issue specific calls for prayer about policy	32.85
Organize prayer events	27.74
At least one prayer activity	64.23
At least one prayer activity among:	
National groups	78.12
State groups	60.00
Denominationally affiliated groups	79.01
Nondenominationally affiliated groups	42.86
N	137

activities, there were significant differences among the different types of prayer activities. Over 51 percent of respondents recalled praying with the leadership of their organization, but only one-quarter to one-third of the respondents recalled any of the other types of prayer activities. While, overall, this suggests that religious interest groups are engaging in a moderate amount of prayer activities, we can demonstrate that the level of prayer activity varies substantially depending upon the characteristics of the religious interest group.

Table 8.2 also reports the percentage of groups that engaged in at least one of the prayer activities broken down by national- and state-level groups. While over 75 percent of national-level groups engaged in at least one prayer activity, only about 60 percent of the state-level groups did. While this finding could be an artifact of the religious traditions found in national- and state-level groups, it could also point to the different environments faced by national- and state-level groups. Though state-level groups may have more opportunities to lobby and mobilize grassroots volunteers by virtue of the smaller geography of a state, national groups seek to connect far-flung members and supporters by engaging them in similar, personal political action in the form of prayer.

Finally, table 8.3 reports the percentage of groups that engaged in at least one of the prayer activities broken down by denominational identity. This is not based on religious tradition. Rather, it distinguishes between those groups that are affiliated with a denomination and those that are nondenominational or made up of a variety of denominations. Groups linked to a denominational identity are far more likely to report having engaged in at least one prayer activity (79 percent) than are those groups not affiliated with a specific denomination (43 percent).

The truly pertinent differences among these groups, however, can be seen in the religious traditions with which they identify. Religious tradition reveals more than just the theological commitments of the groups and their supporters. The different religious traditions in the US— for example, Roman Catholics, mainline Protestants, Jews—embody very different approaches to politics and political issue advocacy. In addition, religious traditions vary widely in their focus on prayer and the importance of prayer in the personal and congregational life of adherents. So, each organization selectively couples with differing audiences. We expect to see differences in how different religious traditions use prayer in political advocacy for both religious and political reasons.

One challenge of our data is that the religious tradition that is recorded measures the religious tradition of the leader respondent. Thus, in some cases, a leader may be of a different overall religious tradition than the organization in which they serve. We believe that this is probably a minor consideration, because the nature of citizen political interest groups makes it difficult for a leader to disagree with the organization's foundational commitments wholesale. Nevertheless, this is a caveat.

Table 8.3 reports the breakdown of religious tradition in our sample of religious interest group leaders. Christian groups dominate the responses, as they do in the world of religious issue advocacy. The second column of table 8.3 shows the percentage of the leaders from each religious tradition who report at least one type of prayer activity taking place in their organization. Catholics have by far the largest percentage, with evangelicals and mainline Protestants following. The Muslim and other non-Christian sample is quite small, but clearly most of these groups are active in using prayer as a communication strategy.

These results give us a good picture of the degree to which groups use prayer as a strategy and how that varies by religious tradition. What these data do not tell us is how prayer fits into their overall advocacy strategy. While groups may use prayer as part of their efforts to change public policy, it may only be a small part of these efforts. Or it could be a major component of the group's overall policy change strategy. One good way to gauge the intensity with which these groups use prayer is to look at the proportion of their advocacy devoted to prayer. We calculated the proportion of prayer activities to other listed advocacy activities for each leader. On average, the proportion was .117, meaning that just over 11 percent of the average group's activities were characterized by prayer. Interestingly, almost 36 percent of respondents reported no prayer activities at all.

Figure 8.1 is a box and whisker plot (with outliers) of the proportions of prayer activities compared to other advocacy activities for each organizational leader organized by religious tradition. Catholics, who were the overall leaders in the percentage of groups engaging in prayer, come in

TABLE 8.3. Prayer Occurrence among Religious Interest Groups by Religious Tradition

Religious Tradition	Percentage of Sample	At Least One Prayer Activity in the Tradition
Catholic	35.29	94.44%
Mainline Protestant	21.56	63.64%
Evangelical Protestant	25.49	84.62%
Jewish	13.73	21.43%
Muslim and other non-Christian	3.92	75.00%
N		137

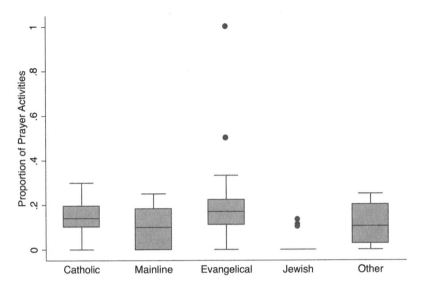

Fig. 8.1. Mean Proportion of Prayer Activities by Religious Tradition (Box Plot with Outliers)

second in proportion with an average of .147. Evangelicals rank first with an average of .209. Figure 8.1 also demonstrates that evangelicals' proportion of prayer compared to other advocacy activities has a unique pattern. Several groups use prayer almost exclusively or as a large part of their attempts to change public policy. Even though other groups exhibit variation in their approach, evangelicals are the most varied in their approach.

These findings mirror our earlier exploration of the ways religious interest groups talk about prayer on their websites. Catholics and evangelicals are more likely to mention and use prayer, while Jews are less likely to do so. But, overall, religious groups encourage and employ prayer as a political strategy—largely mirroring their coreligionists. While we have less explicit evidence about prayer's role among the range of possible political advocacy strategies, we see prayer is rarely used exclusively or even in large proportion to other techniques. And, the larger the scale of the religious interest organization, the less they seem to pray, proportionally speaking.

Discussion and Conclusion

We can think of prayer as an important and unique communication resource used by religious interest groups. Evidence suggests that group leaders certainly do. It is clear from this initial exploration of prayer's role in the arsenal of religious interest groups that these groups approach prayer as both a direct and an indirect resource. Prayer is seen as efficacious in its own right as a means of impacting the direction of public policy. When a lobbyist takes direct action on an issue, she or he aims their advocacy at a specific decision maker. Prayer's use in advocacy operates as direct action in a similar way. Religious people use prayer to ask an ultimate decision maker to impact public policy in their preferred direction (and perhaps also to signal to a secular, earthly decision maker that they are appealing to a higher source).

Prayer also operates as an indirect action in pursuit of policy goals. For interest groups and lobbyists, indirect action is seeking to influence policy makers by impacting public opinion (either generally or by specifically targeting decision makers' constituents). In this case, prayer can be used as an indirect strategy by building constituents' sense of belonging. By asking for prayer from supporters or by hosting events where the goal is to lead supporters in prayer, leaders can mobilize grassroots support. Communicating to supporters the priorities and positions of the group through calls for prayer serves an educational function as well. But mobilization is also encouraged by asking supporters to be part of a larger effort, a solidary benefit, by taking their own individual action at home. Prayer is an almost unique type of mobilizer because it can be done anywhere by oneself or in a group and serves to create a strong connection between people who know they are praying for the same things.

Prayer is one of the ways in which religious interest groups demonstrate their specifically religious dimensions and motivations in politics. To put it simply, nonreligious interest groups do not pray. Our evidence from the groups' websites and the religious interest group leader survey suggests that prayer is used as an additional resource to the other more traditional activities of interest groups. What is not clear is whether prayer is used as a substitute for other kinds of political advocacy. It may be that religious groups that are low in traditional interest group resources use prayer as a strategy because the groups lack access to the other strategies, such as lobbying, campaign donations, or even protest. It may also be that religious groups see prayer as a low-cost boost to their other activities. The website evidence points to this conclusion. Thus, prayer serves as an advocacy multiplier rather than an advocacy trade-off. It is an addition to religious interest groups' repertoire rather than a substitute for other kinds of political activities and serves as a signaling mechanism that reinforces their religious identity and purpose.

This is not to say that the groups themselves, their leaders or their supporters, would describe their approach to prayer in such instrumental terms. While many are comfortable with the dual purpose of prayer as direct advocacy and a vehicle to encourage more solidarity and action by supporters, most would see prayer as a foundational, rather than an ancillary, political strategy. This fits with our approach to religious-political interest groups as hybrid organizations. The organizations selectively couple prayer to more explicit political activities and reap the benefits in both arenas. Even as a foundation, prayer is partnered with more traditional advocacy activities and is rarely used as a strategy on its own.

Our evidence makes clear that the approach to prayer as an advocacy strategy differs greatly across religious traditions. This may be related to prayer's overall role in these traditions or, more specifically, to the tradition's approach to political theology and, thus, the prayer's role in their political advocacy. But not every religious group takes advantage of the unique religious resource of prayer in similar ways. This matters because it demonstrates that we cannot approach all religious motivation in advocacy politics the same way. Religion, overall, is an important factor, but the specific religious tradition strongly impacts the way that religious people are politically involved. While the overwhelming majority of religious political activism in the US is undertaken by Christian groups, the growing presence of religious minorities in both society and politics will make a future difference in these situations.

This initial exploration of prayer's role in religious interest groups' advocacy strategy demonstrates that prayer is a unique communication resource and serves as one of the signal activities of groups with a religious motivation for political involvement. Several other avenues need exploration for us to better understand the difference that prayer makes in religious interest groups' strategic decision-making. First, it is important to understand how religious interest group leaders plan for prayer in their attempts to change policy. Interviews with leadership and observations of group strategy planning processes will lend understanding of the degree to which religious interest groups see their prayer as a direct or indirect issue advocacy form. More importantly, to validate our conclusions about prayer's role in religious interest groups' strategy, scholars need to understand how leaders use previous experiences with prayer to inform their political advocacy plans.

Another important avenue for future research is a comparison of religious interest groups to nonreligious interest groups. While religious groups may not make trade-offs in terms of their prayer and non-prayer activities, it may be that the groups' overall activity differs from their nonreligious counterparts. Prayer is a specifically religious activity, but it may impact the underlying distribution of advocacy activities even if it is not used as a primary strategy. Finally, scholars need to better understand how religious interest groups transform religious resources into traditional political resources. It seems likely that the instrumental benefits of group-oriented prayer are not limited to encouraging membership and group commitment. Prayer likely has an impact on monetary donations and may serve an integral role in convincing members of the interest group's financial integrity and usefulness.

Our focus in this chapter has been on the ways that religious interest groups utilize prayer in their advocacy strategies. Prayer is a unique resource that performs both religious and political functions for groups that lie at the boundary between political activity and personal faith. Taking a broad perspective on prayer as a political communication resource helps us to better identify how prayer is similar to, yet operationally different from, other kinds of political participation.

REFERENCES

Ammerman, Nancy T. 2014. "Finding Religion in Everyday Life." *Sociology of Religion* 75:189–207.

Bade, Mary K., and Stephen W. Cook. 2008. "Functions of Christian Prayer in the Coping Process." *Journal for the Scientific Study of Religion* 47:123–33.

Berger, Peter L. 1969. *The Sacred Canopy: Elements of a Sociological Theory of Religion.* New York: Anchor Books.

Campbell, David E., John C. Green, and J. Quin Monson. 2014. *Seeking the Promised Land: Mormons and American Politics.* New York: Cambridge University Press.

Ebersole, Luke. 1951. *Church Lobbying in the Nation's Capital.* New York: Macmillan.

Giordan, Giuseppe. 2012. "Toward a Sociology of Prayer." In *Religion, Spirituality and Everyday Practice,* edited by Giuseppe Giordan and William H. Swatos Jr., 77–88. Dordrecht: Springer Netherlands.

Grant, J. Tobin, Sandy H. Kim, and Robert Velez. 2014. "Religious Market Interest Groups: Do They Sing with an Upper Class Accent?" In *Mediating Religion and Government: Political Institutions and the Policy Process,* edited by Kevin R. Den Dulk and Elizabeth Anne Oldmixon, 39–58. New York: Palgrave Macmillan.

Hertzke, Allen D. 2009. "Religious Interest Groups in American Politics." In *The Oxford Handbook of Religion and American Politics,* edited by Corwin Smidt, Lyman Kellstedt, and James L. Guth, 299–329. New York: Oxford University Press.

Loveland, Matthew T., David Sikkink, Daniel J. Meyers, and Benjamin Radcliff. 2005. "Private Prayer and Civic Involvement." *Journal for the Scientific Study of Religion* 44:1–14.

Lugo, Luis, Alan Cooperman, Erin O'Connell, and Sandra Stencel. 2011. "Lobbying for the Faithful: Religious Advocacy Groups in Washington, DC." Pew

Forum on Religion and Public Life, November 21. Accessed November 25, 2016. http://www.pewforum.org/2011/11/21/lobbying-for-the-faithful-exec/

McCarthy, John D., and Mayer N. Zald. 1987. *Social Movements in an Organizational Society, Collected Essays*. New Brunswick, NJ: Transaction.

Meadow, Mary Jo, and Richard D. Kahoe. 1984. *Psychology of Religion: Religion in Individual Lives*. New York: Harper & Row.

Pache, Anne-Claire, and Filipe Santos. 2012. "Inside the Hybrid Organization: Selective Coupling as a Response to Competing Institutional Logics." *Academy of Management Journal* 56 (4). https://journals.aom.org/doi/abs/10.5465/amj.2011.0405

Poloma, Margaret M., and Brian F. Pendleton. 1991. "The Effects of Prayer and Prayer Experiences on Measures of General Well-Being." *Journal of Psychology and Theology* 19:71–83.

Sharp, Shane. 2013. "How to Do Things with Prayer Utterances." *Symbolic Interaction* 36:159–76.

Sherkat, Darren E. 2006. "Politics and Social Movements." In *Handbook of Religion and Social Institutions*, edited by Helen Rose Ebaugh, 3–19. New York: Springer.

Stark, Rodney, and Roger Finke. 2000. *Acts of Faith: Explaining the Human Side of Religion*. Berkeley: University of California Press.

Weber, Paul J., and W. Landis Jones. 1994. *U.S. Religious Interest Groups*. Westport, CT: Greenwood Press.

Wuthnow, Robert J. 2011. "Taking Talk Seriously: Religious Discourse as Social Practice." *Journal for the Scientific Study of Religion* 50 (1): 1–21.

NINE

Cue the Backlash

Jason Adkins

One of the core themes of this volume is that religious communication often comes in the form of elite cues. Earlier chapters explored the influence of cues from religious elites outside of the church/denomination structure (i.e., Pat Robertson) and secular political elites wading into policy debates referencing religious groups and history (i.e., Rick Santorum). Earlier chapters also examined the concept of group member prototypicality. I use this chapter to expand consideration of both sets of concepts by assessing the response to religious communication cues to religious elites working in religious contexts—congregations within denominations—among both the members of these denominations and those unaffiliated.

The importance of this topic is rooted as much in the study of religion and communication as it is in the reality of public knowledge levels about politics. Various surveys indicate Americans know little about how American politics functions (Ginsberg et al. 2016). One side effect of this phenomenon is that Americans tend to "rely on trusted experts and political elites to form their opinions on political issues without having to work through the details of those issues themselves" (Gilens and Murakawa 2002, 15). Elite cues come in different forms. Politicians, celebrities, and business leaders are just a few of the many groups that could be considered "elite." The term "elite" can also be used to describe religious leaders, especially leaders of various religious organizations, whether those are leaders of worldwide religious organizations, regional leaders, or leaders of congregations. In considering who is a religious elite, there are various offices or positions that could make a claim of being "elite." For example, leaders within the Roman

Catholic Church include the pope, cardinals, and bishops, who lead either the entire church in the case of the pope or internal church organizations or regional divisions in the case of cardinals and bishops. The Church of Jesus Christ of Latter-day Saints (LDS Church) has a president, his two counselors, and twelve apostles, who serve as the organization's highest leaders, with church members considering those fifteen leaders as "prophets, seers, and revelators." For evangelical Christians, whose local congregations are independent in many respects from a central organization, elites can include ministers such as Billy Graham, Pat Robertson, and Joel Osteen, who do not lead religious organizations but have hundreds of thousands of supporters who have donated money to their respective organizations and/or attended events. However, leaders of organizations like the Southern Baptist Convention can be considered elites who have influence over a wide swath of congregations and individual members.

These elites do more than espouse religious messages. Religious elites from the Catholic Church, Southern Baptist Convention, and LDS Church speak out on political matters with relative frequency. These leaders utilize reverse "God Talk," which consists of coded political cues that only the members of particular religious organizations generally understand and decipher on a regular basis, to sway members of their organizations. Despite the frequency of political cues, direct calls to political action, however, are quite low. The reasons for this have been outlined previously, which include US laws that prohibit religious organizations from making explicit partisan political endorsements as well as religious leaders who worry about potential backlash from their congregants by bringing politics to the pews.

Questions persist regarding the effectiveness of political cues from religious elites. Statements by religious leaders might matter, as opposition could be much higher in the absence of statements. However, it is difficult to assess the impact of statements by religious elites with much precision in survey data and to establish causal links between cues and subsequent political attitudes and behavior. To test these causal links, I fielded an original survey experiment to test how political cues, both explicit and coded, from Roman Catholic and LDS leaders affect political attitudes.

Why Religious Elites Preach Politics

Previous research has indicated that elites have an influence on political attitudes and opinions. In other words, even if we do not think elites have complete control, they shape political discourse and action. Zaller (1992) and Delli-Carpini and Keeter (1996) indicate that elite influence, including that of religious leaders, has a strong potential to shape political attitudes. This coincides with earlier research from the Columbia School that indicates political attitudes are shaped by sociological influences, including family, friends, coworkers, and also fellow members of religious congregations (Berelson, Lazarfeld, and McPhee 1954). Zaller (1992) as well as Delli-Carpini and Keeter (1996) indicate that elite influence, which includes religious leaders, has a strong potential to shape political attitudes.

Members of religious congregations are influenced in political matters for various reasons. While many religious organizations focus on life after death, members of religious organizations also want guidance in how to conduct their everyday lives (Djupe and Gilbert 2003, 2008; Smidt 2004; Jelen 2003; Guth et al. 1997; Huckfeldt, Plutzer, and Sprague 1993; Welch et al. 1993; Wald, Owen, and Hill 1988). Politics becomes a natural extension of day-to-day life, where decisions made by elected and nonelected officials affect others. Some religious leaders also see this connection and seek to tie in religious doctrine to political behavior (Campbell, Green, and Monson 2014; Djupe and Gilbert 2008; G. Smith 2008; Brewer, Kersh, and Peterson 2003). Djupe and Grant (2001, 304) also find that religious elites have an impact, as a "spillover" effect occurs in encouraging members to "live their religion."

Outright partisan political advocacy by religious leaders and organizations is prohibited by the US government as part of the Johnson Amendment, which was enshrined into law in 1965. However, there are many legal gray areas in which religious leaders can operate. Recent moves by the Trump administration have attempted to weaken the Johnson Amendment through both executive action and legislation. In April 2017, Trump issued an executive order directing the Internal Revenue Service to develop new tax regulations that would allow religious organizations to be more active in political affairs.[1] However, attempts to repeal the Johnson Amendment in the 2017 tax reform bill failed. An example of how religious organizations skirt the Johnson Amendment is publishing voting guides that indicate how partisan elected officials vote on matters such as abortion, gay marriage, and school choice (G. Smith 2008, 134; Vinson and Guth 2003, 29; Utter and Storey 2001, 8; Regnerus, Sikkink, and Smith 1999, 1377; Fowler and Hertzke 1995). Such guides are similar to scorecards that orga-

---

1. John Wagner and Sarah Pulliam Bailey, "Trump signs order seeking to allow churches to engage in more political activity," *Washington Post*, May 4, 2017.

nizations such as the National Rifle Association and Planned Parenthood, among many others, put out highlighting voting records of elected officials.

Religious groups will also speak out on nonpartisan issues, such as abortion, same-sex marriage, and school funding.[2] For instance, the United States Conference of Catholic Bishops strongly supports publicly funded school voucher programs that enable children to attend Catholic schools.[3] Roman Catholic bishops have issued public statements to deny communion to elected officials who support abortion rights, which sends a signal to Catholics that they disapprove of abortion.[4] The Southern Baptist Convention passes several resolutions at its annual meetings, which are not binding on individual congregations, regarding the religious organization's position on nonpartisan political issues (Ammerman 2007; O. Smith 2000; Dillon 1995). The fourth-largest religious organization in the US, the LDS Church, also attempts to influence members in political matters. While pledging political neutrality on partisan politics, LDS Church leaders have instructed members which way to vote on initiatives and referendums regarding issues ranging from liberalization of alcohol laws to euthanasia, gambling, legalization of marijuana for recreational use, and same-sex marriage (Campbell, Green, and Monson 2014; Campbell and Monson 2003, 2007; Mauss 1984).

While religious leaders involve themselves in political matters, questions remain of the effectiveness of these elite cues. Existing work on the influence of religious leaders is scarce. Mckeown and Carlson (1987) were among the first to examine the effectiveness of political cues by religious leaders. They used a pastoral letter from the United States Conference of Catholic Bishops that addressed foreign and domestic policy matters. Their experiment utilized a control group that did not receive a cue, a treatment group that received the cue that attributed the source to US Catholic bishops, and another treatment group that was presented with the same letter, but which was attributed to the recently deceased Rev. Billy Graham. Their results indicated cues did not have an effect on political attitudes.

Djupe and Gilbert (2008) argued that the effectiveness of cues depends

---

2. This means "nonpartisan" in the sense that religious organizations will generally advocate for an issue instead of a candidate or a political party.

3. Several statements from Catholic bishops around the country supporting publicly funded school voucher programs can be found at http://www.usccb.org/beliefs-and-teachings/how-we-teach/catholic-education/public-policy/index.cfm

4. Ian Urbina, "Kennedy Discouraged from Communion by Bishop," *New York Times*, November 22, 2009.

on many factors. One factor is issue saliency, in that issues need to be important to individual members of the congregation for them to consider it and become advocates themselves (Krosnick 1990). Other factors that shape influence include the political composition of congregations and opportunities to discuss politics in a congregational environment. Djupe and Gilbert's findings came from surveying Episcopal and Evangelical Lutheran Church in American congregations that separated attitudes of local leaders and rank-and-file congregants.

Cue from religious leaders, though, have been found to be effective in certain circumstances. Adkins et al. (2013) found strong correlations between religious-based cues compared to secular cues on a host of issues. Their experiment used treatment groups where one group received a cue from a religious leader and the secular treatment group received a cue that specifically mentioned "non-religious leaders." The text of the treatment was identical, with the exception of switching out who was issuing the cues, such as "Most Catholic leaders," "Most evangelical backers," and "non-religious leaders" (Adkins et al. 2013, 243–44). A downside to this approach is that it lacks specificity and does not use language produced by religious organizations.

Positive affect toward religious elites may account for the effectiveness of cues (Mulligan 2006). The findings suggest that those "who esteemed" Pope John Paul II were more likely to oppose abortion and the death penalty compared to Catholics with more negative feelings toward the pope (740). Other scholars have found political cues from elites effective in some areas, such as immigration (Nteta and Wallsten 2012). They found that exposure to religious elite cues led to more tolerant attitudes toward increasing immigration, allowing noncitizens to serve in the military, and giving those noncitizens a pathway to citizenship.

Gregory Smith (2008) provided an extensive study of nine Catholic parishes to show the diversity of political cues local priests deliver to Catholics. Part of his argument is that Catholic priests have diverse views and training, since priests attend seminaries throughout the country, and that the political composition of congregations is also diverse. With that context, individual Catholics may not be receptive to dissonant political cues that deviate from existing political attitudes. However, Smith does not address the effects of cues from Catholic priests on rank-and-file Catholics. Catholics also receive political cues from their local bishop, who like their parish priests may have different political views than bishops from other dioceses.

Campbell, Monson, and Green (2014) conducted an original survey experiment to determine if LDS Church leaders are effective in swaying the political attitudes of rank-and-file Mormons. The LDS Church is unique in many respects in that its president is considered a living prophet with sole authority to receive revelation on behalf of the church as a whole. The president along with two assistants (called counselors) form the First Presidency, and all official messages on behalf of the church are approved by that body. Campbell, Monson, and Green (2014, 153) indicate Mormons are influenced by messages from the LDS Church. In their experiment, they asked Mormons about their attitudes on gambling, immigration, and nondiscrimination laws that protect LGBT individuals. A control group did not receive any cue, one treatment group was presented with a message outlining general principles on that given issue before respondents were asked about their attitudes on that issue, and a second treatment group received a specific message regarding the LDS Church's position on that issue before respondents were asked a question regarding their attitudes.

There is also a question of whether cues from religious elites can have an opposite than intended effect. Djupe, Lewis, and Jelen (2016) fielded a survey experiment to determine whether religious leaders were more effective at swaying attitudes among evangelicals who identify as politically conservative compared to other groups, such as those who identify as religious but being politically liberal. Their findings show political cues from religious leaders on religious freedom increase tolerance on other rights-based issues. In essence, cues from religious elites backfire on cue givers. Djupe and Calfano (2013) utilized survey experiments to show how religion influences political attitudes by highlighting how politicians use coded religious messages (God Talk) to garner support. They found that God Talk is effective at garnering support from evangelical Protestants because politicians covertly signal they "are one of them" through the use of carefully constructed language. But an important part of the issue confronting elite cue influence is the prototypicality of the one receiving the message. Having nominal affiliation with a tradition or denomination label is not the same as agreeing with even the core political views espoused by religious leaders. Logically, the more prototypical members are in their preference profile with the religious organization in which they claim membership, the more likely the members should be to rely on cues from the organization leader. But prototypicality is certainly a variable concept, especially in the American religious marketplace. And then there is the returning question of how religious elite cues impact those not intended to receive them. As discussed in the Robertson and Santorum experiments in the volume's early chapters, elites run the risk of alienating constituencies outside their target groups with the cues they communicate. This may present problems if the goal is to motivate voters on referendum issues or candidate choices in an election. Indeed, the backfire effect may be palpable and politically costly.

Analyzing Political Cues from Religious Elites

Following the lead of Campbell, Green, and Monson's (2014) Peculiar People Survey to study Mormon political attitudes, I designed an original survey experiment to test the effects of political cues made by Catholic and LDS leaders on political attitudes. Survey experiments are ideal in that they are able to test for direct causality between treatment exposure and a follow-on response (Druckman et al. 2006; Gerber and Green 2000; Iyengar, Peters, and Kinder 1982). Originally, the survey was going to test the effectiveness of political cues by Southern Baptist leaders, but the number of evangelical Protestants in the sample was extremely small to determine statistical significance. As stated previously, these three religious organizations were selected because they are three of the four largest religious organizations in the US, they deliver political cues on a regular basis, and they also have diverse organizational structures. The LDS Church is heavily centralized, with most financial decisions and leadership decisions made by the First Presidency and the Quorum of Twelve Apostles. All financial contributions collected in individual congregations are sent to LDS Church headquarters in Salt Lake City, Utah. The Catholic Church is decentralized compared to the LDS Church, as Catholic bishops have a large degree of authority over individual parishes, while the Vatican generally does not involve itself in administrative matters at the diocese level. The Southern Baptist Convention represents a heavily decentralized organization, as each congregation is autonomous with full control over its finances, property, and leadership, while the central organization has authority regarding membership of congregations into the organization.

The 2017 Political Attitudes Survey was fielded to students recruited from political science courses at Brigham Young University, Kent State University, Utah Valley University, and York College (Pennsylvania). The usefulness here of drawing subject pools from college student populations is that life cycle theory predicts at least some of those with religious affiliation in college will become less committed to (and, thereby, prototypical of) their group. This built-in variation sets up a useful opportunity to assess how religious elite cues are perceived in that even those holding a nominal religious affiliation in the same group as the elite cue giver may be resistant the communicated messages. A caveat to this study is that surveying just college students may also be problematic in that more educated people may also be able to resist elite cues to a greater extent than those with less education (Delli Carpini and Keeter 1996; Zaller 1992).

Students were provided extra credit or course credit for completing the survey. Out of the 727 students who took the survey, 322 students attended Kent State University, 217 attended Brigham Young University, 55 attended York College, and 38 attended Utah Valley University. The other 95 respondents did not identify their university affiliation. One weakness of the survey is that it did not capture a sufficient number of Southern Baptists or evangelical Protestants, in general, to be able to provide meaningful analysis. However, 269 respondents identified as LDS and 116 as Roman Catholic, which provides a sufficient sample for analysis regarding the influence of Roman Catholic and LDS leaders.

Respondents were asked a series of questions on several matters ranging from the admission of refugees into the US based on religious identification, climate change, immigration, legalization of marijuana, religious freedom for business owners related to providing services to same-sex customers, and transgender bathrooms. These issue-based questions were selected based on recent statements by religious elites within the Catholic Church and LDS Church. LDS respondents were asked about their attitudes toward marijuana legalization, religious freedom for business owners in accommodating LGBTQ customers, and refugee admission into the US based on religion. Catholic respondents were asked questions regarding climate change, immigration, and transgender bathrooms.

Each respondent was asked their religious affiliation, and based on those responses, they were asked questions related to issues that those specific religious organizations have spoken out on in various ways. In addition, the treatment groups received political cues delivered by organizations or leaders of those organizations. For example, Catholic respondents were presented with questions outlining their attitudes on issues that Catholic leaders delivered statements on, and likewise for Baptists and Mormons. Respondents in control groups were not presented with any message from religious elites regarding those issues. Respondents in one treatment group (coded treatment) were presented with a statement from religious leaders outlining that respective organization's principles on a given issue, without providing a clear yes-or-no stance.

Respondents in the second treatment group (explicit treatment) were presented with a statement from religious leaders with a specific political cue regarding that issue. These explicit cues represented a more direct cue than those the coded treatment group received. The presence of political cues from elites also could lead to responses that are more consistent with the stances of a particular religious group (Charters and Newcomb 1952). While there is a concern that such cues may skew the results, the overall goal of cue giving is to change attitudes. The appendix lists the questions and cues presented to respondents.

The ordered logistical regression and logistical regression models were separated into two models per issue.[5] The first model for each issue includes only the treatment variable as an independent variable. In testing how effective political cues from religious leaders are, I created two placebo groups. One dummy variable separates out coreligionists, or those who identify with a religious group that is not the religious organization that religious leaders seek to target with their political cues. A second dummy variable identifies those who do not identify with any religion. The objective of these models is to determine how political cues affect those who identify with different religions and the "nones" who do not identify with any religious group.

Results and Discussion

Results from the survey experiment indicate that political cues from religious elites offer a mixed bag in terms of effectiveness. Regression results in table 9.1 indicate the effectiveness of elite cues for Catholic respondents. The coded treatment in the treatment-only model leads to a higher probability of indicating that climate change exists and is caused by humans, with the coded treatment being statistically significant. In the model with controls for coreligionists and the "nones" included, the effect for Catholics is still statistically significant and larger. For coreligionists, Catholic cues are also effective in swaying attitudes toward the Catholic position. While not statistically significant, the explicit treatment for the "nones" also moved attitudes in the Catholic direction.

As indicated in figure 9.1, political cues from Catholic leaders on immigration lead to split results among Catholic respondents but to backlash among coreligionists and the "nones." The coded treatment is statistically significant in the treatment-only model. While not statistically significant, Catholics who received the coded treatment have a higher probability of believing a border wall with Mexico is necessary, which goes against the

---

5. The question regarding attitudes on transgender individuals' use of restrooms was the only survey question with a binary response and the lone logistic regression model.

intended effect of the cue. This indicates the cue is not effective. However, the explicit treatment has the opposite effect on Catholics, as they have a higher probability of holding attitudes that a border wall with Mexico is unnecessary. For the "nones," the cue is both statistically and substantially significant for those who received either the coded or the explicit treatment in moving attitudes toward believing a border wall is necessary, which indicates a backlash effect is present.

The effect of political cues by religious elites regarding transgender individuals using public restrooms is not statistically significant in either model. While not statistically significant, the treatments lead to a higher probability among Catholics to support attitudes that transgender individuals should use the restroom of the sex they were born with. There is

TABLE 9.1. Catholic Political Cues

	Climate Change		Immigration		Transgender	
	(Treatment)	(Controls)	(Treatment)	(Controls)	(Treatment)	(Controls)
Coded treatment	0.36*	1.34**	−0.33*	−0.61	0.089	0.49
	(0.22)	(0.55)	(0.19)	(0.43)	(0.26)	(0.55)
Explicit treatment	0.036	0.69	−0.22	0.18	−0.091	0.26
	(0.21)	(0.51)	(0.19)	(0.46)	(0.26)	(0.54)
Coreligionists	—	0.46	—	0.23	—	0.59
		(0.37)		(0.35)		(0.47)
Coded treatment * coreligionists	—	−1.18*	—	0.58	—	−0.53
		(0.61)		(0.49)		(0.64)
Explicit treatment * coreligionists	—	−0.84	—	−0.32	—	−0.21
		(0.57)		(0.51)		(0.64)
Nones	—	1.51**	—	2.72***	—	−0.61
		(0.63)		(0.79)		(0.77)
Coded treatment * nones	—	−1.10	—	−1.74*	—	−0.28
		(0.99)		(0.94)		(1.03)
Explicit treatment * nones	—	−0.41	—	−1.98**	—	—
		(0.96)		(0.97)		
/cut1	−2.98***	−2.53***	−2.84***	−2.47***	—	—
	(0.23)	(0.37)	(0.20)	(0.34)		
/cut2	−0.74***	−0.26	−1.37***	−0.97***	—	—
	(0.15)	(0.33)	(0.15)	(0.32)		
/cut3	—	—	−0.41***	0.016	—	—
			(0.14)	(0.31)		
Constant	—	—	—	—	−0.36*	−0.69*
					(0.19)	(0.41)
N	607	607	636	636	363	345
Pseudo R^2	0.0037	0.026	0.0023	0.025	0.00098	0.017

Note: Ordinal logistic regression for climate change and immigration models. Logistic regression for transgender restrooms model. Standard errors in parentheses.

*** $p < .01$, ** $p < .05$, * $p < .1$

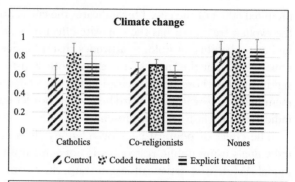

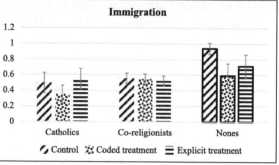

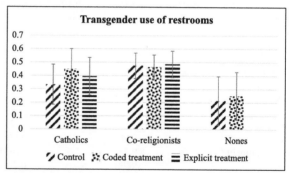

Fig. 9.1. Predicted Probabilities for Catholic Political Cues

Note: Error bars represent 90 percent confidence intervals (two-tailed). Predicted probabilities for climate change are believing climate change is caused by humans. Predicted probabilities for immigration are those who believe a border wall is unnecessary. Predicted probabilities for transgender use of restrooms are based on probability of holding attitude that transgender individuals should use the restroom of the gender they identify with ("nones" excluded due to collinearity).

a backlash effect among coreligionists to the Catholic cue, at least those who received the coded cue. The explicit treatment among the "nones" was excluded from the model due to multicollinearity issues.

For LDS political cues, the effects are not particularly effective to members of the target religious group. As indicated in table 9.2, treatment effects are not statistically significant for the models with controls addressing attitudes toward marijuana legalization, refugee admission in the US, and religious freedom for those who identify as LDS. Regarding marijuana, the results indicate that those who received the coded treatment in the treatment-only model were more likely to support legalization, which goes against the intended effect of the cue. When LDS respondents are considered in the model with coreligionists and the "nones" are separated out, the results are split, as those in the coded group are more likely to support legalization and those in the explicit group are more likely to oppose legalization. For coreligionists, who are already more likely to hold attitudes supporting legalization compared to LDS respondents, the coded treatment has a slight backlash effect. For the "nones," a backlash effect is present for those who received the coded cue; however, the explicit treatment for "nones" in the explicit group is slightly effective in shifting attitudes toward opposing legalization.

The backlash effect toward statements by LDS leaders is not surprising, as other studies have shown attitudes toward Mormons to be the lowest

TABLE 9.2. Regression Coefficients for Catholic Political Cues

	Marijuana		Refugees		Religious Freedom	
	(Treatment)	(Controls)	(Treatment)	(Controls)	(Treatment)	(Controls)
Coded treatment	−0.41**	−0.30	0.071	−0.00068	0.17	0.39
	(0.19)	(0.31)	(0.27)	(0.39)	(0.21)	(0.28)
Explicit treatment	−0.038	0.29	−0.21	−0.16	0.00050	0.072
	(0.19)	(0.29)	(0.26)	(0.38)	(0.20)	(0.28)
Coreligionists	—	−2.11***	—	−1.20***	—	−1.09***
		(0.31)		(0.41)		(0.33)
Coded treatment * coreligionists	—	0.011	—	0.32	—	−0.62
		(0.43)		(0.57)		(0.47)
Explicit treatment * coreligionists	—	−0.51	—	0.27	—	−0.13
		(0.42)		(0.56)		(0.46)
Nones	—	−2.91***	—	0.59	—	−1.72***
		(0.55)		(0.81)		(0.47)
Coded treatment * nones	—	−0.48	—	−0.77	—	−0.55
		(0.85)		(1.03)		(0.76)
Explicit treatment * nones	—	−0.11	—	−1.81*	—	−0.031
		(0.73)		(1.05)		(0.66)
/cut1	0.20	−1.60***	−2.52***	−2.99***	−0.84***	−1.53***
	(0.13)	(0.23)	(0.24)	(0.33)	(0.16)	(0.22)
/cut2	1.78***	0.99***	−2.30***	−2.76***	0.12	−0.43**
	(0.16)	(0.22)	(0.23)	(0.32)	(0.15)	(0.20)
/cut3			−1.21***	−1.63***	1.31***	0.90***
			(0.20)	(0.29)	(0.17)	(0.21)
/cut4			−0.84***	−1.24***	—	—
			(0.19)	(0.28)	—	—
Observations	627	627	397	397	450	450
Pseudo R^2	0.0048	0.17	0.0017	0.031	0.00071	0.061

Note: Ordinal logistic regression models. Standard errors in parentheses.
*** $p < .01$, ** $p < .05$, * $p < .1$

among any Christian denomination. A 2017 Pew Research Center survey from 2017 found that on a scale of 0 to 100, the mean rate toward Mormons was 58. Only atheists (rated 50) and Muslims (rated 48) fared worse. As a comparison, evangelical Christians were rated 61 and Catholics were rated 66. Jews were rated the highest with a mean rating of 67.

Cues from LDS leaders are not effective among LDS respondents regarding attitudes toward refugees, as those in both treatment groups are less likely to support admitting refugees into the US regardless of religious belief. For the refugee model, the only variable that was statistically significant was the explicit treatment for the "nones." The results for both the general and explicit treatment groups indicate a backlash effect is present. While not statistically significant, LDS political cues lead to a slight change among coreligionists in supporting admitting refugees without regard to religious belief. These results are in line with the intent of the cue.

Regarding religious freedom, none of the treatments were statistically significant in either the treatment-only model or the model with controls for coreligionists and the "nones" included. This suggests that LDS cues regarding religious freedom, at least regarding business owners accommodating homosexual couples, are not effective. There are statistically significant differences for coreligionists and the "nones" in the control group compared to LDS respondents in the control group, which indicates that those groups are less sympathetic to business owners regarding religious freedom issues.

Figure 9.2 illustrates the divide more closely. Interestingly, the cues have a slight, albeit not statistically significant, effect on both coreligionists and the "nones." Coreligionists who received both the coded and the explicit treatments are more likely to hold attitudes supporting marijuana legalization compared to coreligionists who did not receive the treatment. The "nones" who received the coded treatment also had a higher probability of holding attitudes supporting marijuana legalization compared to the "nones" in the control group.

Cues regarding the admission of refugees into the US regardless of religious belief did not have any substantive effect on those who identify as LDS. There was backlash with coreligionists and the "nones," as both groups who received the treatments were less likely to hold an attitude that the US needed to admit more refugees without religious screening. Regarding religious freedom, the coded and explicit treatments had a moderate substantive effect on LDS respondents in that they had a slightly higher probability of having more sympathy with business owners' objection to accommodating same-sex couples due to their religious beliefs. There was a backlash effect for coreligionists and the "nones" in that those

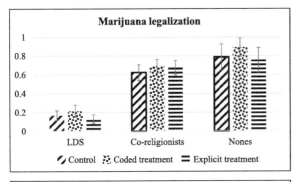

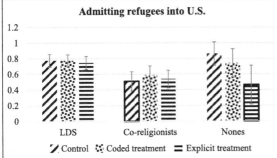

Fig. 9.2. Predicted Probabilities for LDS Political Cues
Note: Error bars represent 90 percent confidence intervals (two-tailed). Predicted probabilities for marijuana legalization are for supporting legalization for both recreational and medicinal uses. Predicted probabilities for refugees are for increasing the number of refugees from the Middle East resettled into the US without any religious screening. Predicted probabilities for religious freedom are those who are very sympathetic to business owners in accommodating same-sex couples who are customers.

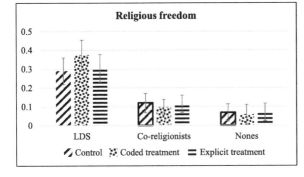

who received either treatment had a slightly lower probability of sympathizing with business owners in accommodating same-sex couples due to religious freedom concerns.

Conclusion

The results of the survey experiment indicate that political cues from religious elites are not particularly effective among the faithful and can spark backlash among those who are not members of those particular religious organizations. This is a provocative, but not entirely unsurprising, finding given prior work on the subject of religious elite influence. The results also speak to the notion that religious identifiers who might, as a whole, be less prototypical of the "ideal" group members (e.g., traditional college-age students) are more resistant to religious elite cues than older group members. Of course, this is a generalization, but one that adds to the complex picture regarding whether religious elite cues are effective.

Assuming these cues have some effect at given times, the next question is for which issues they are effective. For Catholic cues, the only cue that showed effectiveness in the survey experiment was regarding climate change. Cues addressing immigration and transgender issues, which also cross-pressure partisans, as the immigration cue leans liberal and the transgender cue leans conservative, sparked backlash among both coreligionists and the "nones." Why climate change was an effective cue is that it did not address how to treat groups of people. The two other Catholic cues addressed the plights of immigrants and transgender individuals but also may personally affect people as some may fear immigrants or transgender individuals using a woman's restroom. President Trump, for example, has spoken out numerous times about undocumented immigrants committing crimes at a higher rate than citizens or documented immigrants. The transgender "bathroom bills" have stoked fear among some that criminals would claim to be a gender in order to commit crimes in restrooms. Climate change does not elicit fears of others compared to the other two issues, which may be a reason Catholic cues resonate.

All three political cues from LDS leaders suffered a backlash effect. The only issue for which LDS leaders were able to have an intended effect from non-LDS was among coreligionists regarding refugees. That backlash is not surprising due to long-standing issues many coreligionists and "nones" have with the LDS Church. For the "nones," the backlash is not surprising. The LDS Church received criticism for its work organizing support for two ballot initiatives in California banning same-sex marriage, Proposition 22 in 2000 and Proposition 8 in 2008.

There are also a few items to consider regarding the survey sample. The Catholic and LDS samples also differ in that no LDS respondents reported never going to religious services, while nearly 20 percent of Catholics reported never attending. At the higher end of religious service attendance, the difference is even starker, as 80 percent of LDS respondents reported going to religious services on a weekly basis, with only 10 percent of Catholic respondents reporting doing so. Further research using a more representative sample of both Catholic and LDS populations, as well as surveying enough Southern Baptists, would be beneficial in extending the research conducted thus far.

One item that also needs more study is how negative affect toward religious groups might lead to individuals responding in an opposite manner than the intent of the cue. One example that can be seen in the real world is the LDS Church's stance on Proposition 8 in 2008. The LDS Church strongly supported the ballot initiative that would have defined marriage as between one man and one woman. If cues from Proposition 8 led to more people supporting same-sex marriage, this could cause LDS leaders to give pause or even to withdraw from political cue giving if there could be significant backlash. While backlash within religious organizations has been considered, there are many questions regarding backlash from outsiders yet to be answered concerning this aspect of religious elite communication (Welch et al. 1993).

APPENDIX

Climate change

Which of these statements about the Earth's temperature comes closest to your view?

1. The Earth is getting warmer mostly because of human activity, such as burning fossil fuels.
2. The Earth is getting warmer mostly because of natural patterns in the Earth's environment,
3. There is no solid evidence that the Earth is getting warmer.

Coded treatment: In response to the debate regarding global warming, Pope Francis wrote the following: "Humanity is called to recognize the need for changes of lifestyle, production and consumption in order to combat this warming."

Explicit treatment: In response to the debate regarding global warming, Pope Francis said the following: "Global warming continues, due in part to human activity: 2015 was the warmest year on record, and 2016 will likely be warmer still. This is leading to ever more severe droughts, floods, fires and extreme weather events. Climate change is also contributing to the heart-rending refugee crisis. The world's poor, though least responsible for climate change, are most vulnerable and already suffering its impact."

Immigration

Thinking about the issue of immigration, how important of a goal is it to build a wall along the U.S.-Mexico border to stem the flow of undocumented immigrants?

1. Very important
2. Somewhat important
3. Not too important
4. Not all important

Coded treatment: In response to the debate regarding immigration, the United States Conference of Catholic Bishops issued the following: "We call upon all people of good will, but Catholics especially, to welcome the newcomers in their neighborhoods and schools, in their places of work and worship, with heartfelt hospitality, openness, and eagerness both to help and to learn from our brothers and sisters of whatever religion, ethnicity, or background."

Explicit treatment: In response to the debate regarding immigration, Pope Francis said the following: "A person who thinks only of building walls, wherever it may be, and not of building bridges is not Christian. This is not in the Gospel."

Transgender restrooms

Which of the following best matches your position on the use of public restrooms by transgender individuals?

1. Allowed to use the public restrooms of the gender with which they currently identify
2. Required to use the public restrooms of the gender they were born into

Coded treatment: The Catechism of the Catholic Church includes the following passage regarding gender identity: "By creating the human being man and woman, God gives personal dignity equally to the one and the other."

Explicit treatment: In response to the debate regarding gender identity, Pope Francis issued the following regarding the Catholic Church's position: "Beyond the understandable difficulties that individuals may experience, the young need to be helped to accept their own body as it was created, for 'thinking that we enjoy absolute power over our own bodies turns, often subtly, into thinking that we enjoy absolute power over creation.'"

Marijuana legalization

Regarding legalization of marijuana for adults, which of the following best matches your position?

1. Legalization for personal and medicinal use
2. Legalization only for medicinal use
3. Opposed to personal and medicinal legalization

Coded treatment: In response to the debate regarding legalization of marijuana, the Church of Jesus Christ of Latter-day Saints issued the following: "Drug abuse is at epidemic proportions, and the dangers of marijuana to public health are well documented. Recent studies have shed light particularly on the risks marijuana use poses to brain development in youth. The accessibility of recreational marijuana in the home is also a danger to children."

Explicit treatment: In response to the debate regarding legalization of marijuana, the Church of Jesus Christ of Latter-day Saints issued the following: "We urge Church members to let their voices be heard in opposition to the legalization of recreational marijuana."

Refugee admissions based on religion

Which of the following do you think is the best approach for the US to take with refugees from the Middle East?

1. Increase number of refugees from the Middle East resettled into the US without any religious screening
2. Increase number of Christian refugees from the Middle East resettled into the US, but decrease number of Muslim refugees
3. Decrease number of Christian and Muslim refugees resettled into the US
4. Decrease number of Christian refugees and do not accept any Muslim refugees to be resettled into the US
5. Do not accept any refugees from the Middle East into the US

Coded treatment: In response to the debate regarding admitting refugees from the Middle East into the United States, the Church of Jesus Christ of Latter-day Saints issued the following: "We remind Latter-day Saints throughout the world that one of the fundamental principles of the restored gospel of Jesus Christ is to 'impart of your substance to the poor, every man according to that which he hath, . . . administering to their relief, both spiritually and temporally, according to their wants.'"

Explicit treatment: In response to the debate regarding admitting refugees from the Middle East into the United States, the Church of Jesus Christ of Latter-day Saints issued the following statement quoting an 1841 City of Nauvoo ordinance: "Be it ordained by the City Council of the City of Nauvoo, that the Catholics, Presbyterians, Methodists, Baptists, Latter-day Saints, Quakers, Episcopals, Universalists, Unitarians, Mohammedans [Muslims], and all other religious sects and denominations whatever, shall have free toleration, and equal privileges in this city."

Religious freedom

How much, if at all, do you sympathize with businesses regarding laws and regulations requiring them to offer services that may go against their religious beliefs to same-sex couples just as they would to all other customers?

1. A lot
2. Some
3. Not much
4. Not at all

Coded treatment: In response to the debate regarding religious freedom, the Church of Jesus Christ of Latter-day Saints issued the following: "Freedom of religion is a basic principle of the Church of Jesus Christ of Latter-day Saints and a fundamental human right. Moral agency, the ability to choose right from wrong and to act for ourselves, is essential to God's plan of salvation."

Explicit treatment: In response to the debate on religious freedom, the Church of Jesus Christ of Latter-day Saints issued the following: "Religious freedom embraces not only the right to freely worship but also to speak and act based on one's religious beliefs. In a modern revelation, the Lord states that just laws should be 'maintained for the rights and protection of all flesh . . . [t]hat every man may act . . . according to the moral agency which I have given unto him, that every man may be accountable for his own sins in the day of judgment.'"

REFERENCES

Adkins, Todd, Geoffrey C. Layman, David E. Campbell, and John C. Green. 2013. "Religious Group Cues and Citizen Policy Attitudes in the United States." *Politics and Religion* 6:235–63.

Ammerman, Nancy T. 2007. *Everyday Religion: Observing Modern Religious Lives*. New York: Oxford University Press.

Berelson, Bernard R., Paul F. Lazarfeld, and William N. McPhee. 1954. *Voting*. Chicago: University of Chicago Press.

Brewer, Mark D., Rogan Kersh, and R. Eric Peterson. 2003. "Assessing Conventional Wisdom about Religion and Politics: A Preliminary View from the Pews." *Journal for the Scientific Study of Religion* 42:125–36.

Campbell, David E., John C. Green, and J. Quin Monson. 2014. *Seeking the Promised Land: Mormons and American Politics*. New York: Cambridge University Press.

Campbell, David E., and J. Quin Monson. 2003. "Following the Leader? Mormon Voting on Ballot Propositions." *Journal for the Scientific Study of Religion* 42:605–19.

Campbell, David E., and J. Quin Monson. 2007. "Dry Kindling: A Political Profile of American Mormons." In *From Pews to Polling Places: Faith and Politics in the American Religious Mosaic*, edited by J. Matthew Wilson, 105–30. Washington, DC: Georgetown University Press.

Charters, W. W., and Theodore M. Newcomb. 1952. "Some Attitudinal Effects of Experimentally Increased Salience of Group Membership." In *Readings in Social Psychology*, edited by G. E. Swanson, Theodore M. Newcomb, and E. L. Hartley, 415–20. New York: Holt, Rinehart and Winston.

Delli Carpini, Michael X., and Scott Keeter. 1996. *What Americans Know about Politics and Why It Matters*. New Haven: Yale University Press.

Dillon, Michele. 1995. "Religion and Culture in Tension: The Abortion Discourses of the U. S. Catholic Bishops and the Southern Baptist Convention." *Religion and American Culture: A Journal of Interpretation* 5:159–80.

Djupe, Paul A., and Brian R. Calfano. 2013. *God Talk: Experimenting With the Religious Causes of Public Opinion*. Philadelphia: Temple University Press.

Djupe, Paul A., and Christopher P. Gilbert. 2003. *The Prophetic Pulpit: Clergy, Churches, and Communities in American Politics*. Lanham, MD: Rowman and Littlefield.

Djupe, Paul A., and Christopher P. Gilbert. 2008. *The Political Influence of Churches*. New York: Cambridge University Press.

Djupe, Paul A., and J. Tobin Grant. 2001. "Religious Institutions and Political Participation in America." *Journal for the Scientific Study of Religion* 40:303–14.

Djupe, Paul A., Andrew R. Lewis, and Ted G. Jelen. 2016. "Rights, Reflection, and Reciprocity: Implications of the Same-Sex Marriage Debate for Tolerance and the Political Process." *Politics and Religion* 9:630–48.

Druckman, James N., Donald P. Green, James H. Kuklinski, and Arthur Lupia. 2006. "The Growth and Development of Experimental Research in Political Science." *American Political Science Review* 100:627–35.

Fowler, Robert Booth, and Allen D. Hertzke. 1995. *Religion and Politics in America: Faith, Culture, and Strategic Choices*. Boulder, CO: Westview Press.

Gerber, Alan S., and Donald P. Green. 2000. "The Effects of Canvassing, Telephone Calls, and Direct Mail on Voter Turnout: A Field Experiment." *American Political Science Review* 94:653–63.

Gilens, Martin, and Naomi Murakawa. 2002. "Elite Cues and Political Decision-Making." In *Research in Micropolitics*, edited by Michael X. Delli Carpini, Leonie Huddy, and Robert Y. Shapiro, 15–49. Amsterdam: JAI.

Ginsberg, Benjamin, Theodore J. Lowi, Caroline J. Tolbert, and Margaret Weir. 2016. *We the People*. 12th ed. New York: W. W. Norton.

Guth, James L., John C. Green, Corwin E. Smidt, and Lyman A. Kellstedt. 1997. *The Bully Pulpit: The Politics of Protestant Clergy*. Lawrence: University Press of Kansas.

Huckfeldt, Robert, Eric Plutzer, and John Sprague. 1993. "Alternative Contexts of Political Behavior: Churches, Neighborhoods, and Individuals." *Journal of Politics* 55:365–81.

Iyengar, Shanto, Mark D. Peters, and Donald R. Kinder. 1982. "Experimental Demonstrations of the 'Not-So-Minimal' Consequences of Television News Programs." *American Political Science Review* 76:848–58.

Jelen, Ted G. 2003. "Catholic Priests and the Political Order: The Political Behavior of Catholic Pastors." *Journal for the Scientific Study of Religion* 42:591–604.

Krosnick, Jon A. 1990. "Government Policy and Citizen Passion: A Study of Issue Publics in Contemporary America." *Political Behavior* 12:59–92.

Martínez, Jessica Hamar, and Anna Schiller. "Americans Express Increasingly Warm Feelings toward Religious Groups." Pew Research Center for Religion & Public Life, February 17. https://www.pewforum.org/2017/02/15/americans-express-increasingly-warm-feelings-toward-religious-groups/

Mauss, Arnold L. 1984. "Sociological Perspectives on the Mormon Subculture." *Annual Review of Sociology* 10:437–60.

McGuire, William J. 1968. "Personality and Susceptibility to Social Influence." In *Handbook of Personality Theory and Research*, edited by Edgar F. Borgatta and William M. Lambert, 1130–88. Chicago: Rand McNally.

Mckeown, Bruce, and James M. Carlson. 1987. "An Experimental Study of the Influence of Religious Elites on Public Opinion." *Political Communication* 4:93–102.

Mulligan, Kenneth. 2006. "Pope John Paul II and Catholic Opinion toward the Death Penalty and Abortion." *Social Science Quarterly* 87:739–53.

Nteta, Tatishe M., and Kevin J. Wallsten. 2012. "Preaching to the Choir? Religious Leaders and American Opinion on Immigration Reform." *Social Science Quarterly* 93:891–910.

Regnerus, Mark D., David Sikkink, and Christian Smith. 1999. "Voting with the Christian Right: Contextual and Individual Patterns of Electoral Influence." *Social Forces* 77:1375–1401.

Smidt, Corwin E. 2004. *Pulpit and Politics: Clergy in American Politics at the Advent of the Millennium*. Waco, TX: Baylor University Press.

Smith, Gregory Allen. 2008. *Politics in the Parish: The Political Influence of Catholic Priests*. Washington, DC: Georgetown University Press.

Smith, Oran P. 2000. *Rise of Baptist Republicanism*. New York: New York University Press.

Utter, Glenn H., and John Woodrow Storey. 2001. *The Religious Right: A Reference Handbook*. Santa Barbara, CA: ABC-CLIO.

Vinson, C. Danielle, and James L. Guth. 2003. "Advance and Retreat in the Palmetto State: Assessing the Religious Right in South Carolina." In *The Christian Right in American Politics: Marching to the Millennium*, edited by John C. Green, Mark J. Rozell, and Clyde Wilcox, 21–40. Washington, DC: Georgetown University Press.

Wald, Kenneth D., Dennis E. Owen, and Samuel S. Hill Jr. 1988. "Churches as Political Communities." *American Political Science Review* 82:531–48.

Welch, Michael R., David C. Leege, Kenneth D. Wald, and Lyman A. Kellstedt. 1993. "Are the Sheep Herding the Shepherds? Cue Perceptions, Congregational Responses, and Political Communication Responses." In *Rediscovering the Religious Factor in American Politics*, edited by David C. Leege and Lyman A. Kellstedt, 235–54. Armonk, NY: Routledge.

Zaller, John R. 1992. *The Nature and Origins of Mass Opinion*. New York: Cambridge University Press.

TEN

Cues for the Pews

Political Messaging in American Congregations and the Decline of Religious Influence

Paul A. Djupe

American religious history is filled with examples that appear to show religious influence—vibrant public advocacy for a cause, usually about some kind of social vice like drinking, racism, or abortion. This frame is the way that so many investigations of religion and politics begin. But such stories that document religious activity, usually among organizations and elites, are potentially guilty of several academic sins. Correlation is not causation, and the fact that religious variables can be linked to some salient attitude or activity does not mean religion was the cause. From a religious communication perspective, we also cannot assume that where the shepherd leads, the sheep will follow. Indeed, the fact that elites and denominations are active does not necessarily mean their memberships are on board. We need to dig into the mechanisms of communication and influence, not to mention adopt research designs that are more likely to generate causal explanations.

This is no minor academic debate. At stake is the role religion plays in public life. One way to think about religion is that it collects like-minded people and helps to channel their behavior toward some set of goals that members likely share but could not have as easily achieved otherwise. This view of religion as an organizational device solving collective action problems does not place much of any emphasis on its ability to change people's minds through the communication of ideas, norms, and values but focuses merely on its power to aggregate, channel, and mobilize (e.g., McClendon and Riedl 2015; Verba, Schlozman, and Brady 1995). Religious networks, by this mobilization thinking, can be heavily sought after by political organizations as ready-made platoons that simply need deployment toward a particular goal. The degree to which evangelical churches have opened their congregations to the distribution of voter guides from conservative Christian organizations is an example (Beyerlein and Chaves 2003; Djupe 2020).

But, another perspective on religious organizations is that they adhere to a set of values (tied to religious beliefs) that they work toward adopting and applying consistently in their lives and the world. Values act as lodestars, helping provide more or less consistent orientations in decision-making (e.g., Schwartz and Bilsky 1987). Some values are very difficult to implement, such as the near-universal Golden Rule,[1] so they bear constant reminding through sermons and other communication mechanisms. The critical difference in this approach compared to the previous one is the possibility of course corrections. If religion is concerned with living up to a set of standards, then some degree of attitudinal and behavioral change would result from reminders about how adherents and/or institutions are falling short of the ultimate goal. In its most forthright, blunt form, we can think of this perspective as including prophets, figures of great import in the Christian Bible, who communicated messages of judgment and promise.

These perspectives on religion may not be antagonistic. Groups and their representatives may mobilize to witness prophetically to society to live up to the standards the groups have adopted (e.g., end abortion, stop drinking, house the homeless, protect the rivers). Studying the fact of organizational mobilization tells us very little about religious influence, however. We still do not know if the end policy goal was the important thing or if it was some facet of religion that mobilized people. Therefore, the analytically important question is whether religion can change the hearts and minds of followers. If religion cannot do that, it loses its independence and is essentially reduced to a co-optable organizational form—the platoon ready for deployment. If religion's influence is robust, it will maintain independence and will remain somewhat aloof from co-optation from other organizations (such as political parties) that may not live up to expectations set forth by faith communities.

---

1. For instance, in the Christian Bible, it can be found in numerous places, such as Luke 6:31 (Sermon on the Mount); it is found in the Quran and in other commentaries (Qur'an 83:1–6: "be just as you would love to have justice!").

I have a few goals for this chapter. First, I review a communications perspective to establish a cornerstone for evaluating religious influence (for more on this, see Djupe and Calfano 2013, 2019). Without a sense of information exposure and adoption, we cannot hope to have a causal understanding of religion or an accurate description of just what religious actors and organizations are doing. Second, I will review some evidence to document what religious actors have been saying as a way of thinking about how religious actors interface with political parties. This is all in service of making some comments about the overarching project of evaluating religious authority, which by most all intuitions (if not evidence) has declined across time.

The Communications Perspective

Religion is a relational enterprise. It is a system for organizing people around mutual care and a set of beliefs, symbols, values, positions, and identities. For religion to engage the world in coherent ways, instructions need to be coordinated and delivered. Those instructions articulate the content of beliefs, symbols, values, and positions and how they attach to each other and to attitude objects outside of the group (e.g., government, officials, and public policy). People need to be in attendance and attentive to receive those lessons, which people may allow to affect their thinking and acting. This is the essence of religious influence—it involves exposure to communicative acts and adoption processes. There's nothing particularly earth-shattering about this perspective. It lies at the heart of elite and media studies more generally (e.g., Zaller 1992) and is increasingly seen in studies of religion and politics (e.g., Djupe and Gilbert 2009; Leege et al. 2002; McClendon and Riedl 2019; Smith 2019).[2]

It is essential to capture these elements since without them we are left with more questions than answers. For example, let's consider the role of the belief in hard work as a biblical commandment. It is entirely possible that people will reason independently through their belief in working hard (e.g., "Whatever your hand finds to do, do it with your might" Ecclesiastes 9:10) to lead them to oppose the welfare state since it undermines the command to work with all your might. But communication from religious sources, such as clergy, can play a critical role that bears on religious influ-

---

2. A range of other studies have examined what people hear from clergy and why, including Brown et al. (2017); Brown, Kaiser, and Jackson (2014); Hmielowski, Chanjung, and Kim (2015); Nteta and Wallsten (2012); and Scheitle and Cornell (2015).

ence and helps us sketch out a communication-oriented research agenda around exposure and adoption. It could be the case that clergy (and here clergy are an example of a religious information source) preach about that belief and its application to society, highlighting the ills of the modern welfare state or arguing about the failure of capitalism to support this biblical mandate—to give people meaningful work. If clergy successfully fulfill this role, then beliefs do not have an automatic translation to attitudes and may, instead, hinge on elite interpretation.

But it is also possible that a sermon provides both a position on a public problem as well as a religious justification for it (perhaps similar to the revelation of process seen in the Santorum experiment from chapter 3). In such a case, is it truly important that the justification is included? Is it enough for the position to have come from a presumably credible source? It is also possible that the policy position comes without a specific biblical grounding and perhaps the person stumbles upon Ecclesiastes later. Obviously, political position taking is in the driver's seat in this scenario and religion or religious justification is entirely endogenous (a result of politics and not its cause). There are further complications to consider, of course, but these are enough to demonstrate the importance of studying exposure to information from religious sources. The timing and content of communication are critical to knowing whether religion is a critically active or redundant force in public life.

Adoption is dependent on exposure. Ideas do not come from the void but are supplied for consideration. Without a convincing dose of exposure, we cannot be sure that religious influence over adoption is true. And even then, in a highly mediated world, we still may not be sure that a religious source was the influential one; the source could easily have been secular in nature—a politician, the mass media, or someone else. At the very least, it is possible to say that holding a belief or attitude is consistent with confident exposure.

Adoption is not an automatic consequence of exposure. The simple stereotype of religious people, that they adopt whatever their clergy say, is far from reality. Instead, research with independent measurements of what clergy say has found little to no influence (Djupe and Gilbert 2009; Smith 2008), though experimental studies are more likely to have found effects (e.g., Condra, Isaqzadeh, and Linardi 2019; Wallsten and Nteta 2016; but there are limits: Djupe, Neiheisel, and Olson 2015).

It is not necessary to study only policy communication from religious elites. In fact, the finding that clergy had so little persuasive influence motivated the study of alternate routes to policy influence, most notably through priming beliefs and values. Priming is essentially a reminder, which could be subtle or overt, that raises some information into your thought processes. Priming a belief that God is in control, for instance, has been found to increase support for income redistribution (Be'ery and Bloom 2015) and foreign policy interventions (Glazier 2013).

There are several ways of gaining more confidence in exposure that dovetail with our desire to define the limits of religious influence. First, we can strategically pick issues that are new, and, hence, citizens are likely to have no well-developed priors that would compete with new information and arguments. We can also look for examples of religious organizations advocating for policy (and hence looking for attitudinal) change. So, when the National Association of Evangelicals took a stance in favor of environmental protection in 2003, it was an example of advocating for a change from the previous antagonism or indifference they had asserted toward the environment. Of course, by 2003 evangelical identifiers already had opinions about environmental protection (and mostly opposed), so the new line of argument competed with those established views, which allows us to gain a measure of religious influence (see Djupe and Gwiasda 2010).

Given the difficulty of capturing exposure confidently, certain research designs recommend themselves to assess adoption processes. Randomized experiments are an obvious choice (for reviews, see Djupe and Calfano 2013; Djupe and Smith 2019). Naturally, experimenters can be confident about exposure since they supply some stimuli themselves (though, of course, some participants may not be paying attention). Then, given the controlled exposure, researchers can be confident that it affected the attitude or behavior of interest. It is important to note that participants may not be cognizant of what the exposure was even as it influenced them in some way. This means that simply asking them what they've been exposed to is no silver bullet for pursuing the communicative perspective to religious influence. In fact, Djupe and Gilbert (2009) document the widespread misperception that individuals have about what political issues their own clergy have talked about recently. Still, perceptual measures are often a necessary and useful shortcut, even as they will necessarily fail to capture the actual amount of exposure. There are many possible avenues of the communications perspective to explore. For now, I'll move through some types of exposure data that are seldom shown to help us think about the likely role of religion in society, as discussed at the chapter's beginning.

Questions appropriate to tap a relational view of religion are not often asked in national surveys, which overwhelmingly focus on individual religious beliefs and behaviors. Originally inspired by clergy surveying (e.g.,

Guth et al. 1997), I have been regularly inserting batteries of questions asking if citizens have heard their clergy talking about various public policy issues and political figures. I was also curious to get a sense of how supportive congregations and clergy are of President Donald Trump. These questions were asked in a fall 2016 panel survey, a May 2017 survey, and another conducted in May 2018.[3] I focus here on the three largest Christian traditions so the estimates are more reliable given their larger sample size. I will also consult data from a clergy survey that Brian Calfano and I conducted in 2014.

Perceived Reception of Political Communication

So, what are congregants hearing and how has it changed over time? Figure 10.1 shows the percentage of each white Christian group that reported hearing their clergy talk about each issue. It is immediately clear, with a few exceptions, that reports have declined since 2016—the high-water mark. Multiple issues show a 10 percent drop from 2016, including abortion, Donald Trump, religious freedom, and gay rights. This is surprising given the reluctance of religious groups, for the most part, to engage in electoral politics. But it's more surprising given the issues salient across this time period that touched deep cultural nerves: the "Muslim ban," the continued aftermath of the *Obergefell* decision legalizing same-sex marriage (as conservative Christians have refused to serve LGBTQ Americans in a variety of contexts), and continued controversy about immigration, including a border wall and family separation. The most commonly heard issue by evangelicals, aside from participating in politics, was religious freedom, which peaked at 42 percent in May 2017. Evangelicals were also more likely to hear clergy discuss religious freedom and gay rights together—just over double the rate that Catholics and mainline Protestants reported.

But, some of the most contentious issues in American politics over this period were heard by very small numbers of congregants. Islam in America, which would presumably capture any discussion of Muslims, was heard by 10 percent or fewer Americans in these religious groups. Immigration was only heard by less than 20 percent of all groups, and that proportion declined over time.

---

3. For these surveys, we contracted with Qualtrics Panels to supply respondents. This means the data are not the result of random sampling. But, after placing representative gender and region quotas, the distributions look very close to the general population. In any event, I only examine group experiences, focusing on partisanship and religious traditions.

On this basis, what should we make of polling results that describe evangelicals' attitudes about immigration? For instance, Burton (2018) reports that 75 percent of white evangelicals believed the crackdown on undocumented immigrants was a positive thing and 68 percent thought that the US had no responsibility to take in refugees. It would be easy to assume that religious figures, following the Evangelical Advisory Council's lead, were following the Trump administration's line on this. But, at least from the perspective of people in the pews, their clergy were essentially silent. That means that white Christians are effectively ceding the communications field to partisan and media elites or national religious elites like Rev. Robert Jeffress, who publicly backed Trump's immigration policies (Young 2018).

That's a striking finding on its own that resonates with 1960s-era complaints from sociologists that the clergy were too quiescent, too silent on the pressing issues of the day (Stark et al. 1971). One of the reasons why clergy were silent during that period is that their colleagues who spoke up often faced considerable headwinds from their congregants who did not want to hear liberal advocacy on civil rights and the Vietnam War (and there is reason to suspect a similar dynamic exists today, even among clergy with substantial institutional protections—see Calfano, Michelson, and Oldmixon 2017). As a result of such advocacy efforts, many congregants reduced their participation and giving or simply left (Hadden 1969; Quinley 1974). Disagreement still drives at least marginal affiliates out of congregations (Djupe, Neiheisel, and Sokhey 2018), so it is no surprise that clergy engage in political communication reluctantly given the risks.

But this pattern reveals perhaps an even more dire story about religious influence. People develop defenses against the prophetic politics of clergy, which urges people to have a change of heart. Very few clergy are talking about immigration politics despite a political environment that is saturated with it; and white Christians have adopted political views that are in line with the Republican Party's current positioning. So not only does this mark a rejection of where evangelical elites might want to lead their denominations (e.g., Moore 2011; see also Evangelical Immigration Table 2019), as well as a failure of congregational clergy to try, but it also suggests that whatever religious beliefs and values are present have not undermined support of the family separation policy, opposition to refugee hosting, and embrace of a position that sees immigration as a net negative for the country.

It is important to assess how a perceived agenda from clergy lines up with partisanship. If religious communication is driving partisan decision-

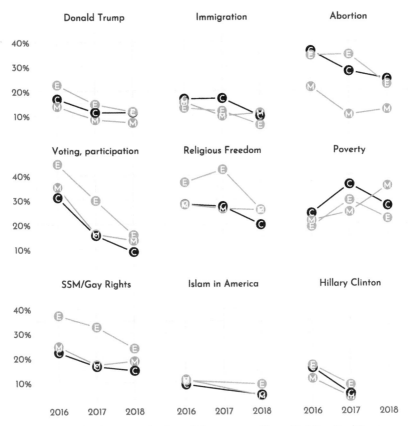

Fig. 10.1. Perceived Communication of Clergy across Three Christian Traditions, 2016–18

making, which was polarized on many issues in 2016, then we would expect to see sizeable differences in issue communication between partisan groups. Instead, figure 10.2 shows generally small differences. On most issues—immigration is a prime example—partisans report the same percentage of their clergy discussing the issue. That's true about culture war issues as well. There is a small, less than 10-point gap between Democrats and Republicans reporting their clergy addressing gay rights and only a slightly larger gap on abortion – abortion has the largest gap in this collection of issues.

Figure 10.2, using data collected during the 2016 election in September and November, also shows that there is no issue discussed by a majority of clergy, though substantial minorities discussed several key items: civility, religious freedom, and the importance of political participation. While

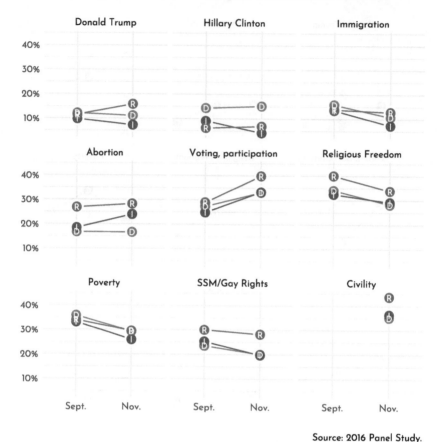

Source: 2016 Panel Study.

Fig. 10.2. How Partisans Report Clergy Issue Communication, 2016 Panel Data

religious freedom was an important politicized issue in the wake of the 2015 *Obergefell* decision and state and organizational reactions to it (Wilson and Djupe 2020), the others might be said to define the boundaries of citizenship. While I do not know exactly what was said with respect to civility, Trump's campaign behavior certainly centered that topic of conversation. Political participation is clearly of perennial importance, and clergy regularly exhort their congregants to be involved (Djupe and Gilbert 2003; Guth et al. 1997).

Note the low levels of mentioning particular candidates. Clergy tend to be loath to connect their ministries to particular candidates. There was an uptick in mentions of Trump during the general election among Republicans, but the numbers are quite low (16 percent). That helps confirm that clergy would like to maintain some distance from political parties. The evidence also suggests a few other tentative conclusions. Religious communication is not closely aligned with partisanship, which probably means that religious organizations are largely passengers on partisan trains rather than their conductors. Only further evidence involving what clergy think and say will help us build this story with more confidence.

How Clergy Talk about Issues

But where do clergy actually stand on immigration policy? To this point, these data have only shown whether clergy talked about immigration and not where they stood. I'll pivot away from congregant perceptions to what clergy actually report thinking *and* saying in 2014. We tried to gather some of the more common frames available in the immigration debate of that time in the Obama administration, which almost produced bipartisan immigration reform, and offered them to clergy, asking, "We'd like to ask if you have MENTIONED each argument in public discussion (or something like it—please be generous to our wording) and if you AGREE with each argument (generally speaking)." This measurement approach helps us know which arguments were most common, whether clergy argued in favor of or in opposition to arguments, and how diverse their argumentation was. It's an incredibly rich set of data.

Figure 10.3 shows how often clergy mentioned each frame and what portion of the sample agreed with each argument. We need to now dispense with the assumption that clergy will make their opinions public. There are many frames that most clergy in this sample agree with, but few communicated them in public. For instance, there is widespread support (68 percent) for the Evangelical Immigration Table talking point that "We need an immigration policy that is tough, fair, and practical." But only 26 percent reported mentioning it. This is not a surprise in some ways, because most of this sample (94.5 percent) reported having no idea what the Evangelical Immigration Table was (Djupe 2017b).[4]

The most commonly reported frames (frames 11–13) were also the most platitudinous. They define the bare minimums of an immigration policy—that they treat people with respect, with dignity, and consistent

---

4. The Evangelical Immigration Table is a well-funded evangelical elite organization that advocates for immigration reform very similar to the policy that passed the (Democratically controlled) Senate in 2014. It ran radio ads, provided educational materials, and engaged in other traditional forms of advocacy. It is still in existence in 2019.

with the Golden Rule. This is not getting in the weeds of the immigration debate. Instead, it provides evidence consistent with how Alexis de Tocqueville ([1835] 1945) thought that religion functioned in the 1830s-era US. Religion worked indirectly to "confine the imagination of the Americans within certain limits." Rather than advocating directly, "religion exercises but little influence upon the laws and upon the details of public opinion; but it directs the customs of the community, and, by regulating domestic life, it regulates the state."

But clearly there are (a few) clergy who do get in the weeds. The average level of engagement in this sample is the mention of four frames, and many of those include reminders to treat people with dignity and respect. But there is a distinct minority that mentioned more. Fully 10 percent reported mentioning ten or more of these frames, while 40 percent mentioned five or more. On the flip side, 25 percent of this sample reported mentioning none of these frames in public.

It is perhaps notable that relatively few clergy in this sample agree with or have mentioned something close to Republican talking points—that immigrants are a drain on government services, take away jobs, and undermine local culture. To be sure, I examined how partisan clergy stand on the frames—figure 10.4 shows the level of agreement among Democratic and Republican clergy in the sample (independents, not shown, floated in between them, sometimes closer to Democrats, sometimes closer to Republicans).

There is no doubt that Republicans and Democrats have their differences, but they hold quite a bit in common as well. Consistent with Tocqueville's expectations, both partisan clergy groups agree in overwhelming proportions with the baseline conditions of treating people with dignity. But they also agree with the principle of protecting the family, respecting the rule of law, and treating the stranger as yourself. The clergy here tend to disagree about more traditional political ideology, such as whether immigrants deserve access to basic government services (though, it is important to note, a slim majority of Republican clergy agree). The greatest disagreement comes over whether illegal immigration needs to be stopped, but clergy are also divided over whether to crack down on businesses and individuals, as well as whether immigrants take away jobs. While there are gaps on the Republican talking points (bottom three items), Republican clergy are themselves divided on them, and only the perceived negative effect of immigration on the supply of jobs enjoys (slim) majority support.

That's a key insight because it is precisely the argument space where

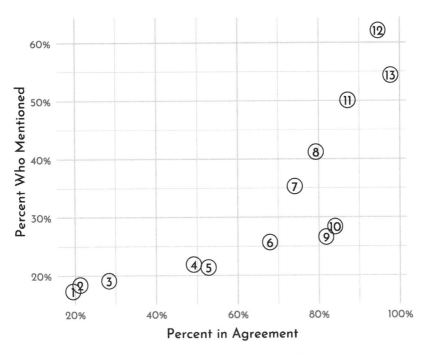

Fig. 10.3. Distribution of Clergy's Mention and Agreement with Various Immigration Frames

Republican clergy could push back against the party line. As it stands, however, these are the least frequently mentioned arguments in the list (see arguments 1–3 in fig. 10.3). The problem is compounded when we dig a bit deeper. There is no difference in the amount of mentions by agreement among Democrats—20 percent of those who agree or disagree mentioned the argument "Immigrants drain our community of scarce resources." However, the gap among Republicans is huge—26 percent of those who agree with it (which 39 percent did) mentioned the argument, but only 8 percent of those who disagreed with it (61 percent) mentioned the argument. This highlights the degree to which the political environment inhibits religious witness—clergy are often not secure enough in the religious marketplace to challenge the dominant political status quo in the community. Instead, there's some evidence that they change their tune to conform with the community when they face pressure over membership (Smith 2016) or face disagreement in the pews (Djupe and Friesen 2018).

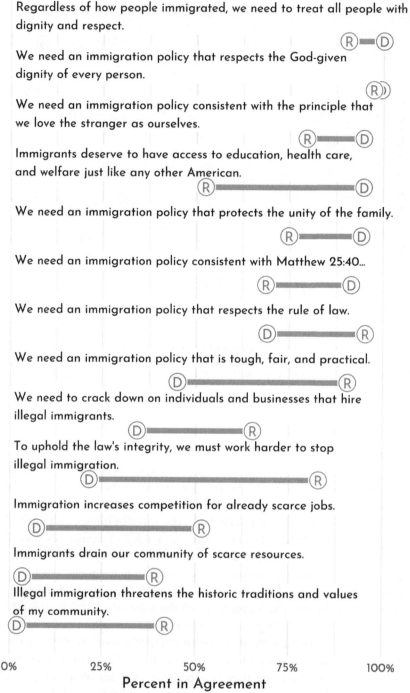

Regardless of how people immigrated, we need to treat all people with dignity and respect.

We need an immigration policy that respects the God-given dignity of every person.

We need an immigration policy consistent with the principle that we love the stranger as ourselves.

Immigrants deserve to have access to education, health care, and welfare just like any other American.

We need an immigration policy that protects the unity of the family.

We need an immigration policy consistent with Matthew 25:40...

We need an immigration policy that respects the rule of law.

We need an immigration policy that is tough, fair, and practical.

We need to crack down on individuals and businesses that hire illegal immigrants.

To uphold the law's integrity, we must work harder to stop illegal immigration.

Immigration increases competition for already scarce jobs.

Immigrants drain our community of scarce resources.

Illegal immigration threatens the historic traditions and values of my community.

0%   25%   50%   75%   100%

Percent in Agreement

Source: 2014 Clergy Survey

Fig. 10.4. How Partisan Clergy View Immigration Frames: Some Daylight but Few Chasms

White Christians Take on Trump

If there was ever a time for religious witness, it was with Trump's candidacy. That's hyperbole, of course, because there are a great many injustices in the world that call out for someone to notice and provide a call to action. Trump is a morally flawed human who ran a morally flawed campaign. There were many reasons for conservatives to back his candidacy, including his promise to appoint conservative judges and pursue an end to abortion in America. That does not mean, of course, that his personal story and conduct on the campaign trail did not invite critical reflection.

Brian Calfano and I were in the field a week before the election, surveying just over one thousand white Christians about the election, with a focus on what they were hearing in their congregations. The survey began with an experiment involving a portion of an op-ed by the editor of *Christianity Today*, a widely known evangelical news and commentary outlet. On October 10, editor Andy Crouch (2016) took the following position:

> We are not indifferent when the gospel is at stake. The gospel is of infinitely greater importance than any campaign. There is hardly any public person in America today than Trump who has more exemplified the "earthly nature" that Paul urges the Colossians to shed: "sexual immorality, impurity, lust, evil desires, and greed, which is idolatry" (3:5). Enthusiasm for a candidate like Trump gives our neighbors ample reason to doubt that we believe Jesus is Lord.

At this late stage of the campaign, the experiment had no effect on attitudes toward Trump or about his electability (compared to a control with no statement).

This isn't surprising given that people had long before decided who they would vote for primarily because that decision was dictated by partisanship. Republicans support Republican candidates, and Democrats support Democratic candidates. In this heavily polarized environment, with quite a lot of social distance between the parties, it is not surprising that there is little room for political heresy committed by religious elites who argue, "Evangelicals, of all people, should not be silent about Donald Trump's blatant immorality" (Crouch 2016).

The experiment ensured that some people were exposed to a #NeverTrump-style argument that our chapter in *The Evangelical Crackup* (Djupe and Calfano 2018) indicated might be a rare event. To what extent were clergy in these white Christian traditions addressing Trump in their congregations? I'm turning back to perceptual data—self-reports of people providing their perception of what their pastor said and where they stand on Trump. But I want to issue a caveat first. These perceptions are filled with error due to faulty memory, projection of their own views, lack of attendance to hear the available cues, and misperception of disagreement. Still, they give us a sense of whether people can report clergy communication about Trump.

Only 18 percent of the sample (among churchgoing, white Christians) reported hearing their clergy addressing Trump. The figures were a bit different among the three Christian traditions: 17 percent of Catholics, 23 percent of evangelicals, and only 14 percent of mainline Protestants reported their clergy addressing Trump. Therefore, it was simply not a common thing to do.

Figure 10.5 reports how supportive clergy were perceived to be of Trump. In each case, there was some variation in support for Trump among those who addressed him, but the average was consistently (and significantly) higher by ten to fifteen points among those who addressed Trump versus those who did not. Note that the majority of mainline Protestants and Catholics saw their clergy as less than fully supportive—their median is below 50 on the 0–100 scale. Only among evangelicals do they see their clergy as supportive, on balance, but those who addressed Trump in some way were clearly the most supportive (mean of 62, median of 70).

> These results reinforce the story from the clergy data discussed above. Clergy are reticent about taking on political issues and candidates when they disagree with them, especially if that stance would set them apart from the congregation and community. The costs of lost or waning membership and the problems it may make for outreach to new potential members are simply too great to bear. One might argue that this is simply a case of clergy thinking it inappropriate to address political candidates, though I found a similar result above using immigration attitudes that did not explicitly involve a candidate.

Clergy are not the only source from which people in the pews receive political information from a religious source. They are surrounded by information sources. There are numerous ways in which political cues are available in congregations, from knee-level surveys of the parking lot (bumper stickers) to discussion at coffee hour after a service to formal group

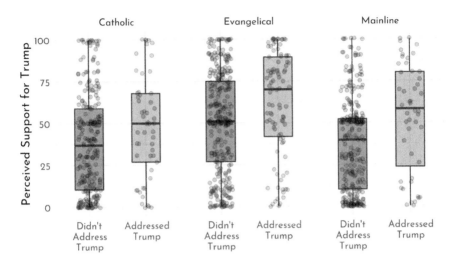

Source: Week Prior to the 2016 Election Survey

Fig. 10.5. Minority of Clergy Who Addressed Trump Were More Supportive of Him

involvement where social and political issues are discussed (e.g., Djupe and Gilbert 2009; Schwadel 2005). It is also quite likely that people map their own and the community's political distribution onto their congregation.

The upshot is that clergy are, in effect, competing with hundreds of other people for attention and influence. That leads to two propositions. First, it is unlikely that clergy will run up hard against the congregation, so they will soft-pedal their views or simply not pedal them at all. Second, it may be difficult for congregants to perceive accurately the views of clergy that do not resonate with the congregation. As such, certainty of the perceived views of the clergy should hinge on whether they line up with the congregation for both exposure and adoption reasons.

Figure 10.6 shows just this, but let me walk you through this, as there are a number of moving parts.[5] The y-axis shows the level of certainty (1 = very uncertain, 5 = very certain) congregants have about their perceptions of their clergy's support for Trump. The x-axis shows their perception of how supportive the congregation is of Trump. The dashed line is for clergy

_____

5. This analysis is from a different survey of 957 people that was run just after the 2016 election, gathered with Anand Sokhey and Amanda Friesen.

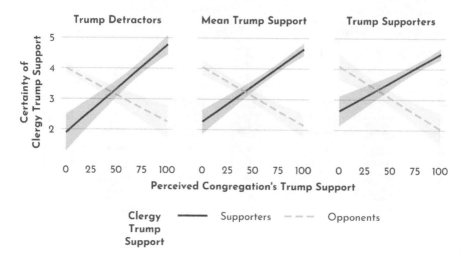

Fig. 10.6. Certainty about Their Clergy's Support Level for Trump Was Highest at the Poles

who are perceived to be unsupportive of Trump (support level of less than 50), while the solid line is for clergy who are supportive (>50). Finally, the panels show the survey respondent's support level collapsed down to opponents and supporters (in the same way the clergy were parsed).

Certainty about the clergy's views does not shift based on the respondents' views—we see the same pattern across the three panels. Instead, they fluctuate drastically given how the clergy's perceived views resonate with the perceived congregation's views toward Trump. In each graph panel, certainty is highest when clergy opponents are in congregations least supportive of Trump; certainty about clergy as Trump opponents declines as the congregation is seen as more supportive of Trump. The reverse is true of clergy supportive of Trump—certainty is highest in Trump-supportive congregations.

I find the same basic pattern when looking at reports of clergy addressing Trump as well—clergy are perceived to have addressed him when they have supportive congregations (evidence not shown). Again, the precise reasons for these patterns are opaque. We can't be completely certain whether these patterns are produced by clergy tailoring their communication to their audience or as the result of perceptual screens. The truth is surely that some of each is in play, and both serve to undermine even the possibility of religious influence.

Discussion

Trump's 2016 election with enormous levels of support from white evangelicals was a gift to the social scientific study of religion (Djupe and Claassen 2018). Here was a candidate who did not provide any credible evidence that he was religious (let alone evangelical) or display any developed sense of a personal morality. Evangelicals flocked to him, not without dissent from a few, and embraced not just his politics but him as well. They did not "hold their noses" and vote for his promises to end abortion—they actually liked him (e.g., Djupe 2017a). On top of that is one of the more remarkable about-faces that I have seen in polling. According to polling from the Public Religion Research Institute, 30 percent of white evangelicals in 2011 agreed that "an elected official who commits an immoral act in their personal life can still behave ethically and fulfill their duties in their public and professional life." By fall 2016, fully 72 percent of white evangelicals agreed (Kurtzleben 2016). The reversal is all the more dramatic given that the pivot is clearly meant to protect their support for Trump and because it runs counter to what has been the center of evangelical thought about humanity, let alone leadership. It can be shown in the widespread support among evangelicals for the "individualist" notion that bringing society to Christ will cure social ills (e.g., Guth et al. 1997).

Therefore, I propose that it is the *lack of engagement* (e.g., the lack of communication) of evangelical clergy that paved the way for the close ties between white evangelicals and Trump. To be sure, this process was not a creation of 2015–16 and has been going on for quite a while, despite increasing political involvement of evangelicals (e.g., Guth et al. 1997). Here's my argument in one (long) sentence: Idiosyncratic issue discussion and a reticence to challenge the politics of their flocks, combined with an individualist social theology that people know what is right given their faith commitments, enable external organizations (e.g., political parties) offering consistent frames, a directed sense of threat, and specific collective action steps to sway believers. It seems clear at this juncture that evangelicals are, on average, loyal Republicans, more committed to their candidates than they are to the faith tradition.

Of course, this is a distinctive time in American politics, marked by deep polarization, wide gulfs in political ideology (at least on an American scale), and consistent minority control by Republicans. Ongoing demographic diversification and urbanization continue to sound warning bells to white Americans, as do rapidly changing standards with respect to LGBTQ rights, that their influence is waning. This is to say that the political envi-ronment is placing enormous pressure on white Christians through out-group threat amped by ingroup partisan communication and identity that provides little room for religious organizations to maneuver. This is not the only time in history when these pressures have come together, but it is important to note that it has not always been this way.

I promised I would lay out a communications perspective on religious influence, show some seldom-seen evidence about who hears what and who says what, and then reflect on what this evidence has to say about the role of religion in society. Obviously, there is not just one role but many pos-sible roles. That said, I can venture some thoughts about what the weight of the evidence has to say at this point.

From the perspective of people who attend white Christian congrega-tions in the US, they hear relatively little about public policy. Given ever-shrinking attendance rates among most everyone aside from evangelicals, the average affiliate is simply not present to hear most of what clergy say. Congregants also suffer from biased attention and recall, which works against hearing, especially, disagreeable information. Substantial minorities hear clergy talk about some issues that tend to be salient in campaigns—civility, religious freedom, and getting involved in 2016. This is appropri-ate, but it also means that cues from religious sources are competing with those from the saturated political environment. The content of their cues is up for debate but from this limited analysis seems to suggest consider-able self-censoring, especially on issues in play (see also Brown et al. 2017).

Congregations in the US continue to supply their congregants with opportunities to work face-to-face with others and to practice valuable skills that can boost congregant political involvement. But without an organization and its elites assertively promoting their independence, it is relatively easy for party organizations to co-opt religious networks for their own purposes (see also Mantilla 2021). My read of the evidence is that religion in the US has a very difficult time asserting its independence. Given its competition for members of the community, congregations are reticent to challenge the status quo and will promote individualism (live and let live) before religious elites try to change hearts and minds. This is arguably less true with the Catholic Church, which stubbornly continues to advocate issue positions that cross partisan lines and provides institu-tional backing for clergy to take less than popular stands (Calfano 2009; Calfano, Oldmixon, and Gray 2014; but see Holman and Shockley 2017). But it certainly seems to hold for evangelicals (and perhaps mainline Prot-estants who are not widely engaging in prophetic politics), who appear not to challenge their members to live up to and hold policy positions consistent with long-standing ideals that may conflict with their political party.

REFERENCES

Be'ery, Gilad, and Pazit Ben-Nun Bloom. 2015. "God and the Welfare State - Substitutes or Complements? An Experimental Test of the Effect of Belief in God's Control." *PLoS ONE* 10 (6).

Beyerlein, Kraig, and Mark Chaves. 2003. "The Political Activities of Religious Congregations in the United States." *Journal for the Scientific Study of Religion* 42 (2): 229–46.

Brown, R. Khari, Angela Kaiser, and James S. Jackson. 2014. "Worship Discourse and White Race-Based Policy Attitudes." *Review of Religious Research* 56:291–312.

Brown, R. Khari, Angela Kaiser, Lara Rusch, and Ronald E. Brown. 2017. "Immigrant-Conscious Congregations: Race, Ethnicity, and the Rejection of Anti-Immigrant Frames." *Politics & Religion* 10:887–905.

Burton, Tara I. 2018. "The Bible Says to Welcome Immigrants. So Why Don't White Evangelicals?" Vox, October 30. https://www.vox.com/2018/10/30/180 35336/white-evangelicals-immigration-nationalism-christianity-refugee-hond uras-migrant

Calfano, Brian R. 2009. "Choosing Constituent Cues: Reference Group Influence on Clergy Political Speech." *Social Science Quarterly* 90:88–102.

Calfano, Brian R., Melissa R. Michelson, and Elizabeth A. Oldmixon. 2017. *A Matter of Discretion: The Politics of Catholic Priests in the United States and Ireland.* Rowman & Littlefield.

Calfano, Brian R., Elizabeth A. Oldmixon, and Mark Gray. 2014. "Strategically Prophetic Priests: An Analysis of Competing Principal Influence on Clergy Political Action." *Review of Religious Research* 56:1–21.

Condra, Luke N., Mohammad Isaqzadeh, and Sera Linardi. 2019. "Clerics and Scriptures: Experimentally Disentangling the Influence of Religious Authority in Afghanistan." *British Journal of Political Science* 49:401–19.

Crouch, Andy. 2016. "Speak Truth to Trump." *Christianity Today*, October 10. https://www.christianitytoday.com/ct/2016/october-web-only/speak-truth-to -trump.html

Djupe, Paul A. 2017a. "Did Evangelicals Hold Their Noses and Vote for Trump?" Religion in Public, July 27. https://religioninpublic.blog/2017/07/27/did-evan gelicals-hold-their-noses/

Djupe, Paul A. 2017b. "What Is Religious Influence? Perspectives on the Legacy of the Evangelical Immigration Table." Religion in Public, January 26. https://reli gioninpublic.blog/2017/01/26/what_is_religious_influence/

Djupe, Paul A. 2020. "Religion in the Trump Era: The End to Religious Influence or the Beginning?" In *Interest Group Politics*, 10th ed., edited by Allan J. Cigler, Burdett A. Loomis, and Anthony J. Nownes. Lanham, MD: Rowman & Littlefield.

Djupe, Paul A., and Brian R. Calfano. 2013. *God Talk: Experimenting with the Religious Causes of Public Opinion*. Philadelphia: Temple University Press.

Djupe, Paul A., and Brian R. Calfano. 2018. "Evangelicals Were On Their Own in the 2016 Elections." In *The Evangelical Crackup? The Future of the Evangelical-Republican Coalition*, edited by Paul A. Djupe and Ryan L. Claassen. Philadelphia: Temple University Press.

Djupe, Paul A., and Brian R. Calfano. 2019. "Communication Dynamics in Religion and Political Behavior." In *Oxford Encyclopedia of Politics & Religion*, edited by Paul A. Djupe, Mark Rozell, and Ted G. Jelen, 209–24. New York: Oxford University Press.

Djupe, Paul A., and Ryan L. Claassen. 2018. *The Evangelical Crackup? The Future of the Evangelical-Republican Coalition*. Philadelphia: Temple University Press.

Djupe, Paul A., and Amanda J. Friesen. 2018. "Moralizing to the Choir: The Moral Foundations of American Clergy." *Social Science Quarterly* 99:665–82.

Djupe, Paul A., and Christopher P. Gilbert. 2003. *The Prophetic Pulpit: Clergy, Churches, and Communities in American Politics*. Lanham, MD: Rowman & Littlefield.

Djupe, Paul A., and Christopher P. Gilbert. 2009. *The Political Influence of Churches*. New York: Cambridge University Press.

Djupe, Paul A., and Gregory W. Gwiasda. 2010. "Evangelizing the Environment: Decision Process Effects in Political Persuasion." *Journal for the Scientific Study of Religion* 49:73–86.

Djupe, Paul A., Jacob R. Neiheisel, and Laura R. Olson. 2015. "Carriers of the Creed: The Effect of Urging Tolerance on Persuasion." In *Religion and Political Tolerance in America: Advances in the State of the Art*, edited by Paul A. Djupe, 183–99. Philadelphia: Temple University Press.

Djupe, Paul A., Jacob R. Neiheisel, and Anand E. Sokhey. 2018. "Reconsidering the Role of Politics in Leaving Religion—The Importance of Affiliation." *American Journal of Political Science* 62:161–75.

Djupe, Paul A., and Amy Erica Smith. 2019. "Experimentation in the Study of Religion and Politics." In *Oxford Encyclopedia of Politics & Religion*, edited by Paul A. Djupe, Mark Rozell, and Ted G. Jelen, 337–56. New York: Oxford University Press.

Glazier, Rebecca A. 2013. "Divine Direction: How Providential Religious Beliefs Shape Foreign Policy Attitudes." *Foreign Policy Analysis* 9:127–42.

Guth, James L., John C. Green, Corwin E. Smidt, Lyman A. Kellstedt, and Margaret M. Poloma. 1997. *The Bully Pulpit: The Politics of Protestant Clergy*. Lawrence: University of Kansas Press.

Hadden, Jeffrey K. 1969. *The Gathering Storm in the Churches*. Garden City, NY: Doubleday.

Hmielowski, Jay D., K. Chanjung, and S. Kim. 2015. "Engaging the Congregation: Examining the Conditional Indirect Effects of Religious Leaders' Cues on Environmental Behavior." *Journal of Communication and Religion* 38:51–66.

Holman, Mirya R., and Kristen Shockley. 2017. "Messages from Above: Conflict and Convergence of Messages to the Catholic Voter from the Catholic Church Hierarchy." *Politics & Religion* 10:840–61.

Kurtzleben, Danielle. 2016. "POLL: White Evangelicals Have Warmed to Politicians Who Commit 'Immoral' Acts." NPR, October 23. https://www.npr.org/2016/10/23/498890836/poll-white-evangelicals-have-warmed-to-politicians-who-commit-immoral-acts

Leege, David C., Kenneth D. Wald, and Brian S. Krueger. 2002. *The Politics of Cultural Differences: Social Change and Voter Mobilization Strategies in the Post-New Deal Period.* Princeton: Princeton University Press.

Mantilla, L. Felipe. 2021. *How Political Parties Mobilize Religion: Lessons from Mexico and Turkey.* Philadelphia: Temple University Press.

McClendon, Gwyneth H., and Rachel B. Riedl. 2015. "Religion as a Stimulant of Political Participation: Experimental Evidence from Nairobi, Kenya." *Journal of Politics* 77:1045–57.

McClendon, Gwyneth H., and Rachel B. Riedl. 2019. *From Pews to Politics: Religious Sermons and Political Participation in Africa.* New York: Cambridge University Press.

Moore, Russell. 2011. "Immigration and the Gospel." Russell Moore (website), June 17. https://www.russellmoore.com/2011/06/17/immigration-and-the-gospel/

Nteta, Tatishe M., and Kevin J. Wallsten. 2012. "Preaching to the Choir: Religious Leaders and American Opinion on Immigration Reform." *Social Science Quarterly* 93:891–910.

Quinley, Harold E. 1974. *The Prophetic Clergy: Social Activism among Protestant Ministers.* New York: Wiley.

Scheitle, Christoher P., and Nicole Cornell. 2015. "Hearing Clergy Speak about Social and Political Issues: Examining the Effect of Religious Tradition and Personal Interest." *Social Science Quarterly* 96:148–60.

Schwadel, Philip. 2005. "Individual, Congregational, and Denominational Effects on Church Members' Civic Participation." *Journal for the Scientific Study of Religion* 44:159–71.

Schwartz, Shalom H., and Wolfgang Bilsky. 1987. "Toward a Universal Psychological Structure of Human Values." *Journal of Personality and Social Psychology* 53:550–62.

Smith, Amy E. 2016. "When Clergy Are Threatened: Catholic and Protestant Leaders and Political Activism in Brazil." *Politics & Religion* 9:431–55.

Smith, Amy E. 2019. *Religion and Brazilian Democracy: Mobilizing the People of God.* New York: Cambridge University Press.

Smith, Gregory A. 2008. *Politics in the Parish: The Political Influence of Catholic Priests.* Washington, DC: Georgetown University Press.

Stark, Rodney, Bruce D. Foster, Charles Y. Glock, and Harold Quinley. 1971. *Wayward Shepherds: Prejudice and the Protestant Clergy.* New York: Harper and Row.

Tocqueville, Alexis de. (1835) 1945. "Indirect Influence of Religious Opinions Upon Political Society in the United States." In *Democracy in America*, volume 1, chapter 17. New York: Alfred A. Knopf.

Verba, Sidney, Kay Lehman Schlozman, and Henry E. Brady. 1995. *Voice and Equality: Civic Voluntarism in American Politics.* Cambridge, MA: Harvard University Press.

Wallsten, Kevin, and Tatishe M. Nteta. 2016. "For You Were Strangers in the Land of Egypt: Clergy, Religiosity, and Public Opinion toward Immigration Reform in the United States." *Politics & Religion* 9:566–604.

Wilson, Angelia R., and Paul A. Djupe. 2020. "Communicating in Good Faith? Dynamics of the Christian Right Agenda." *Politics & Religion* 13 (2): 385–414.

Young, Stephen. 2018. "Bonus Jeffress: The Pastor Talks to the *Observer* about Trump's Child-Separation Policy." *Dallas Observer*, June 19. https://www.dalla sobserver.com/news/first-baptist-dallas-robert-jeffress-on-child-separation-10 811842

Zaller, John R. 1992. *The Nature and Origins of Mass Opinion.* New York: Cambridge University Press.

ELEVEN

Considering the Future Paths of Religious Communication Research

Brian Calfano

As the volume's introductory chapter established, religion, in the way it is interpreted and lived out through the experiences of both religious elites and laypeople, is variable in its motivating orientations, emphases, and effects. In addition, an overlooked, yet highly consequential aspect of religion is the nature with which it is communicated. An equally important point is that the link between religion and politics is embedded in the exposure and adoption processes inherent in communication. The previous nine chapters have focused on questions of communication exposure and adoption in novel ways.

The major theme uniting these chapters is that religious communication can take several forms and communication effects are variable. But behind this perspective is the notion that religion's influence as a motive for political perspectives and behavior is not a foregone conclusion. Indeed, religion's influence is conditional and, as scholars have begun to explore through assessments of how faith may be co-opted by secular politics, may not wield influence at all. Yet, this is not the same as saying religion is unimportant for political study or that the voting habits of some faith communities (e.g., white evangelicals) portend an end faith as a fertile empirical area for political scholars. In fact, if one adopts this volume's general perspective that religion exists as a context-specific, mediating influence of varying strength and relevance, the possibilities for driving new and insightful research agendas are virtually endless.

In looking ahead from the insights provided in the previous chapters, the purpose of this concluding chapter is twofold. The first is to attend to the scope and methods most appropriate for advancing questions of both broad and narrow interest on religious communication as it relates to politics. Second, and building on this volume's insights, this chapter is a vehicle to consider what future directions in religious communication research might entail. The goal is to provide the reader with both a general summary of the prior chapters and a look ahead at the questions that will typify a new generation of religion and politics research.

Scope and Methods of Religious Communication Research

When discussing "scope and methods," the "scope" usually comes first to signal the envisioned breadth of investigation. But in regard to religious communication, which stands at a crossroads of topics ranging from the humanities to the social sciences, it seems more efficient to first talk about methods (leaving the discussion of scope to be driven by what the methods can empirically demonstrate). In terms of what qualifies as "demonstrate," we should aim for wide parameters since not all questions about religious communication are answerable through a single research method. But the methodological shifts within political science and religion and politics research also suggest that not all methods are equally equipped to provide insight on questions of interest.

Randomized experiments of varying modes (e.g., survey embedded, field, etc.) should have pride of place in the arsenal of research methods that scholars leverage in pursuing these religious communication research agendas (Djupe and Calfano 2013; Calfano and Lajevardi 2019). This is because, if we assume that people are generally unreliable in their ability to recall political and religious experiences (see Bradburn, Rips, and Shevell 1987; Ansolabehere and Iyengar 1994), that what they indicate about their attitudes may be artifacts of survey question wording (see Bishop 2005), and that endogeneity exists between recall and attitudes (partisan or religious based), reliance on observational data alone represents inherent disadvantages. Randomized experiments can give us insight on exposure-based effects for various religious communication examples.

But this is not to suggest that randomized experiments are a panacea, particularly in situations where experiments lack mundane realism (see Hovland 1959; McDermott 2002). Furthermore, it is impossible to gain useful leverage on some research questions using random assignment. For example, if one's goal is to test for the causal forces at work in moving denominations toward more progressive theological stances on LGBTQ issues, randomized experiments would help in explaining lay- and elite-level views (see Calfano, Michelson, and Oldmixon 2017). But a randomized design would be hard-pressed to explain small-group elite-level decisions about affecting denominational policy changes in a general assembly meeting or similar situation.

The same goes for any elite-level decision where researchers want to get inside the black box of small-group interactions, much less in regard to a single elite's actions. Indeed, we are likely never to leverage randomized experiments to understand the decision calculus of Jerry Falwell Jr. or Robert Jeffries in offering their kind of religious communication on political topics. Neither would an experiment be useful in mining the vast troves of behavior-based data about religious-oriented communication on social media. In these instances, the sheer "bigness" of those data produces compelling insights, even if scholars are unable to lift the proverbial hood in isolating direct causal relationships.

An additional word of caution even in cases where random assignment is feasible: a single experiment is unlikely to overcome the problems of exposure, effect, and message recall. To piece together insights on religious communication effects in various religious, social, and political contexts, scholars will need to adopt the kind of incremental knowledge building that Kuhn (1962) described as "normal" science. Social science is generally considered weakest in terms of established paradigms (see Rosenberg 2012), so, by extension, the study of religion and politics is at a stage where scholars are matching observed facts with theory while progressing toward an established paradigm of well-tested causal stories.

Perhaps the drawback of fitting a Kuhnian definition of science on top of the study of religious communication is the problem of irreconcilable paradigms in Kuhn's (1962) approach. Realistically, religion and politics—and all of political science, for that matter—is not at a stage where paradigms can be considered incompatible. Indeed, recognizing a paradigm of politics, or of politics and religion, would be a welcome development in itself. This is why advancing the study of religious communication may be best accomplished through Lakatos's (1970) view of science as cumulative progress toward improved explanations and predictions focusing, in part, on more modest challenges to existing theory (i.e., the axillary hypotheses). This means that religious communication as the blending of various subfields in political science (and related disciplines) benefits from the kind of pluralistic methodological approach that the scholars in this volume employed.

But as discussed in the volume's opening chapter, while perhaps not a paradigm, approaching the study of religious communication from the communication exposure standpoint suggests that acceptance (and follow on action) provides a useful opportunity to properly situate the refined theories. This returns us to the consideration of scope in extending religious communication research beyond this volume.

Exposure and Adoption: Elite Cue Efficacy

The scope of the exposure and adoption assessments in this volume spans elite cues, the prevailing political contexts whereby religion constructs narratives, and the institutional and organizational settings in which religion helps coalesce identity and behavior. Given the centrality of elite cues to the act of religious communication, the first and last sets of empirical chapters examined them for, among other things, their effects on intended (and even unintended) audiences. Chapters 2, 3, and 4 dealt with exposure and adoption from the standpoint of elite cue giving and the transmission of incongruent cue information specifically. These chapters' key theoretical insight is that both religious and secular elite cues can overcome incongruence with targeted groups and effectively move audience attitudes in the cue's intended direction. The core mechanism behind this influence was the revelation of decision process language reflecting religious considerations, suggesting that decision process language has a potential effect beyond religious identity ingroups targeted for elite cues.

The possible research question extensions from these chapters' findings are as expansive as their political implications. This is because the research designs in chapters 2 and 3 were, like most experiments, narrowly tailored in scope. This means that, for example, we do not know how audiences might perceive other types of incongruent cues focusing on different policy considerations (and featuring different elite voices). We also do not know what exactly it was about the religiously oriented decision process information that affected both prototypical and nonprototypical audiences to align their stated attitudes on (1) LGBTQ rights and (2) US foreign policy toward Iran. A general hunch might be that subjects respected that the elite showed respect by explaining, albeit briefly, part of what went into his stated perspective in the treatments (i.e., religious consideration). This explanation finds support in the literature (see Djupe and Calfano 2013), but even this insight merely scratches the surface of the effectiveness of religious process cues. After all, there are other means of communicating religious decision process. And, all processes might not be equal.

For instance, and assuming that both the targeted and the untargeted audiences responding to the elite cues in the Robertson and Santorum experiments also did so out of recognition that each person (even an elite) has a right to use faith to form and communicate political views, would the decision process have been as effective if it claimed a direct, divine revelation from God? Furthermore, what about decision process claiming that the cue offered "the truth" about a situation (as religious rhetoric is apt to do). These are interesting questions that put the term "religious communication" in an entirely different light, and one that is not without precedent in American politics. Not only are religious elites, including Pat Robertson, known for making public statements roughly like "God told me that he wants ____ to be in office, or ____ policy to be enacted," but secular political elites have started mimicking this approach too.

The question for future research will be whether this revelation of divine knowledge, which is clearly a form of religious decision process, moves targeted and/or untargeted audiences in directions not envisaged by the elite cue givers. Whereas the decision process featured in prior chapters may be considered reasonable across audiences of different religious identities (and even those without a religious affiliation), cues based on claims of divine revelation may have an altogether different effect across audiences.

Then there are the issue domains that the elite cues address. That subjects aligned their attitudes to match elite incongruence on two issues with clear cultural identity dimensions seems promising in generating insights about audience acceptance of elite messages. It remains for scholars to assess whether these cues might work on what could be described as less culturally contentious issues, including, for example, infrastructure spending, the funding of public sector pensions, or the intricacies of federal monetary policy. It might be that religious cues, incongruent or not, have their greatest impact on policy areas with a clear identity base or cultural dimension that audiences already care about. But scholars should take the time to demonstrate this rather than assume it away. This is particularly true as political elites continue to merge the sacred and the secular in their official acts. It may be increasingly likely that religious publics see faith arguments as central to a broader range of policies than researchers have traditionally examined.

The types of policies are but one aspect of assessing religious elite cues.

It is unlikely that elite cues on contentious, cultural issues are communicated in a vacuum where incongruent cues go unchallenged by other elites. These elites may call into question both the messenger's prototypicality (relative to a targeted ingroup audience) and the judgment of those electing to follow the incongruent cue. This is where experiments on cue effects can fall into problems with mundane realism. Ideally, cue experiments include competing statements, some of which challenge incongruent views and give subjects a choice of which elite cues to follow. The challenge with the type of design, however, is not in formulating multiple cue treatments but in garnering large enough subjects to provide adequate statistical power. Any useful experiment will represent a simplified version of the real-world communication environment. Advancing our understanding of cue effects, therefore, might require an acceptance of certain existing findings from the literature. This would then allow newer designs to become more specific with their tests without having to nail down every competing explanation in an experiment.

But researchers will need to speak to the larger literature on information exposure, processing, and acceptance in forging these new paths. Two topics recommend themselves for their centrality in the communication process—the nature of exposure and the potential for backlash. There are strong theoretical reasons to expect that the audiences targeted for religious communication engage in specific cue selection (or resistance). Generally, those with the strongest preferences are the most likely to seek information that aligns with existing beliefs (Bennett and Iyengar 2008; Stroud 2011; Arceneaux, Johnson, Murphy 2012). There is reason to expect that this same type of resistance maps onto refusal or acceptance of elites' communication, especially in cases where political issues and policies are at the forefront.

Several key studies on exposure effects used what Benedicts-Kessner et al. (2019) refer to as a forced choice design, which presents subjects with a single randomized stimulus (from which researchers measure reaction) (see, e.g., Feldman 2011). The elite cue experiments in this volume all followed this forced exposure approach. This is not a problem from an internal validity standpoint, but, in a nation where people are free to pick and choose which leaders (secular or religious) they listen to, forcing a single cue on audiences has clear external validity drawbacks. Therefore, expanded understanding of elite cue effects requires audience opportunity to engage in a free selection of cues (Arceneaux, Johnson, Murphy 2012) (and, ideally, the more cue options they can select from the better).

Then there is the ever-present possibility of backlash effects from elite cues, especially on issues with strong partisan alignments. Dating as far back as Lazarsfeld, Berelson, and Gaudet (1944), researchers noticed an audience tendency to move opinions in directions opposite of information presented. Zaller's (1992) seminal theory refined the backlash expectation somewhat by locating the people capable of backlash as those most highly informed. These highly informed persons are, arguably, the highly pro-totypical group members who may be the most hostile to countervailing or incongruent elite cues (see also Kuklinksi et al. 2001). Others argue that audience responses are subconscious and emotion laden and therefore backlash likely happens when information triggers affective responses (see, e.g., Redlawsk 2002). There is also a view of backlash as a rational response to shoring up one's group identity when a group-dominant perspective is threatened by incongruent cues (Kahan 2012). With the increasing close-ness of religious and political identities, preferences, and outlooks, it is likely that one (or perhaps all) of these processes undergirds responses to elite religious communication. But curiously, we did not observe much in the way of backlash to the incongruent cues offered in the elite cue experi-ments in chapters 2 and 3, even though the subject pools were composed of self-identifying evangelicals (i.e., those who might have the strongest rea-sons to resist cue incongruence). We did find more evidence for backlash in chapter 9's college student subject pool.

There may be several reasons for this lack of effect, not the least of which could be an overstatement of backlash potential based on earlier research design choices (see Guess and Coppock 2020 for a discussion of field experiment findings). It might also be that, at least concerning chap-ter 3's Santorum experiment, audiences were not motivated by a strong enough set of preferences to erect cognitive walls to resist elite calls to reconsider any anti-Iranian/anti-Persian views. And, it might also be that religious decision process of the type featured in those experiments packs an effective antidote to any backlash potentials. Yet, in understanding more about the lack of backlash (so to speak), scholars should replicate and refine the experiments presented in these previous chapters. The outcomes may be as sensitive to differences in theoretical perspective as they are to design choice and modality.

One case where backlash seemed more likely at work was in chapter 4's Georgy experiment, which also addressed the question of what kind of elite the public is willing to accept (and be influenced by). The Georgy experiment was an example of finding elite plausibility bounds. Whereas the incongruent cues offered in the Robertson and Santorum studies were attributed to white male Christians, Georgy was variably described as having one scrutinized outgroup identity (and in some cases two such identities). In those results, being Arab was less of a liability than being Muslim (or Arab Muslim), but the general implications are the same: elites—even those signaling the practice of well-worn "American" political behaviors—are not perceived positively by the public and may be subject to backlash effects. And, not surprisingly, there is no benefit in perception to the scrutinized identity group when an elite of the same identity signals alignment with socially dominant behavior.

Religious Communication in Prevailing Contexts

The ramifications of this finding spill into chapter 5's consideration of the delegitimization of Muslims as an identity group outside of the randomized experiment context. Jenkins and Williams focused on what they termed "dominant interpretations" of religious minorities and suggested that, unless shifts to these metanarratives occur, it likely will not matter what behaviors elites and members of these dominated religious minorities undertake. These minorities will not make headway in shifting public perceptions. Indeed, if dominant views of religious outgroups are typified by suspicion and fear, the signaling of dominant social values and practices, as seen in the Georgy experiment, will not make much headway. And, as Jenkins and Williams rightly point out, a phenomenon like Islamophobia is very much alive in the world's two largest secular democracies.

Here, we note that religious communication in the form of negative narratives about a dominated religious group like Muslims is but one example of how established, socially accepted narratives of mobility intersect with religious motives and rhetoric. But the groups on the receiving end of these abuses are not always the same in cross-national comparisons. After all, in states like Egypt, where Coptic Christians are a minority, some may use Islam as the state's official religion to construct dominant and oppressive narratives affecting those outside the religious majority. Yet the nature and effects of religious communication are much more likely to be conditional and nuanced than overt and deterministic. Again, using Egypt as an example, the nationalistic lens through which much of the country views contemporary issues suggests that secular politics, not religion, unites Egyptians of different faith identities around a set of priorities and concerns. That said, much of what happens "on the ground" in any communication environment is as much a matter of perspective as it is of measurement. To get a firm handle on expectations about how religion is (or is not) used to advance political agendas, scholars need to engage in careful study of the total societal context. The takeaway point, therefore, is that advancing religious communication research from a comparative politics lens should mimic the type of "deep dive" into the subnational, national, and regional environments that the authors used in chapter 5.

Chapter 6 makes the full transition into consideration of religious communication from an institutional standpoint, while speaking effectively to the findings presented in prior chapters. One of the key items recommended for future scholarly attention by Wagner and Friesen's analysis is the notion that denominational context—and the sense of institutional identity brought forth through congregational involvement—matters in how congregants organize their sense of religious and political self. One clear implication of this finding is that scholars are well advised to look for ways to collect data in situations where congregational and denominational influence is most salient—in the houses of worship themselves. This is, of course, often easier said than done. Outside of chapter 6's focus group data, there are scant examples of data collected on religious communication topics using subjects physically located in their house of worship while providing their survey response (but see Djupe and Calfano 2013). But the challenges to this type of research design notwithstanding, scholars attempting to understand group prototypicality variance and its effects need to find ways to better incorporate a target audience's sense of group identity.

From a religious standpoint at least, there is no better way to incorporate group identity than to surround subjects with a physical reminder of where their sense of collectiveness comes from. Admittedly, situating surveys and experiments in houses of worship may not produce much in the way of effects for those who are atypical members of their denominations. But chapter 6 reminds us that denominational and congregation-level identity can be critical in understanding audience responses to varying types of religious communication. It may be that, as Djupe and Gilbert (2009) forcefully argue, denominational effects are heterogeneous across local congregations within these larger institutions, thereby creating pockets of response difference to religious stimuli. Such a finding does no violence to the possibility of institutional-specific effects, however. Instead, it shows outcomes related to religious identity and communication exposure to be contextually variable (which a large portion of the religion and politics literature already demonstrates).

If understanding how audiences perceive religious messages is the goal, not only are institutional effects critical but, as Burge reported in chapter 7, so is appreciation of what broader identity terms like "evangelical" mean to (and how they are used by) the public. Burge shows that Tweet content associated with the term "evangelical" is highly political in nature—suggesting that the general public does not view evangelicalism as a religious movement but, rather, as an adjunct of Republican Party politics. Aside from this finding's spiritual and theological implications, scholars should probe for increased insight into the nature of evangelical identity's political characteristics. Margolis's (2018) work provides a useful template in understanding how people may use political lodestars to guide their reentrance to faith practice. But, from a religious communication perspective, it will be important to gain greater leverage on questions relating to when (and to what extent) evangelicals separate religious values and other conceptions from partisan preferences.

It may not always be that evangelicals have the same degree of association with secular politics as Burge reports. It is also possible for other faiths to be activated along partisan lines in a similar manner. At issue is the nature of the religious/political connection in determining which of the two reacts and which is causal and under what conditions. The experiment results of chapters 2 and 3 suggest that by revealing their decision process, religious and secular elites can sway evangelical policy views, even on social issues like LGBTQ rights. This suggests that religion maintains some effect on the political, at least in terms of religious elite cues of political consequence. We would not expect issue positions on topics like abortion to be malleable (or at least not to the extent found in the reported experiments), but abortion may be the exception rather than the rule when it comes to evangelicals. Other Christian traditions are a different story in that their ideological and partisan views are more heterogeneous, so we should expect the association between political and religious terms to be more variable. Regardless, and with the sheer amount of data generated by social media platforms—indeed, internet-based data more generally—there is every reason to expect that scholars have opportunities to advance Burge's work.

Chapter 8 moves into a different take on religious communication by combining elements of institutional, individual, and spiritual components related to prayer as a communication resource. Conger and Grant examine the extent to which religious organizations mention prayer as a mobilizing and identity resource. This characterization of prayer may be useful as an example of topics that scholars can tap to test similar communication phenomena. Prayer is but one of the activities that can bind individuals in groups and organizations. Reading the Bible, attending religious services, and participating in organization-sponsored meetings or retreats are other ways that elites can use appeals to engage and motivate individuals to develop and deepen connections to a cause or movement. Granted, prayer is perhaps unmatched as an example of personal religious communication, but the larger point from Conger and Grant's work is that the activities inherent in religious communication can be a tie that binds, helping to perpetuate more religious communication in the process.

Elite Cue Redux

Adkin's work in chapter 9 transitions back toward a focus on religious elite communication, but with a specific emphasis on elites in religious denominational contexts (something that Robertson did not qualify as in the chapter 2 experiment). But unlike the general effectiveness found for the elite cues in chapters 2 and 3, elite cues coming from leaders ensconced in religious institutions either are not persuasive on targeted audiences or cause a backlash effect among audiences not intended to receive the cue. That this cue effect pattern was found across religious traditions on an array of public policy issues suggests that, while the public might be willing to think carefully about elite cues posed outside of religious denominations, those operating inside these institutions are looked upon in a substantially different manner.

Direct comparisons with the Robertson and Santorum experiments are not possible given that those experiments occurred on distinct subject pools and the chapter 9 experiment did not test either the impact of incongruent cue information or religious decision process cues (something that scholars should consider in future iterations of experiments assessing cue impact). But, in the end, the lack of effect (or the backlash effect) found in chapter 9 may be more indication that religious elites operating in religious institutions are hemmed in when it comes to public impact.

But, as Djupe reports in chapter 10, the issue may not simply be due to the rejection of religious elite cues. Rather, it may be an unwillingness of religious elites working in churches and denominations to take independent (and contrasting) positions on salient public policy issues. Simply put, the same elites who need the buy-in of congregants to provide monetary support to keep the institution running may avoid speaking prophetically in a manner that challenges congregationally dominant political thinking. This trend seems primed to continue, especially as politics takes a greater role in determining the public's level of religious engagement.

This cursory review of the analyses of the volume's chapters reveals a topical scope with enough breadth to power several new and expanded religious communication research agendas. In addition, the studies featured herein point to a litany of alternatives hypotheses for investigation. In essence, the scope of religious communication research is broad enough to support a robust exchange of perspectives on the variable influence of exposure and adoption of religious stimuli across disparate contexts. And, though a dominant paradigm of religious communication may be out of reach for now, the future discoveries inherent in updating our understanding of this critical aspect of meaning making help us envision exciting possibilities across social science disciplines.

REFERENCES

Ansolabehere, Stephen, and Shanto Iyengar. 1994. *Going Negative: How Attack Ads Shrink and Polarize the Electorate*. New York: Free Press.

Arceneaux, Kevin, Martin Johnson, and Chad Murphy. 2012. "Polarized Political Communication: Oppositional Media Hostility and Selective Exposure." *Journal of Politics* 74:174–86.

Benedicts-Kessner, Justin De, Matthew A. Baum, Adam J. Berenski, and Teppei Yamamoto. 2019. "Persuading the Enemy: Estimating the Persuasive Effects of Partisan Media with the Preference-Incorporating Choice and Assignment Design." *American Political Science Review* 113.

Bennett, W. Lance, and Shanto Iyengar. 2008. "A New Era of Minimal Effects? The Changing Foundations of Political Communication." *Journal of Communication* 58:707–31.

Bishop, George F. 2005. *The Illusion of Public Opinion: Fact and Artifact in American Public Opinion Polls*. Lanham, MD: Rowman and Littlefield.

Bradburn, Norman M., Lance J. Rips, and Steven K. Shevell. 1987. "Answering Autobiographical Questions: The Impact of Memory and Inference on Surveys." *Science* 236:157–61.

Calfano, Brian R., and Nazita Lajevardi. 2019. *Understanding Muslim Political Life in America: Contested Citizenship in the Twenty-First Century*. Philadelphia: Temple University Press.

Calfano, Brian R., Melissa R. Michelson, and Elizabeth A. Oldmixon. 2017. *A Matter of Discretion: The Politics of Catholic Priests in the United States and Ireland*. Lanham, MD: Rowman and Littlefield.

Djupe, Paul A., and Brian R. Calfano. 2013. *God Talk: Experimenting with the Religious Causes of Public Opinion*. Philadelphia: Temple University Press.

Djupe, Paul A., and Christopher C. Gilbert. 2009. *The Political Influence of Churches*. New York: Cambridge University Press.

Guess, Alexander, and Andrew Coppock. 2020. "Does Counter-Attitudinal Information Cause Backlash? Results from Three Large Field Experiments." *British Journal of Political Science* 50: 1497–1515.

Hovland, Carl I. 1959. "Reconciling Conflicting Results from Experimental and Survey Studies of Attitude Change." *American Psychologist* 14:8–17.

Kahan, Dan M. 2012. "Ideology, Motivated Reasoning, and Cognitive Reflection: An Experimental Study." *Judgment and Decision Making* 8:407–24.

Kuhn, Thomas S. 1962. *The Structure of Scientific Revolutions*. Chicago: University of Chicago Press.

Kuklinski, James H., Paul J. Quirk, Jennifer Jerit, and Robert F. Rich. 2001. "The Political Environment and Citizen Competence." *American Journal of Political Science* 45:410–25.

Lakatos, Imre. 1970. "Falsification and the Methodology of Scientific Research Programmes." In *Criticism and the Growth of Knowledge*, edited by Imre Lakatos and Alan Musgrave, 91–196. New York: Cambridge University Press.

Lazarsfeld, Paul F., Bernard Berelson, and Hazel Gaudet. 1944. *The People's Choice: How the Voter Makes Up His Mind in a Presidential Campaign*. New York: Columbia University Press.

Margolis, Michele L. 2018. *From Politics to the Pews: How Partisanship and Political Environment Shape Religious Identity*. Chicago: University of Chicago Press.

McDermott, Rose. 2002. "Experimental Methodology for Political Science." *Political Analysis* 10:325–42.

Redlawsk, David. 2002. "Hot Cognition or Cool Consideration? Testing the Effects of Motivated Reasoning on Political Decision Making." *Journal of Politics* 64:1021–44.

Rosenberg, Alexander. 2012. *Philosophy of Social Science*. 4th ed. New York: Routledge.

Stroud, Natalie Jomini. 2011. *Niche News: The Politics of News Choice*. New York: Oxford University Press.

Zaller, John R. 1992. *The Nature and Origins of Mass Opinion*. New York: Cambridge University Press.

Contributors

Jason Adkins is Assistant Professor of Political Science at the University of Montana, Billings. His research focuses on elite political cues in religious contexts.

Ryan Burge is Assistant Professor of Political Science at Eastern Illinois University. His work examines measurement approaches to religious identity, opinion, and behavior.

Brian Calfano is Professor of Political Science and Journalism at the University of Cincinnati. His research focuses on religion and politics, marginalized groups, and media and politics.

Kimberly H. Conger is Associate Professor of Political Science at the University of Cincinnati. Her research examines state politics, religion and politics, and public administration topics.

Paul A. Djupe is Professor of Political Science at Denison University and the former editor of *Politics and Religion*. His research focuses on social networks, political participation, and democratic deliberation.

Amanda Friesen is Associate Professor of Political Science at Indiana University–Purdue University Indianapolis. Her work investigates political psychology, gender and politics, and religion and politics topics.

J. Tobin Grant is Professor of Political Science at Southern Illinois University and the editor of the *Journal for the Scientific Study of Religion*. His research encompasses political methodology, public opinion, and religion and politics.

Laura Dudley Jenkins is Professor of Political Science and Faculty Affiliate, Asian Studies and Women's, Gender, and Sexuality Studies at the University of Cincinnati. Her current research focuses on religion and politics, international women's rights, and women in political science.

Nazita Lajevardi is Assistant Professor of Political Science at Michigan State University. Her work examines political identity, media coverage of marginalized groups, and race and ethnic politics.

Melissa Michelson is Professor of Political Science and Dean of Arts and Sciences at Menlo College. Her research investigates marginalized groups, GOTV campaigns, and race and ethnic politics.

Salvatore James Russo is Associate Professor of Political Science at California State University, Dominguez Hills. His work focuses on religion and politics and legal issues.

Alexis Straka is a marketing analyst at Nielsen. Her academic research assesses religion and gender stereotypes and their impacts on political participation.

Michael W. Wagner is Professor of Journalism and Mass Communication at the University of Wisconsin, Madison. His research encompasses political communication, public opinion, and political psychology.

Rina Verma Williams is Associate Professor of Political Science, and Faculty Affiliate in Asian Studies and Women's, Gender, and Sexuality Studies at the University of Cincinnati. Her research focuses on religious/conservative women and politics, religion, gender and nationalism in Bollywood cinema, and oral histories of women in political science.

Index